Tort Law in Belgium

Tort Law in Belgium

Marc Kruithof

This book was originally published as a monograph in the International Encyclopaedia of Laws/Tort Law.

Founding Editor: Roger Blanpain
General Editor: Frank Hendrickx
Volume Editor: Britt Weyts

Wolters Kluwer

Published by:
Kluwer Law International B.V.
PO Box 316
2400 AH Alphen aan den Rijn
The Netherlands
E-mail: international-sales@wolterskluwer.com
Website: lrus.wolterskluwer.com

Sold and distributed in North, Central and South America by:
Wolters Kluwer Legal & Regulatory U.S.
7201 McKinney Circle
Frederick, MD 21704
United States of America
Email: customer.service@wolterskluwer.com

Sold and distributed in all other countries by:
Air Business Subscriptions
Rockwood House
Haywards Heath
West Sussex
RH16 3DH
United Kingdom
Email: international-customerservice@wolterskluwer.com

Printed on acid-free paper

ISBN 978-94-035-0063-8

e-Book: ISBN 978-94-035-0064-5
web-PDF: ISBN 978-94-035-0065-2

This title is available on www.kluwerlawonline.com

Printed in the United Kingdom.

The Author

Marc Kruithof was born on 25 April 1960 in Wilrijk (Antwerp), Belgium.
He studied at Ghent University in Belgium and obtained a Licentiate (nowadays called a Master's) in Law *summa cum laude* in 1983 and a Licentiate (nowadays called a Master's) in Economic Science *magna cum laude* in 1985. In 1986, he obtained a Master of Laws (LLM) from the Yale Law School in New Haven, Connecticut, USA. In 2009, he was awarded a PhD in Law by Ghent University with a dissertation on the legal (private law) and regulatory (public law) treatment of conflicts of interest financial institutions can face when providing investment services.
From 1988 until 1991, he was Assistant for commercial, economic and financial law at Ghent University Law School. From 1991 until 2011, he was Professor at Ghent University College, where he taught law courses for students in the academic bachelor and master programs in Commercial Sciences (Business Administration) and Public Administration and Non-profit Management. In 2002, he spent the spring quarter at the University of Chicago Law School as a Visiting Professor, where he taught a course on the Creation of the European Common Market. Since 2011, he has been full time Professor of Civil Liability (Torts) and Comparative Law at Ghent University Law School.

The Author

Table of Contents

Table of Contents

List of Abbreviations

AM	*Auteurs et média—Auteurs en Media*
Arr.Cass.	*Arresten van het Hof van Cassatie* (official Dutch publication of decisions of the Court of Cassation since 1967, available at the website of the Court at https://justitie.belgium.be/nl/rechterlijke_orde/hoven_en_rechtbanken/hof_van_cassatie and older volumes available at http://bib.kuleuven.be/rbib/collecties-en-zoeken/arresten-van-het-hof-van-cassatie)
Arr. Verbr.	*Arresten van het Hof van Verbreking* (older official Dutch publication of decision of the Court of Cassation until 1961, available at http://bib.kuleuven.be/rbib/collecties-en-zoeken/arresten-van-het-hof-van-cassatie)
Bull.Ass.	*Bulletin des assurances*
CA	Court of Appeal (*cour d'appel—hof van beroep*)
C.Arb.	Court of Arbitration (*Cour d'arbitrage—Arbitragehof*), since 2007 called the Constitutional Court
Cass.	Court of Cassation (*Cour de cassation—Hof van Cassatie*)
CC	Belgian Civil Code (*Code civil—Burgerlijk Wetboek*)
CEL	Code of Economic Law (*Code de droit économique—Wetboek van Economisch Recht*)
CFI	Court of First Instance, Civil Court (*tribunal de première instance—rechtbank van eerste aanleg*)
Comm.	Commercial Court (*tribunal de commerce—rechtbank van koophandel*)
Con.	Belgian Federal Constitution, coordinated on 17 February 1994 (*Constitution coordonnée—Gecoördineerde Grondwet*)
Con.C.	Constitutional Court (*Cour constitutionnelle—Grondwettelijk Hof*)
Corr.	Court of First Instance, Correctional Court (*tribunal correctionel—correctionele rechtbank*)
CoS	Council of State (*Conseil d'état—Raad van State*)
CRA	*Circulation, Responsabilité et Assurance—Verkeer, Aansprakelijkheid, Verzekering*

Crim.Pro.	Code of Criminal Procedure (*Code d'instruction criminelle—Wetboek van Strafvordering*)
ECA	(Federal) Employment Contracts Act of 3 July 1978 (*Loi relative aux contrats de travail—Wet betreffende de arbeidsovereenkomsten*)
ECHR	Convention for the Protection of Human Rights and Fundamental Freedoms, Rome, 4 November 1950, also called the European Convention on Human Rights
ECJ	EU Court of Justice
ECR	European Court Reporter
ECtHR	European Court of Human Rights
MHIA	(Federal) Coordinated Mandatory Health Insurance Act of 14 July 1994 (*Loi relative à l'assurance obligatoire soins de santé et indemnités coordonnée—Wet betreffende de verplichte verzekering voor geneeskundige verzorging en uitkeringen*)
IAA	(Federal) Industrial Accidents Act of 10 April 1971 (*Loi sur les accidents du travail—Arbeidsongevallenwet*)
JC	Judicial Code (*Code judiciaire—Gerechtelijk Wetboek*)
JCt	Court of First Instance, Juvenile Court (*tribunal de la jeunesse—jeugdrechtbank*)
JLMB	*Revue de jurisprudence de Liège, Mons et Bruxelles*
JPC	Justice of the Peace Court (*justice de paix—vredegerecht*)
JT	*Journal des tribunaux*
LC	Labor Court (*tribunal de travail—arbeidsrechtbank*)
MVIA	(Federal) Mandatory Motor Vehicle Insurance Act of 21 November 1989 (*Loi relative à l'assurance obligatoire de la responsabilité en matière de véhicules automoteurs—Wet betreffende de verplichte aansprakelijkheidsverzekering inzake motorrijtuigen*)
NJW	*Nieuw Juridisch Weekblad*
Pas.	*Pasicrisie belge* (official French publication of decisions of the Court of Cassation)
PC	Penal Code (*Code pénal—Strafwetboek*)
PLA	(Federal) Product Liability Act of 25 February 1991 (*Loi relative à la responsabilité du fait des produits défectueux—Wet betreffende de aansprakelijkheid voor produkten met gebreken*)
Pol.	Police Court (*tribunal de police—politierechtbank*)
RDC	*Revue de droit commercial belge—Tijdschrift voor Belgisch Handelsrecht*

List of Abbreviations

RW	*Rechtskundig Weekblad*
RGAR	*Revue générale des assurances et des responsabilités*
TMR	*Tijdschrift voor Milieurecht*

List of Abbreviations

General Introduction

§1. General Background of the Country

I. Geography

1. Belgium is a small country, located in the middle of the western coast of continental Europe, covering an area of 30,528 square kilometers. The country shares its northern border with The Netherlands, its eastern border with Germany and the Grand Duchy of Luxemburg, and its southern border with France. Its western border is the North Sea coast, consisting mainly of large sand beaches exploited for tourism. The northern half of the territory is flat, lying between 0 and 150 meters above sea level, while the southern half of the territory is more uneven, containing the smaller mountain range called the Ardennes, with the highest point at almost 700 meters above sea level. The capital of the country is Brussels, which also holds the seat of several international organizations, among which the European Union and the North Atlantic Treaty Organization (NATO).

2. On January 1, 2017, Belgium had an officially registered population of 11,303,528, of which 6,509,894 live in the northern region of the country, called Flanders, 3,610,089 live in the southern region of the country, called Wallonia, and 1,183,545 live in the centrally located Brussels Capital Region.[1] This Capital Region, which consists of one urbanized area, administratively actually consists of nineteen separate municipalities, with in the center the city of Brussels, which only has a population of around 175,000. This means that Antwerp, housing the second largest port of Europe and having a population of around 520,000, is actually the largest city in Belgium. Other relatively large cities are Ghent with around 260,000 inhabitants and Liège with around 200,000 inhabitants.[2] The northern and middle part of the territory of Belgium, including all these cities, form the most densely populated region in continental Europe. The total population shows a yearly increase of 0.5%, which for four-fifth is the result of immigration numbers being higher than emigration numbers.[3] Around 11.5% of the inhabitants do not hold the Belgian nationality.

---

1. Numbers based on the inhabitants registered in the State Registry (*Rijksregister—Registre national*), available at the website of the Federal Department of the Interior, at www.ibz.rrn.fgov.be.
2. Numbers also available at www.ibz.rrn.fgov.be.
3. AD Statistiek—Statistics Belgium, FOD Economie, K.M.O., Middenstand en Energie, Press Release of 8 June 2016, available at http://statbel.fgov.be.

3. Most inhabitants living in the north of the country use Flemish as their main language. Flemish is a variety of the Dutch language, using some different vocabulary and a different pronunciation, although people from Flanders and The Netherlands can perfectly understand each other if they do not use local dialect or purely regional pronunciation. In the southern part of the country, the main language is French, as the original Walloon language has almost disappeared. In the border area between the north and the south, and particularly in the region of Brussels, both languages are used, although more people speak French than Flemish. In the east of the country, a small area that in the past has been part of Germany has a population of around 60,000 using German as its main language.

The many recently immigrated citizens, who are mostly living in the larger cities, use many other languages. This has turned the Brussels area into a true multilingual area, with over the last decades English being more and more used as a *lingua franca* by the expat community and the Belgian professionals working for larger companies and institutions.

The fact that Belgium lies on the border between the southern Romanic and northern Germanic cultural areas in Europe make it an interesting place sharing characteristics of both, which also causes some internal cultural friction.

II. History

4. Belgium, with its present territory, is a relatively recent phenomenon.[4] During most of its history since the middle ages, this territory either consisted of several smaller separate political entities, or was unified but then together with other territories that today are part of The Netherlands, France and the Grand Duchy of Luxembourg.

5. After the division of the Carolingian empire by the treaties of Verdun (843) and Meersen (870), the territory west of the river Scheldt became part of West Francia (which later became France), while the territory east of this river first became part of Middle Francia and later of Lotharingia. At the end of the ninth century, however, the western part became an autonomous principality under the counts of Flanders. This part, that today is invoked as the historic basis for a Flemish entity predating Belgium, only covered the two most western provinces (called West Flanders and East Flanders) of the five provinces that form the present day region of Flanders, but also included the northwestern part of what is today France ("*la Flandre française*") and part of today's Dutch province of *Zeeland* south of the river Scheldt. The other part of today's Belgian territory, including the other three nowadays "Flemish" provinces called Antwerp, Limburg and Flemish Brabant and the five Walloon provinces called Hainaut, Namur, Liège, Luxembourg and Walloon Brabant, remained a part of the Duchy of Lotharingia until the eleventh century, when it also disintegrated and became dominated by local rulers. Thus, in the twelfth and thirteenth centuries, what today is called Belgium was a patchwork of autonomous principalities.

4. This historic overview is largely based on D. Heirbaut, "The Belgian Legal Tradition: Does It Exist?" in M. Kruithof & W. De Bondt (ed.), *Introduction to Belgian Law*, 2d ed., Alphen aan den Rijn: Kluwer Law International, 2017, 1–24, including a useful selected bibliography for those interested in further reading.

From the end of the fourteenth century on, the dukes of Burgundy brought most of these principalities under their control, and their successors, the Habsburgs, completed the process of unification in the sixteenth century. The territory of this unified region, however, did not only include what is now Belgium, it also included what is now The Netherlands and the Grand Duchy of Luxembourg and part of northern France. Even though one can find sources of this territory being called Belgium at the time, this term apparently applied to what today is called the Low Countries.

6. At the end of the sixteenth century, the Low Countries revolted against their Habsburg overlord, Philip II, King of Spain, for religious and other reasons. The Protestants managed to obtain the northern part, which became independent and known as the United Provinces, the predecessor of today's The Netherlands. The southern part remained under Habsburg catholic rule. Cultural and economic elites that were protestant moved from the leading southern cities (the sixteenth century is often referred to as the "golden century" for Antwerp) to the liberated north, resulting in a boost of cultural and economic life in Dutch cities (the seventeenth century is called the "golden century" for The Netherlands). By the eighteenth century, the southern part of the Low Countries had been passed from the Spanish to the Austrian Habsburgs. At that time, the territory did not include the principalities of Liège and Stavelot-Malmédy, which had remained autonomous under the rule of a bishop and an abbot, but did include the whole of today's Luxembourg, and the northern part of France.

7. At the end of the eighteenth century, the French revolution resulted in an annexation of both the southern Habsburg and the northern independent part of the Low Countries by France. The Low Countries, the north and south united, became independent in 1815 in the United Kingdom of the Netherlands (hence, the use of the plural which in Dutch means "the low countries"). At that time, the names *De Nederlanden* in Dutch and *Belgique* in French were still used for the whole territory, and the inhabitants were called *Nederlanders* in Dutch and *Belges* in French.

However, the reunification turned out to be short-lived, as the population of the north and the south had estranged in the course of the preceding two centuries. The cultural-religious differences between the mostly catholic south and politically dominantly protestant north, and the language tensions between the more Dutch-speaking north and more French-speaking south, resulted in the southern part breaking away in 1830. The new independent country continued to call itself *Belgique* in French (Belgium), and the north continued to call itself *Nederland* in Dutch (The Netherlands).

8. Apart from the economic, social and political evolution Belgium has shared with most West-European countries in the two centuries since its independence, Belgium also underwent a particularly important specific development. At the time of its creation and much throughout the nineteenth century, the cultural and economic elites of the country used French as their language.[5] Educated people, that is to say those who could actually read and write, in fact did so in French, the language that had replaced Latin in schooling. The language of the less fortunate was local: in what today is called Flanders, different local dialects were used that were related to the Dutch language. In the southern part of the country, Walloon was used, one of the *langues d'oïl*. The evolution of social emancipation during the nineteenth century, resulting in an increasing participation in economic and political life by the formerly called lower and middle

5. It nowadays is often forgotten, but also the Dutch elites were historically French speaking.

classes, therefore also resulted in important language tensions. In the southern part of the country, Walloon was in fact mostly replaced by French. In the north, however, resistance to French was stronger and the different Flemish dialects were more and more considered variants of the Dutch language. During the twentieth century, this resulted in the cultural and economic elites in the north using less and less French and becoming Dutch speaking.

9. Generalizing, one could say that the law in the territory that now forms Belgium consisted mostly out of customary law until well into the eighteenth century. Relatively little had been legislated. As a result, the French codifications, which became applicable in the Belgian territory, as it was applicable to all annexed departments, form the historic basis for the written law in the country. The Napoleonic Civil Code of 1804 has remained in force in Belgium, even though many amendments and additions have been added to it by the Belgian legislature since 1830. For much of the nineteenth century, Belgian civil law developed closely linked to French law. From the end of the nineteenth century on, however, the dependence on France has diminished. Today, one can say that although French-speaking authors still cite French sources and literature regularly, Dutch-speaking authors no longer consider French law as any more relevant for Belgium as the law of the other neighboring states. While Belgian tort law is still based on the same statutory provisions as French tort law, the bulk of the substance of this branch of law has been elaborated by the courts, which over the last century have not felt obliged to adhere to the French interpretation of the same statutory texts. Therefore, it would be a serious mistake to assume that Belgian and French civil liability law have the same content.

10. Starting in 2015, the federal government has launched an attempt to modernize Belgian legislation and particularly the codes.[6] The Justice Minister has appointed working groups consisting of academics and asked them to prepare a draft for a new civil code.[7] At present, the result of this effort has not yet been published, so it is too early to tell whether the proposals with relation to civil liability law will be limited to codifying existing law as it has been developed by the courts or will try to introduce major changes.

III. Political System

11. Originally, Belgium was created as a so-called unitary state. Apart from local government at the municipal and provincial level, there was only one central government with full jurisdiction over the entire national territory. The Belgian Constitution of 1831 stood out as a model for parliamentary monarchies, with strongly formulated individual liberties. The system is based on democracy, with an elected Parliament and the King having no powers to act on his own. For every act in the performance of his constitutional function, he needs the approval and backing by a

6. *See* the plan of the federal Justice Minister K. GEENS, *De sprong naar het recht voor morgen—Le saut vers le droit de demain*, s.l., 6 December 2016, available at www.koengeens.be.
7. *See* Ministerial Decree of 30 September 2017, *Moniteur belge—Belgisch Staatsblad*, 9 October 2017, p. 91,600.

minister,[8] who is politically responsible to Parliament.[9] The King and more broadly the executive branch has no powers apart from those explicitly granted by the Constitution or by specific legislation.[10]

12. During the course of the twentieth century, however, the cultural and economic differences between the northern and the southern part of the country, which became more and more compelling as social emancipation diminished the relative importance of French-speaking elites in the north, rendered this unitary system unworkable. With political opinions on crucial policy matters sometimes diametrically opposed between the north and the south, the only way to keep the country together was to gradually introduce a system with, apart from a national government with diminishing powers, also separate centralized governments for the north and the south of the territory as well as for the Dutch and the French-speaking parts of the country.

13. Nowadays, Belgium is a federal state with very distinctive characteristics.

At the *national level*, there is an executive branch consisting of the King,[11] assisted by his ministers, a legislative branch consisting of the Federal Parliament together with the King,[12] assisted by his ministers, and a judicial branch consisting of the regular courts.[13] Although the text of the Constitution states that the Federal Government only has jurisdiction over matters that have been specifically delegated to it by the Constitution or by statute based on the Constitution,[14] this provision has not entered into effect yet. At present, the Federal Government has the so-called residual powers, meaning it has full jurisdiction except for matters that the Constitution or statutes based on the Constitution have specifically granted to the governments of the federated entities.

The particularity of the Belgian federal model, is that there are two types of federated entities, which territorially overlap.

First, the national territory is divided into three *regions*: the northern region called Flanders, the southern region called Wallonia, and the central metropolitan area of Brussels, called the Brussels Capital Region, which actually includes the relatively small municipality called Brussels (i.e., the actual city of Brussels) and eighteen other surrounding municipalities. Each region's government has an executive branch, consisting of a council of ministers, and a legislative branch, consisting of a directly elected regional parliament and the council of ministers. The regional ministers are politically responsible to the regional parliament. Each regional government has jurisdiction over listed policy matters that have a territorial link, such as the economy, employment policy, energy, agriculture, the environment, transport and public works, traffic safety, urban planning, housing, and local government.[15]

Second, the territory of the country is also divided into three *communities*, which are superimposed on the regions: the Flemish Community, which has jurisdiction in

8. Article 106 Con.
9. Article 88 Con.
10. Article 105 Con.
11. Article 37 Con.
12. Article 36 Con.
13. On the judicial branch, *see infra* General Introduction, §2, I.
14. Article 35 Con.
15. Article 6, §1, Special Act of 8 August 1980 Reforming the Institutions.

the territories of the region of Flanders but also in the Brussels Capital Region,[16] the German Community, with as its territory a collection of nine municipalities in the eastern part of Wallonia, bordering Germany,[17] and the French Community, which has jurisdiction in the Brussels Capital Region and in the French-speaking part of the region of Wallonia, that is in Wallonian territory minus the nine municipalities which are recognized as German speaking.[18] The government of each of these three communities has its own executive branch, consisting of a community council of ministers, and a legislative branch, consisting of a community parliament and the council of ministers. The community parliament, however, is not directly elected. It consists of elected members of the regional parliament for the regional territories that fall within the powers of the community. The community ministers are politically responsible to the community parliament. The parliaments of the Flemish Region and the Flemish Community have been merged into one Flemish Parliament, and the executives of the Flemish Region and the Flemish Community have been merged into one Flemish Council of Ministers. Each community government has jurisdiction over listed policy matters that have a cultural or a personal link to the person subject to it, such as culture, education, the use of languages, and certain issues directly related to persons, such as health issues, personal assistance, family policy, integration of immigrants, senior citizens, and juvenile protection.[19]

The complicated result is that Belgium consists of many political governance levels: at the basis, the local municipalities, at the middle level ten subordinate provinces, and at the central level no less than six parliaments and six councils of ministers.

14. Direct elections for members of the different parliaments are based on proportionate representation, so in general, no party is able to obtain an absolute majority. This results in coalition governments at all levels, following relatively strict governance accords reached between the cooperating parties in the coalition. The parliamentary majority, consisting of the members of the political parties in the coalition, supports the coalition council of ministers and approves the bills it introduces, as long as they remain within the boundaries set by the governance accord. As a result, political life in Belgium is more dominated by the political parties and their leaders, than by the actual members of the parliaments.

In the second half of the twentieth century, the traditional three political parties that dominated the country were the (relatively centrist) Christian democrats, the (relatively right wing) liberals, and the (relatively left wing) socialists. Originally, there was one party of each ideology in the country, at the national level, but as the interests of the electorate in the north and the south of the country became more and more opposed, all three parties were split up in a separate Flemish and a separate Walloon party, leaving no federal political parties. This meant that, while a coalition government at the federal level before usually needed only two parties, it now needed at least four parties participating. Although this is not legally required, federal

---

16. *See* Arts. 127, §2, 128, §2, and 129, §2, Con.
17. Article 3, (federal) Act of 31 December 1983 Reforming the Institutions for the German Community.
18. *See* Arts. 127, §2, 128, §2, and 129, §2, Con.
19. Articles 127, §1, 128, §1 and 129, §1, Con. and Arts. 4 and 5, Special Act of 8 August 1980 Reforming the Institutions.

governments tended to be symmetric, meaning that the coalition contained parties from the same ideologies from both the north and the south. Moreover, coalitions tended to have a majority in parliament in both language groups, meaning the federal coalition had political backing in both the north and the south.

Near the end of the twentieth century and in the first two decades of the twenty-first century, the three traditional parties lost ground and were reduced to each representing less than 20% of the electorate. New political parties emerged such as the (relatively left wing) green parties and an (extreme right wing) Flemish nationalist and anti-immigration party, and some older smaller groups became more popular such as the traditional (relatively right-of-center) Flemish nationalist party, which in the elections of 2014 became the largest party in the country. As a result, a coalition could no longer always be formed with just the traditional parties, and the tradition that the federal coalition was symmetrical was given up as well. Moreover, the last two federal coalitions were supported by a majority in parliament but did not have a majority in both language groups within parliament. The result is that government at the federal level is clearly becoming less stable than it used to be.

15. As opposed to in some other federal systems, federal law does not overrule regional or community law in Belgium. The constitutional system assigns subject matter jurisdiction to the different types of governmental level—i.e., the federal State, the regions or the communities—and each has supreme power within its jurisdiction. These competences are considered exclusive, so as opposed to in most other federal systems, Belgium does not know concurrent competences. Federal statutes cannot deal with matters for which the regions or communities have jurisdiction, regional statutes cannot touch issues for which the federal State or the communities have jurisdiction, and community statutes cannot regulate subjects for which the federal State or the regions have jurisdiction. In this system, federal statutes (*loi—wet*) and community or regional statutes (*décret—decreet*) have identical legal value. Any conflict between two of these types of legislation inherently means one of the legislatures has exceeded its constitutional powers. The Constitutional Court has the power to arbitrate in such conflicts and annul federal, regional or community statutes that exceed jurisdiction.[20]

16. Belgium is one of the six original Member States of the European Union. The Constitution explicitly recognizes that a federal statute or treaty can grant international institutions the jurisdiction to exercise certain governmental powers.[21] EU law is recognized to be supreme to national law, which means that citizens can rely on EU law if the relevant provisions have direct effect, even if there is conflicting national law.[22] Civil liability as such is not a field for which the EU has legislative jurisdiction, but specific liability issues can come within EU competence as part of another matter for which the EU has jurisdiction, such as the creation of the internal

20. Article 142 Con.
21. Article 34 Con.
22. *See infra* para. 25.

market[23] or assuring that EU law has *effet utile* by imposing government liability for losses caused by the failure to comply with EU law.[24]

IV. Economic and Social Values

17. Belgium adheres to the traditional continental Western European model of a market economy with strong social corrections. While after World War II, reconstruction and development was advanced through important foreign investment but also the mechanisms of a mixed economy, with public intervention in several sectors including transport, utilities but also banking, the role of government as an active participant in the production of goods and services has significantly decreased. Since the last two decades of the twentieth century, the general move has been to privatize public enterprises. However, the public budgets of all government levels combined still spend over 50% of the gross national product,[25] showing that the public sector remains very important.

18. Private property enjoys constitutional protection against expropriation,[26] and citizens have a fundamental right of association.[27] General freedom of enterprise is legally protected,[28] although several types of activities may be regulated and for some activities, a license is required. Freedom of contract is recognized, although some types of contracts are subject to mandatory rules.[29] Free competition is protected by legal rules that closely follow the EU model.[30] The labor market is relatively strictly regulated, giving the Belgian employees relatively strong protection. There is a very broad system of social security, including pensions, disability benefits, compensation for industrial accidents and professional diseases, child support, unemployment benefits for an unlimited period of time, and mandatory mutual health insurance covering almost the entire population.[31]

23. On this basis the EU has harmonized the law relating to product liability. *See infra* Part III, Ch. 2.
24. *See infra* para. 117.
25. Specific data can be found at http://ec.europa.eu/eurostat/statistics-explained.
26. Article 16 Con.
27. Article 27 Con.
28. Article II.3, CEL.
29. The basis underlying principles of Belgian contract law are very clearly discussed in I. Claeys, "Contract Law", in: M. Kruithof & W. De Bondt (ed.), *Introduction to Belgian Law*, 2d ed., Alphen aan den Rijn: Kluwer Law International, 2017, 227–242.
30. Book IV of the Code of Economic Law (CEL).
31. For a concise overview of Belgian labor and social security law, *see* W. Van Eeckhoutte, "Labour and Social Security Law", in: M. Kruithof & W. De Bondt (ed.), *Introduction to Belgian Law*, 2d ed., Alphen aan den Rijn: Kluwer Law International, 2017, 353–380.

§2. Legal System

I. Position of the Judiciary

19. In Belgium, the judicial function is exercised by two types of courts:[32] ordinary courts, which belong to the judicial branch of the federal government,[33] and administrative courts, which are part of the executive branches of the federal or the federated governments.

20. Of each type of administrative court there is only one, with jurisdiction over the whole territory of the federal or federated entity that established it. The ordinary courts mostly have territorially limited jurisdiction, based on a division of the national territory in several areas.

At the most local level, the subdistricts (*canton—kanton*), there is a justice of the peace court (*justice de paix—vredegerecht*),[34] which has jurisdiction over small claims and claims about matters closely related to local circumstances, including for instance many real estate and neighborly disputes.

At the district level (*arrondissement—arrondissement*) there are several types of courts. The most important one is the court of first instance (*tribunal de première instance—rechtbank van eerste aanleg*),[35] which includes correctional court (*tribunal correctionel—correctionele rechtbank*), a family and juvenile court (*tribunal de la famille et de la jeunesse—familie- en jeugdrechtbank*) and a civil court (*tribunal civil—burgerlijke rechtbank*),[36] and which has general criminal and civil jurisdiction. For civil liability disputes, another important court at the district level is the police court (*tribunal de police—politierechtbank*),[37] which has criminal jurisdiction over all misdemeanors but which also has exclusive jurisdiction over all criminal and civil disputes relating to traffic violations and traffic accidents.

At the higher level, the national territory is divided into five areas (*ressort—rechtsgebied*), with in each area one court of appeal (*cour d'appel—hof van beroep*),[38] a commercial court (*tribunal de commerce—rechtbank van koophandel*) and a labor court (*tribunal de travail—arbeidsrechtbank*),[39] and a labor court of appeal (*cour du travail—arbeidshof*).[40]

At the top of the pyramid, there is one Court of Cassation (*Cour de cassation—Hof van Cassatie*) for the whole territory of Belgium, sitting in Brussels.[41]

---

32. For more information, *see* P. Taelman & C. Van Severen, "The Judicial System and Civil Procedure", in: M. Kruithof & W. De Bondt (ed.), *Introduction to Belgian Law*, 2d ed., Alphen aan den Rijn: Kluwer Law International, 2017, 81–127.
33. Article 40 Con. There is no judicial branch of government at the level of the federated entities in Belgium.
34. Articles 59 and 61 JC; Art. 2 JC Supplement.
35. Article 73 JC; Art. 3 JC Supplement.
36. Article 76 JC.
37. Articles 60–61 JC; Art. 3 JC Supplement.
38. Article 156 Con.
39. Article 73 JC; Art. 4 JC Supplement.
40. Article 73 JC; Art. 103 JC.
41. Article 147, para. 1, Con.; Art. 6 JC Supplement.

21. In general, civil procedure includes potentially three instances.

Only small claims are heard in first and second instances at once.[42] Against most decisions, however, appeal is possible to a higher level court without restriction. Thus, appeals against judgments from the justice of the peace court and the police court are heard by a court of first instance or a commercial court, depending on whether the subject matter is commercial or not. Appeals against first instance judgments of the court of first instance and the commercial courts are brought before a court of appeal. Appeals against judgments from the labor courts go to a labor court of appeal. Appeal is not limited to points of law: also, questions of fact can be retried at the appellate level, resulting in an overload of casework for the appellate level courts.

After the second instance at the appellate level, there is no general third instance available. Only a petition for cassation is available at the Court of Cassation. This Court does not have jurisdiction to find facts or decide on factual disputes.[43] It can only decide whether a decision by a lower fact-finding court is consistent with the law. If it finds a lower decision to violate the law, it will annul this judgment and send the case to another lower court of the same level, which then will decide on the facts and the law again. However, since mid-2017, this lower court is bound by the decision of the Court of Cassation.[44] The Court of Cassation therefore functions as the keeper of unity in the interpretation of the law in all courts belonging to the judicial branch of government.

22. All career judges and justices in the judiciary are appointed for life (i.e., until they reach the retirement age)[45] by the King, under political responsibility of the Minister of Justice, on the nomination of the High Council of Justice,[46] an institution created in the Constitution that does not belong to any of the three branches of government, and which functions to depoliticize the appointment of judges.[47] This High Council consists of representatives of judges, elected by their peers, and non-judges are appointed by the federal Senate.[48] The labor and commercial courts, however, also have lay-judges, which are representatives of the respective professional fields. Judges and justices are independent in the exercise of their adjudicative powers.[49] This independence is reinforced by a statutory immunity from civil liability. Only in cases of fraud, when a judge refuses to decide a case, or when a statute specifically imposes liability, recourse can be had against a judge.[50]

23. The division of adjudicative jurisdiction among the ordinary courts and the administrative courts is based on the type of dispute that has to be decided. First, a distinction is made between what are called subjective and objective disputes. Subjective

42. Article 617 JC, setting the limit at EUR 2,500 for decisions of courts of first instance and commercial courts and at EUR 1,860 for decisions of justice of the peace courts and police courts.
43. Article 147, para. 2, Con.
44. Article 1110, para. 4, JC, as inserted by (federal) Act of 7 July 2017.
45. Article 152 Con.
46. Article 259*bis*/9 JC.
47. Article 151 Con.
48. Article 259*bis*/2, §§1–2, JC.
49. Article 151 Con.
50. Article 1140 JC.

disputes involve a claim by a person or legal entity based on a subjective right, demanding a specific action or attitude from another legal subject. Objective disputes involve a demand for the court to judge on the validity of acts of government. Second, within the category of subjective disputes, a distinction is made between disputes involving claims based on what are called civil rights and claims based on political rights.

The ordinary courts have exclusive jurisdiction over subjective disputes involving civil rights.[51] This includes criminal proceedings and most types of civil disputes, irrespective of the type of parties involved.[52] These courts can also hear cases involving political rights, but for such disputes the federal, regional and community legislatures can create separate administrative courts, which are not part of the executive branch of government.[53]

The ordinary courts can decide on the legality of acts of administration from the executive branch of government. However, while the judiciary must refuse to apply administrative acts that are illegal or unconstitutional,[54] they cannot annul such acts, as this is considered part of the executive function that the Constitution has granted to the executive branch of government. For objective disputes involving a claim to annul an act of administration, special administrative courts have been created. The most important is the federal Council of State (*Conseil d'état—Raad van State*).[55] Recently, an amendment to the Constitution has made it possible for the legislature to grant jurisdiction to the Council of State to decide also on the consequences under civil law of its decisions finding a governmental act to be illegal.[56] This has been implemented, so citizens that suffer losses caused by an illegal administrative act can now not only try to recover damages based on civil liability in a court belonging to the judicial branch, but also based on an administrative compensation option in the Council of State.[57]

24. The ordinary and administrative courts do not have jurisdiction over the constitutionality of statutes.[58] For such rulings, the Constitutional Court (*Cour*

51. Article 144 Con.
52. Disputes between a private person and a public entity or the government that are based on subjective civil rights are also adjudicated by the ordinary courts. Belgium does not know a system of a separate court or courts for proceedings against the government.
53. Article 145 Con. Examples are the federal Council for Disputes regarding Aliens (*Conseil du contentieux des étrangers—Raad voor vreemdelingenbetwistingen*; *see* www.rvv-cce.be), which decides on disputes under the (federal) Act of 15 December 1980 on the Entrance to the Territory, Stay, Residency and Removal of Foreigners, and the Flemish Council for Disputes regarding Permits (*Raad voor Vergunningsbetwistingen*; *see* www.dbrc.be/raad-voor-vergunningsbetwistingen), which decides disputes about zoning and urband planning permits (Art. 4.8.1 Flemish Zoning and Urban Planning Codex; Art. 105 Flemish Zoning Act of 25 April 2014; Flemish Act of 4 April 2014 on the Organization and Procedure of Some Flemish Administrative Courts).
54. Article 159 Con.
55. Article 160 Con.; (federal) Coordinated Act of 12 January 1973 on the Council of State.
56. Article 144, para. 2, Con.
57. *See infra* para. 114.
58. Already in Cass. 27 June 1845, *Pas.* 1845, 392, the Court held that Arts. 1382 et seq. CC are not applicable to statutes.

constitutionnelle—Grondwettelijk Hof)—formerly the Court of Arbitration (*Cour d'arbitrage—Arbitragehof*)—has exclusive jurisdiction.[59] It can hear cases directly brought by a petition for the annulment of a specific federal, regional or community statute,[60] but it can also provide preliminary rulings on the constitutionality of certain statutory provisions, after hearing a preliminary reference from another ordinary or administrative court.[61] In the latter type of procedure, the unconstitutional provision is not annulled, but the ordinary or administrative court is given the permission to ignore it.

25. Consistent with EU law,[62] Belgian law allows any court to ignore a rule of national law if it conflicts with a rule of EU law that has direct effect, even if the national rule is statutory.[63] Belgian courts regularly reference for a preliminary ruling by the EU Court of Justice (hereinafter "ECJ") on issues of interpretation of rules of EU law.[64]

II. Distinction Between Public and Private Law

26. The classic continental European *summa divisio* between public and private law can be found in the curricula of law schools in Belgian universities, in the organization of books in law libraries and in the titles and subject matter delineations of treatises. In its simple laymen's form, the distinction is explained as if private law contains the rules applicable to relations between private citizens, while public law contains the rules applicable to relations between public or governmental entities and citizens or between public entities among themselves. This, however, does not correctly reflect Belgian law as it is applied, nor as it is understood by lawyers.

During the first half of the nineteenth century, there were court decisions that excluded the application of rules of private law to public or governmental entities, based on the idea that rules of private law are only applicable to relations between private citizens.[65] However, from 1852 on, the Court of Cassation has made it clear that civil law—and by extension more generally private law—is of general application and therefore also applicable to public entities and government, except when a statute provides otherwise or when the act of the public entity to which the rule of private

59. Article 142 Con.
60. Articles 1–25 Special Act of 6 January 1989 on the Constitutional Court.
61. Articles 26–30 Special Act of 6 January 1989 on the Constitutional Court.
62. ECJ, *NV Algemene Transport- en Expeditie Onderneming van Gend & Loos v. Netherlands Inland Revenue Administration*, Case No. 26-62, ECLI:EU:C:1963:1, decision of 5 February 1963, ECR 1963, 3; ECJ, *Flaminio Costa v. E.N.E.L.*, Case No. 6/64, ECLI:EU:C:1964:66, decision of 15 July 1964, ECR 1964, 1141.
63. Cass. 27 May 1971, *Arr.Cass.* 1971, 959, *Pas.* 1971, 886, usually referred to as the *Fromagerie Le Ski* decision.
64. For statistics, *see* the Annual Reports on Judicial Activity of the EU Court of Justice at CURIA (https://curia.europa.eu/jcms).
65. *See* Cass. 23 February 1850, *Pas.* 1850, 163, at p. 172, refusing the application of the rule of vicarious liability in Art. 1384, para. 3, CC to losses caused by government personnel, because this rule, as part of civil law, is only applicable to master-servants relations between citizens for private purposes.

law has to be applied is a public act.[66] Whether an act of government is public or private in nature depends on the characteristics of the act itself, and not the purpose of the public entity engaging in it. In other words, when a public entity engages in acts that a private person could also engage in, the rules of private law are applicable. This legal reality means that while public law can be defined as those rules that specifically govern the relations between a public entity and private entities and the relations between public entities amongst each other, private law must be defined as those rules that govern the relations *that can exist* between citizens or private entities.

27. Although this classic terminology is still widely used, one can also detect that it is not based on a generally accepted underlying concept, as specific areas of the law are not categorized in the same manner by all authors. Some branches of the law are difficult to place within one of the two categories, because they contain both rules that have a private nature and rules that have a public nature. Social law is a good example: this branch of the law includes both rules applicable to relations that can exist between private employers and employees but also contain rules that specifically govern the relation between private entities and the government or quasi-governmental entities. Economic law is another branch of the law containing rules applicable to relations that can exist among private persons but also rules that are public in nature.

More damaging for the *divisio*, however, is the fact that a classic branch of the law such as civil procedure is brought under the umbrella of private law by many authors because it contains the rules applicable to judicial proceedings between private parties, while of course this branch of the law contains the rules that apply to the exercise of the quintessential public judicial function of the government. Its content can also be viewed as the law implementing constitutional principles for the judicial function of the government in much the same way as administrative law implements constitutional principles for the executive function of the government, making it quintessential public law.

28. The distinction between private and public law is also much less relevant for Belgian positive law as it works in reality than one might think, because through the mechanism of the so-called unity theory, which considers any illegality or breach of a statutory or regulatory rule of conduct as a civil wrong leading to civil liability for the losses it causes,[67] rules of public law applicable to the relation between a private entity and a public entity become also relevant in the relation between the private entity that violates such rules and another private entity that suffers a loss because of it. What is more, procedural mechanisms such as a petition for an injunction, prohibiting behavior of a private citizen that violates certain statutory rules, can under certain conditions be instituted by other private entities. In this way, rules of policing public law that prohibit certain behavior in fact become part of the law applicable to the relation between private parties among themselves.

66. *See* Cass. 27 May 1852, *Pas.* 1852, 370, at p. 391.
67. *See infra* Part I, Ch. 1, §3.

III. Legislation Versus Case Law

29. The classic narrative of Belgian law wants us to believe that law is made by the legislature(s) and that courts only interpret and apply the law to particular cases. Thus, statutes and codes are considered to be the primary sources of legal rules—as if most rules would be created by legislatures—and to be the highest rules in the hierarchy, supreme over any ruling by a court.[68] Courts are supposed to decide actual cases, but not allowed to impose rules.[69]

30. This classic positivistic rendition of Belgian law does not faithfully and completely reflect legal reality.

First, legislation is only legally valid if it is consistent with the Constitution. The Constitutional Court has the exclusive power to decide on the constitutionality of statutory provisions, so in that sense, this Court sets the hierarchically highest rules, which the legislature has to obey. Of course, the Constitutional Court is limited in its freedom by the text of the Constitution that it interprets, but as is well known, present day principles of constitutional interpretation allow this Court to in reality to a large extent set the boundaries of the legislative freedom of the legislature.

Second, statutory rules only receive their true legal content when they are applied to a specific case by courts. Thus, the statutory rule in legal reality means what the courts say it means. As Belgian courts tend to interpret statutory rules rather freely,[70] not feeling too restricted by the specific wording of the text and often choosing for a meaning based on the rationale or the function of the provision, again the courts tend to have a much more important role in actual law making than the classic narrative would have one think.

31. Courts rule on individual cases, and do not have the power to legislate. This does not only mean that one court is never bound by the interpretation of the law given by another court in another case[71]—there is no formal system of legal precedent in Belgian law—but it also means that the legal value of a court decision does not reside in its specific wording or text. The legislature makes rules, and does so by pronouncing certain specifically formulated abstract texts. This text is a legal formant, and has itself a legal value. The courts, when interpreting and applying this text, are bound in the sense that they can only give the statute a meaning that can be reconciled with the text. The courts, however, are specifically prohibited from doing this: they can only

68. *See* M. Van Hoecke & S. Vandenbogaerde, "Basic Features of the Belgian Legal System", in: M. Kruithof & W. De Bondt (ed.), *Introduction to Belgian Law*, 2d ed., Alphen aan den Rijn: Kluwer Law International, 2017, 25–48, at pp. 27–28.

69. Article 6 JC forbids judges to decide cases by general orders that apply as a rule.

70. *See* M. Van Hoecke & S. Vandenbogaerde, "Basic Features of the Belgian Legal System", in: M. Kruithof & W. De Bondt (ed.), *Introduction to Belgian Law*, 2d ed., Alphen aan den Rijn: Kluwer Law International, 2017, 25–48, at p. 29, stating that Belgian courts tend to eclectically follow the method of interpretation—grammatical, systemic, intentional, historical or teleological—that in the particular case is able to underpin the result that is desired on other, mostly not explicitly stated (policy) grounds.

71. As was mentioned, the lower court that has to decide after referral by the Court of Cassation is since mid-2017 bound by the decision of this supreme court. *See supra* para. 21.

take specific individual decisions.[72] They cannot pronounce an abstract, binding text. Only the content of their actual or concrete decision is binding, not the formulation of it or the wording used. However, given that the principle of equal protection is part of Belgian positive law,[73] and the courts have to obey this principle as well,[74] the consistent manner in which courts decide certain cases becomes to a certain extent binding on the courts. This is not because a specific rule has been pronounced by a court or the courts, but because their actual decisions reveal a certain systematic treatment of a type of case, which has to be maintained in future cases because of the requirement of equal treatment of citizens by the government. The legal rules as they actually govern disputes, i.e., positive law, are therefore the principles that *a posteriori* can be derived from the actual decisions courts take in like cases, not in the words courts use or the rules courts explicitly invoke to justify the decisions they actually take.

32. However, in spite of this legal reality, Belgian courts tend to use the phrasing and vocabulary of legal positivism. From the Court of Cassation, this can be understood as a way to legally justify its decisions. The Court of Cassation has limited jurisdiction: it can only annul decisions of lower courts when they violate rules that are part of the so-called written law, i.e., rules imposed by the Constitution, federal, regional or community statutes, regulations from all governmental levels, and rules contained in international instruments such as treaties, EU regulations and directives.[75] Strictly speaking, the Court cannot overrule a decision of a lower court because it violates customary law, case law or legal tradition. In reality, however, the Court does base its decisions also on legal rules that are not really imposed by written law, but it feels compelled to always invoke a specific statutory provision as a basis for such decision. This leads to sometimes rather artificial reasonings in the Court's decisions, basing relatively plain legal rules that are generally recognized and as such not disputed on specific statutory provisions which historically have nothing to do with this rule and/

72. Article 84 Con. states that only the legislature can give the "authentic interpretation" of statutes, and Article 6 JC forbids judges to decide cases by general orders that apply as a rule.
73. Articles 10–11 Con.
74. Already a long time ago, the Court of Cassation confirmed that the courts have to interpret statutes if possible consistent with the Constitution. *See* Cass. 20 April 1950, *Pas.* 1950, 560, *Arr. Verbr.* 1950, 517. The Constitutional Court also accepts this principle. *See* Con.C. No. 9/90 of 7 February 1990; Con.C. No. 71/92 of 18 November 1992; Con.C. No. 16/99, 10 February 1999; Con.C. No. 201/2005 of 21 December 2005, para. B.4.3; Con.C. No. 180/2011 of 24 November 2011, para. B.4.2.3. The Constitutional Court does not have jurisdiction to review judicial decisions on their constitutionality, but the Court does use its power to review the constitutionality of statutes to indicate to the judicial courts that a statute is in itself not unconstitutional if several interpretations are possible and one of them does not violate the constitution. *See* e.g. Con.C. No. 32/96 of 15 May 1996; Con.C. No. 29/97 of 21 May 1997; Con.C. No. 67/97 of 6 November 1997; Con.C. No. 92/2010 of 29 July 2010, para. B.4.2; Con.C. No. 7/2017 of 25 January 2017.
75. Article 608 JC.

or which contain text which cannot be read to include such rule either.[76] Of course, the Court could solve this problem by explicitly admitting that its jurisdiction includes reviewing court decisions under any rule of law, but as this would be admitting openly that the courts are not restricted to interpreting and applying rules imposed by the legislature, this apparently is not an option.

IV. Sources of Tort Law

33. The core of Belgian civil liability law is still formulated as rules based on the six articles the Civil Code (available online)[77] devotes to the subject. These articles have remained largely unchanged since their version in the 1804 Napoleonic Code.[78]

However, these provisions are extremely vague, and leave most of the task of deciding the content of the rules that can actually decide cases to the courts. If one wants to know what specific rules these articles impose, one can only find out by either researching the case law or consulting literature of authors that have done so. In this sense, the most important source of Belgian tort law in the sense of the place where the content of this branch of the law can be found, are in practice the overviews of case law that are systematically published about every five to ten years in law journals.[79]

34. Case law is not only the place where the rules of Belgian civil liability can be found, it is also in reality the most important source of civil liability law in the sense that most of the actual specific liability rules originally were created by the courts. Interestingly, the case law reveals many liability rules that actually predate the Napoleonic codification and that, although nowadays formally presented as if they were based on these statutory provisions, are in fact much older rules that are based on tradition. Over the last century and a half, the courts have also expanded on the

76. Examples include the Court of Cassation's decision to base the tort of nuissance, which in reality is part of traditional law, on Art. 544 CC, the provision which defines the subjective right of property (Cass. 6 April 1960 (two decisions), *Pas.* 1960, 920, *Arr. Verbr.* 1960, 722), but also the Court's decision to base the rule imposing product liability on professional sellers, which based on the principle *spondet peritiam artis, et imperitia culpae adnumeratur* has been part of the law long before the Napoleonic codification, on Art. 1645 CC, a provision which historically only relates to the liability of sellers that act in bad faith, knowingly selling defective goods (Cass. 4 May 1939, *Pas.* 1939, 223). An example of a newly introduced legal rule which the Court artificially based on a statutory provision which historically did not have this meaning is the strict liability for losses caused by defective goods, which the Court linked to Art. 1384, para. 1, CC (Cass. 26 May 1904, *Pas.* 1904, 246).

77. The Civil Code in its present content can be found at www.ejustice.just.fgov.be/loi/loi.htm, choosing "Code civil" in the pull down menu called "Nature juridique."

78. Only two amendments have been made. In 1935, a sixth provision was added to deal with the liability of the mentally ill (Art. 1386*bis*), which recently underwent a minor change in terminology (amended by (federal) Act of 5 May 2014 on Involuntary Commitment, in effect since 1 October 2016), and in 1977, Art. 1384, para. 2, was modernized to place the vicarious liability of fathers and mothers for damage caused by their minor children on equal footing.

79. These overviews, written by different authors, are published in the Flemish *Tijdschrift voor Privaatrecht* (available online at www.tpr.be) and in the French *Journal des Tribunaux* and *Revue critique de jurisprudence belge*.

principles enumerated in the Civil Code and developed several *torts*, i.e., separate bases for civil liability, outside of the law as it existed at the beginning of the nineteenth century. Examples are a strict liability for losses caused by defective goods,[80] a liability for nuisance,[81] and most recently a governmental liability for suffering an unequal share of the burden of public intervention.[82]

One says, therefore, that civil liability law is a branch of the law where Belgian law to a significant extent functions as if it were a *common law* system and not a classic *civil law* system in the sense that the legal rules are *a priori* and in the abstract formulated by the legislature and do not come about as a result of the actual decisions of several specific cases.

35. Over the last 200 years, the legislature of course has also added to the arsenal of liability rules.[83] First, some separate statutes, outside of the Civil Code, systematically deal with and regulate particular civil liabilities. Examples include liability for losses caused by fire or explosion in facilities that are open to the public,[84] liability for nuclear accidents,[85] and liability for losses caused by personnel of public entities[86] and members of local government.[87] Second, many statutes or even codes regulating another area of the law include some provisions dealing with civil liability in that area. To list only a few examples, the civil liability of corporate officers is dealt with in the Companies Code,[88] prospectus liability is regulated in the statute regulating IPO's and admission of financial instruments to a regulated market,[89] and liability of architects is regulated in the statute dealing with the rules of that profession.[90]

36. Civil liability in general is a subject matter not specifically attributed by the Constitution to the regions, so it remains a federal matter.[91] However, the Constitutional Court has ruled that in the absence of a constitutional provision stating otherwise, the regions have complete legislative jurisdiction in the matters within their constitutionally

80. *See infra* Part III, Ch. 1.
81. *See infra* Part I, Ch. 2, §5.
82. *See infra* para. 119.
83. Statutory law can be found at www.ejustice.just.fgov.be/loi/loi.htm, choosing the type of legislative act in the pull down menu called "Nature juridique" and filling out the date of promulgation.
84. (Federal) Act of 30 July 1979 on the Prevention of and Liability for Fire and Explosions, which introduced a strict liability of the person exploiting the public facility.
85. *See* e.g. the (federal) Act of 9 August 1963 on the Liability of the Person Exploiting a Nuclear Ship; the (federal) Act of 22 July 1985 on the Statutory Liability in the field of Nuclear Energy.
86. Act of 10 February 2003 on the Liability of and for Personnel of Public Entities.
87. Act of 4 May 1999 on the Civil Liability of Mayors, Members of Municipal Governments and Members of Provincial Governments.
88. *See* H. DE WULF, "Company Law" in M. KRUITHOF & W. DE BONDT (ed.), *Introduction to Belgian Law*, 2d ed., Alphen aan den Rijn: Kluwer Law International, 2017, 309–351, pp. 344–346.
89. Article 61, §2, (federal) Act of 16 June 2006 on the Public Offering of Investment Instruments and the Admission of Instruments to Trading on a Regulated Market.
90. (Federal) Act of 20 February 1939 on the Protection of the Title and of the Profession of Architect.
91. *See supra* para. 13.

attributed competences.[92] This means that the regions can introduce rules of private law that deviate from the rules in the Civil Code as long as these rules fit in their policy on issues within their subject matter jurisdiction.[93] It is therefore accepted that the Flemish region, having jurisdiction in matters of environmental protection, can introduce a statutory rule rendering the holder of a license for underground storage of carbon dioxide liable for all losses caused by activities under this license.[94] However, a generally applicable regional rule of strict liability for industrial activities would be unconstitutional, as this would exceed the specific subject matter jurisdiction attributed to the regions. If a region has introduced specific liability rules, they will cumulatively apply on top of the federal liability rules.[95]

The number of regional liability rules is relatively limited, but growing. Several relate to the attribution of costs for environmental cleanup operations undertaken by the administration.[96] Some regional statutes render the regional government immune from liability[97] or limit the liability of certain civil servants.[98]

37. Of course, Belgian civil liability law undergoes the influence of international law, just like the law of any other modern nation participating in globalization. There are several liability rules part of Belgian national law that are the national implementation of liability principles agreed in international treaties. For instance, environmental liability is significantly set at an international level.[99] The European Convention for the Protection of Human Rights and Fundamental Freedoms of 1950, as amended and with additional protocols (in short the "European Convention on Human Rights" or "ECHR") has an important influence on the content of civil liability law,[100] and can in particular serve as a basis for government liability in cases of violations of fundamental rights.

EU law is of growing importance for civil liability, not only because some specific liability issues are harmonized at the level of the internal market, such as for instance

92. C.Arb. No. 61/2004 of 31 March 2004, para. B.4.1.
93. C.Arb. No. 61/2004 of 31 March 2004, para. B.4.1 and B.4.2; Con.C. No. 101/2008 of 10 July 2008, para. B.23.1; Con.C. No. 8/2011 of 27 January 2011, para. B.6.1.5.
94. *See* Art. 62, Flemish Act of 8 May 2009 on the Deep Underground.
95. C.Arb. No. 61/2004 of 31 March 2004, para. B.6.3.
96. *See* Arts. 16, 25 and 134 of Flemish Act of 27 October 2006 on Soil Cleanup and Soil Protection.
97. *See* e.g. Flemish Act of 16 June 2006 on the Guiding Shipping on Maritime Entrance Routes and the Organization of the Maritime Rescue and Coordination Center; Flemish Act of 14 March 2008 on the Information on Underground Cabels and Pipelines.
98. *See* e.g. Flemish Act of 24 December 2008 on the Organisation of the Public Welfare Centers, the Flemish Act of 23 January 2009 amending the Flemish Municipalities Act and the Flemish Act of 30 April 2009 amending the Flemish Provinces Act.
99. For example, International Convention on Civil Liability for Oil Pollution Damage of 29 November 1969, as amended; Convention on Third Party Liability in the Field of Nuclear Energy of 29th July 1960 and the Brussels Supplementary Convention of 31 January 1963; the Convention on the International Liability for Damage Caused by Space Objects of 29 March 1972, UNTS Vol. 961,1-13810, the European Convention on the Liability of Hotel-keepers concerning the Property of their Guests of 17 December 1962, ETS No. 041.
100. *See* the recent PhD of S. Somers, *Aansprakelijkheidsrecht en mensenrechten: kruisbestuiving in een meergelaagde rechtsorde*, Antwerp: Intersentia, 2016.

product liability,[101] but also because the liability of EU for losses caused by its institutions or by its servants in the performance of their duties,[102] as developed by the case law of the ECJ, also serve as the basis for the civil liability of Member States for losses caused by a violation of EU law.[103]

38. Doctrine in legal literature is probably more important as a source in the field of civil liability than in other branches of law in Belgium. There are relatively few treatises or handbooks that cover the whole field of civil liability without covering a wider range, such as the whole field of the law of obligations.[104] Most scholarly or academic contributions are published as articles or chapters in conference books and in some law journals, although most publications in Belgian law journals tend to be very descriptive, more comparable to publications in professional journals in the US and not scholarly or academic such as the publications in the major law journals in the USA. More in depth academic contributions can be found in the Dutch *Tijdschrift voor Privaatrecht* and the French *Revue critique de jurisprudence belge*.

§3. Function of Civil Liability Law

39. The function of a social phenomenon is the need it is intended to fulfill.[105]

Civil liability is a source of obligations. Once liability (*responsabilité—aansprakelijkheid*) is established, one party—the victim (*victime—slachtoffer*)—has a claim for restoration of his harm against the other party—the person held liable (*le responsable—de aansprakelijke*). Because liability law (*droit de la responsabilité—aansprakelijkheidsrecht*) in many cases that are brought before the courts results in

101. Council Directive 85/374/EEC of 25 July 1985 on the approximation of the laws, regulations and administrative provisions of the Member States concerning liability for defective products, as amended, is implemented in Belgium by the (federal) Act of 25 February 1991 on the Liability for Defective Products. *See infra* Part III, Ch. 2.

102. Article 340 of the Treaty on the Functioning of the European Union.

103. *See* O. Dörr (ed.), *Staatshaftung in Europa. Nationales und Unionsrecht*, Berlin/Boston: De Gruyter, 2013; K. Oliphant (ed.), *The Liability of Public Authorities in Comparative Perspective*, Cambridge: Intersentia, 2016.

104. In Dutch there are two to mention, the treatise by T. Vansweevelt & B. Weyts, *Handboek Buitencontractueel* Aansprakelijkheidsrecht, Antwerp: Intersentia, 2009, 935 p. and the handbook by H. Bocken & I. Boone with M. Kruithof, *Inleiding tot het Schadevergoedingsrecht. Buitencontractueel Aansprakelijkheidsrecht en Andere Schadevergoedingsstelsels*, Bruges: die Keure, 2014, 270 p. In French, there is no recent treatise or handbook just covering noncontractual civil liability. There is a looseleaf collection of articles on the different topics in civil liability: *Responsabilités: Traité théorique et pratique*, Waterloo: Kluwer. The most important older treatise is R.O. Dalcq, *Traité de la responsabilité civile*, 2 vol., Brussels: Larcier, 1959 and 1962, 667 and 821 p. The only recent books cover the broader field of the law of obligations, including also contracts, such as P. Van Ommeslaghe, *Les obligations*, 3 vol., Tome II in *De Page Traité de droit civil belge*, Brussels: Bruylant, 2013, 2814 p., and P. Wéry, *Droit des obligations*, 2 vol., Brussels: Larcier, 2011 and 2016, 1044 and 1016 p.

105. *See* E. Durkheim, *De la division du travail social*, Vol. I, 1893, digital edition based on the 8th edition published by Les Presses Universitaires de France, Paris, 1967, 55 (available via http://classiques.uqac.ca).

liability, most Belgian scholars that write about tort law assume without much analysis that the function of liability law is to compensate victims for their losses.

Even though it is generally accepted in Belgian legal literature, this view neglects the legal reality that the most basic rule of liability law is that *the loss lies where it falls*. Only when all constituent elements of liability are present, liability law grants the victim a right to compensation and imposes a duty to compensate on the person held liable. When the constituent elements of liability are not met, however, the intended result of liability law is to deny the victim compensation. Even though there are more court cases ending in liability than in a denial of liability, there are in legal reality many more instances—i.e., "cases" including those disputed and those not disputed—in which liability law results in no liability. Shifting the financial burden of an existing loss from the victim to another person in certain circumstances by declaring this person liable and leaving the burden of the loss for the victim in other circumstances are therefore both part of the function of liability law.

So while the function of *liability*—which is only one of the possible results of the application of liability law—may be to compensate victims for losses suffered, the function of *liability law* itself is not to compensate for losses suffered but rather to determine whether liability will attach. Therefore, the function of liability law is more properly stated as the allocation and/or distribution of the financial burden of losses between victims and other persons that in some way can influence the occurrence of the loss.[106]

Unfortunately, most Belgian authors do not make the distinction between the function of liability and the function of liability law, and some continue to argue for victim-friendly interpretations of rules of liability law based on the sole argument that their function is to compensate victims. Some courts also seem to have sympathy for such reasoning, resulting in a relatively claimant friendly climate in Belgium.

40. The limitations of liability as a system for compensating victims in today's industrialized and consumerist welfare society—where people are vulnerable to more types of risks causing greater harm but at the same time are less prepared to accept misfortunes and have increased expectations to be shielded from losses—have resulted in the creation of alternative compensation mechanisms in the course of the twentieth century. First, the development of a system of social security, including generalized, mutualized and partially publicly financed health insurance, provides compensation for medical costs irrespective of their cause and for lost income in the form of benefits.[107] Second, the popularization of commercial first party insurance means that victims often can shift the financial burden of harm to their insurer. Third, the legislature has created compensation mechanisms for certain risks—such as industrial accidents, traffic accidents and recently medical accidents.[108] As a result, a large fraction of harm

106. Alternative loss compensation systems which shift the burden of certain losses from the victim to another person who is in no way connected to the causation of the loss, such the general system of compensation for certain losses caused by traffic accidents (*infra* para. 167), accidents in the workplace (*infra* para. 281), and certain medical accidents (*infra* para. 87), do not result in "liability" and are therefore not considered to be part of liability law in the true sense.
107. (Federal) Coordinated Mandatory Health Insurance Act of 14 July 1994, here in short "MHIA."
108. *See infra* paras. 87, 167 and 281.

is shifted from the victim to insurance companies, the social security system and different compensation funds.

Many of these institutions are statutorily subrogated in the victim's right to restoration based on civil liability to the extent they have compensated the harm. While civil liability may today in practice be less the primary basis for compensation of victims, it thus remains crucial as the system of allocation of the ultimate financial burden of the compensation of harm.

As nowadays third-party insurance is increasingly used—the legislature has even made such insurance mandatory for certain types of risk[109]—the person held liable can shift the financial burden of this liability to his insurer. Under Belgian law, a victim has a direct claim for compensation based on his own right against the liability insurer of the person liable for his harm.[110] In practice, therefore, civil liability law is more and more a matter relevant for disputes among insurers, appearing both as (subrogated) claimants and as defendants in many of the court cases that have elaborated the principles of this branch of law.[111]

41. Several authors recognize that liability law also has preventive effects. On the one hand, this can be the result of a court ordering the person held liable to take specific measures to undo the factual situation which caused the initial loss for the victim.[112] In that case, the court decision that orders specific restoration for losses already suffered in effect also prevents future losses from occurring. On the other hand, liability has, of course, also the general effect of internalizing the costs of losses, which are externalities of the actions causing them. This creates incentives to avoid behavior that results in liability, and thereby has at least theoretically the effect of preventing losses from occurring.

In general, however, while Belgian authors recognize that liability law has this preventing *effect*, they more rarely invoke the prevention of losses as the *function* of liability law. One does not find many Belgian court decisions or scholarly pieces arguing that an existing rule of liability should be interpreted in a certain way because that meaning serves to optimally prevent losses by providing the proper incentives. While the law and economics literature has received some attention in Belgian academia, one has to acknowledge that so far legal practice and the content of existing Belgian positive law has not yet been significantly influenced by this view. To the contrary, many courts and legal scholars remain relatively hostile or at least skeptical about the view that liability law serves to enforce efficient behavior.

42. Recently, more attention has been paid by scholars to the potential punitive function of liability. In certain instances of persistent lucrative faults—i.e., faults that result in a gain for the wrongdoer that is larger than the losses caused to the victims,

109. For a list of mandatory insurance in Belgium, *see* the website of the Financial Services and Markets Authority (FSMA), the government agency supervising the insurance market and insurance products (www.fsma.be).

110. Article 150 (federal) Insurance Act of 4 April 2014.

111. Even if the defendant in a suit is the person allegedly liable, it often is his insurer that in fact is leading the defense, as Art. 143, para. 2, Federal Insurance Act of 4 April 2014 grants the liability insurer the exclusive power to lead the defense in cases where the potential obligation to compensate the claimant falls within the insurance guarantee.

112. *See infra* paras. 217–218.

leaving the wrongdoer with a net profit even after compensating the victim for his losses—claimants and courts are looking for ways to impose sanctions that can provide sufficient incentives to avoid the wrongful behavior. Some authors have pleaded for the introduction of the possibility for judges to impose punitive damages, i.e., damages that are higher than the amount of losses actually suffered. Most authors, however, remain hostile to the idea that the victim could profit from the liability, and therefore seem more sympathetic to the idea of a system of punitive damages that are paid to the government instead of to the victim.

There are no court decisions yet that openly impose punitive damages. The Court of Cassation has stuck to the traditional position that damages based on liability have to correspond to actual losses suffered by the victim because of the fact for which the person held liable is responsible. In an important ruling, the Court has reversed a decision of the Court of Appeal of Liège that had awarded the holder of an infringed intellectual property right extra damages in the amount of 25% over the amount of the unlawfully avoided licensing fee. The Liège Court had based this decision on the argument that such extra damages are necessary to finance the global battle against violations of intellectual property and to provide for an incentive for third parties to seek the permission of the right holder before exploiting an idea protected by an intellectual property right. The Court of Cassation pointed out that these arguments do not justify a finding that these extra damages serve to compensate for actual losses caused by this particular infringement, which is what the law in its view requires.[113]

43. However, one cannot ignore the reality that there are typical case settings, such as cases involving the bad faith infringement of personality rights among which the right to privacy and the right to one's image by the media for commercial purposes,[114] and cases involving bad faith infringement of intellectual property rights,[115] in which lower courts in reality tend to grant "damages" which cannot really be explained as mere compensation of losses actually suffered. One can, however, wonder whether these decisions should be understood as based on liability, which would mean one has to recognize that liability can lead to noncompensating remedies, even though this is inconsistent with generally accepted basic principles. It is the view of the author of this overview, that these decisions should not be understood as examples of noncompensatory remedies based on civil liability, but rather as examples of the courts ordering disgorgement of profits as a distinct remedy against bad faith infringements of subjective rights, i.e., a remedy not based on civil liability but based directly on the infringed subjective right itself.[116] This view explains why such awards that in fact grant more than compensation can only be found in court decisions on cases where the fault

113. Cass. 13 May 2009 (P.09.0121.F), No. 314, *Pas.* 2009, 1167, *Arr.Cass.* 2009, 1254.

114. *See infra* para. 106.

115. *See* e.g. CA Ghent 19 January 2009, *AM* 2009, 384; CA Antwerp 13 October 2008, *AM* 2009, 391. *See also* the examples of more recent not (yet) published decisions reported in J. Deene & L. De Cort, "Intellectuele rechten kroniek 2011", *NJW* 2012, 438–452, at p. 443, No. 31, and in J. Deene, "Intellectuele rechten kroniek 2010", *NJW* 2011, 442–449, at p. 449, No. 49.

116. *See* M. Kruithof, "Disgorgement of Profits in Belgian Private Law", in: E. Hondius & A. Janssen (ed.), *Disgorgement of Profits. Gain-Based Remedies throughout the World*, Cham: Springer, 2015, 89–120.

consisted in the infringement of intellectual property rights and personality rights, and not in cases involving other types of lucrative faults.

§4. Relationship Between Civil Liability and Criminal Liability

44. As will be discussed later, under Belgian liability law a person who is culpable of a violation of a legal rule that imposes or prohibits certain specific behavior without any ground of justification, has committed a fault, rendering him civilly liable for all losses caused by this act.[117] As a criminal offense under Belgian law always involves the violation of a legal rule imposing or prohibiting certain behavior,[118] all criminal offenses are per se civil wrongs. The opposite is not true: most civil wrongs that can lead to civil liability are not sanctioned by criminal sanctions. A civil wrong can also consist in behavior that is not even prohibited by law,[119] which by its nature cannot be the case for a criminal offense.[120]

45. The victim of a criminal offense can claim compensation for his loss based on civil liability as a "civil party" in the criminal proceedings against the offender before the criminal court.[121] If the victim chooses this procedural route, he has the advantage that the effective burden of proof of the fault will rest on the public prosecutor, who has more means at his disposal. This is important, as the burden of proof of every constituent element of the offense,[122] including the required intent, lies with the claimant when the alleged civil wrong is a criminal offense. Also, in cases of civil wrongs that are also a criminal offense, the defendant only has to make it plausible that a ground of justification or of nonculpability might be present for the claimant to have the burden to prove that no ground of justification is present and the defendant is culpable for his acts.[123] In practice, this is an important rule, as any civil fault, even mere negligence, that results in physical injury is a criminal offense.[124]

The victim can intervene in the criminal proceeding at the preliminary stage, when the criminal investigation is still going on, or at the trial stage, directly before the criminal court.[125] After the criminal trial has ended and a verdict has been pronounced, the victim can also bring its civil claim before the same criminal court, as the criminal

117. *See infra* Part I, Ch. 1, §3.
118. More even: Art. 12, para. 2, and Art. 14 Con. provide that no one shall be prosecuted except in the situations provided by statute and that no punishment shall be introduced and applied save by virtue of a statute (*nulla poena sine lege, nullum crimen sine lege*).
119. *See infra* Part I, Ch. 1, §2.
120. Negligence only constitutes a criminal offence if it results in physical injury to a person, such as in the case of involuntary manslaughter (Art. 419 PC) and criminal negligence causing bodily harm or unlawful wounding (Art. 420 PC).
121. Article 4 Preceding Title to Crim.Pro.
122. Cass. 14 June 1971, *Pas.* 1971, 1971, *Arr.Cass.* 1971, 1022.
123. Cass. 18 September 1972, *Pas.* 1973, 60, *Arr.Cass.* 1973, 65; Cass. 14 December 2001 (C.98.0469.F), No. 705, *Pas.* 2001, 2129, *Arr.Cass.* 2001, 2200; Cass. 11 June 2010 (C.09.0178.F), No. 419, *Pas.* 2010, 1844, *Arr.Cass.* 2010, 1761.
124. *See* Art. 418 PC, defining the offences of unlawful wounding and unintentional killing.
125. Articles 63–67, Crim.Pro.

judgment will not have closed the case for civil purposes.[126] In cases of criminal offenses that are not the most serious crimes, the victim can even initiate the criminal proceedings against the alleged offender by bringing its claim before the criminal court if the public prosecutor has not brought any criminal charges yet or has decided not to bring any charges.[127]

46. The victim can also bring his civil claim against the offender separately before a civil court. The civil court will be bound by what a criminal court has decided in the same matter. However, the principle of res judicata is only applicable to issues directly decided by the criminal court and is only binding between parties that were represented before the criminal court.[128] This means that an offender who unsuccessfully defended his innocence before the criminal court that convicted him cannot claim that he did not commit a fault before the civil court that has to decide on the civil claim based on the same offense. However, the civil court can find that an alleged offender who was found not guilty by a criminal court did in fact commit the criminal offense that constitutes a fault in civil proceedings brought by a victim that was not represented in the criminal proceedings.

47. If the victim initiates a separate civil suit while the criminal proceedings are still pending or if criminal charges are brought while the victim's claim for compensation is still pending before the civil court, the civil proceedings are suspended until the criminal court has reached a final judgment on the criminal charges.[129] This principle is usually referred to as *le criminel tient le civil en état*. The purpose of this principle is to avoid potential inconsistencies between the criminal and the civil judgments.[130] To make sure this principle does not preclude the victim from obtaining effective compensation, the period of limitation for the civil claim, which is set by the rules of civil law,[131] will not lapse before the criminal prosecution has prescribed.[132]

This procedural rule causes enormous delays for civil claims in cases involving personal injuries that could be caused by a fault, which is almost always a criminal offense.[133] As a result, victims of disasters or accidents of a large scale had to wait years before they received any compensation. To improve the situation of such victims, the legislature has recently amended the law to allow the civil proceedings based on strict (i.e., no-fault) liability to move ahead even if there is a criminal proceeding pending for an alleged wrong in the same matter.[134] Also, a special compensation fund

126. Article 4, paras. 2–4, Preceding Title to Crim.Pro.
127. Articles 145 and 182 Crim.Pro.
128. Cass. 15 February 1991, No. 322, *Arr.Cass.* 1990–1991, 641, *Pas.* 1991, 572; Cass. 24 June 2002, *NJW* 2002/10, 353; Cass. 24 April 2006 (S.05.0075.N), No. 233, *Arr.Cass.* 2006, 949, *Pas.* 2006, 933.
129. Article 4, para. 1, Preceding Title to Crim.Pro.
130. Con.C. No. 113/2008 of 31 July 2008.
131. *See infra* Part IV, Ch. 1.
132. Article 26, Preceding Title to Crim.Pro.
133. Articles 418–420 PC; *see supra* footnote 120.
134. Article 4, para. 1, *in fine*, Preceding Title to Crim.Pro., added by (federal) Act of 8 June 2017 on the Coordination of Expert Investigation and the Acceleration of the Procedure concerning certain forms of Strict Liability, which also added Arts. 1385*quinquiesdecies–octiesdecies* to the Judicial Code, organizing specifics of the civil proceedings on the strict liability in such cases.

has been created for victims of large disasters caused by human fault or technical failure, in order to help solve these practical problems.[135]

§5. Relationship Between Contractual and Delictual or Tortious Responsibility

48. In Belgian law, precontractual liability is based on extracontractual liability, not on contractual liability. In principle, a party that commits a fault during the negotiations for a contract is liable for the losses caused to the other party. Whether a party has committed a fault in negotiating has to be decided taking into consideration the freedom of contract, which is recognized as a general principle of law. According to general rules of private law, one is not required to enter into negotiations when one receives an offer. Entering into negotiations also does not create a duty to complete the negotiations and conclude a contract. However, a party that abuses its freedom of contract, can be held liable based on Article 1382 of the Civil Code.[136] Such abuse can consist of entering into negotiations with no intention to eventually enter into a contract but with another purpose, for instance to obtain certain confidential information, but can also consist of abruptly breaking off ongoing negotiations without legitimate motive while having created a reasonable expectation that a contract would be concluded. The damages courts award in such cases are most often limited to a compensation for costs and expenses already made (reliance interest), and will generally not include compensation for the lost profits that could have been made if the contract would have been concluded (expectation interest), but there are instances where courts apparently are prepared to also award damages for lost profits. The fault can also consist in not having provided necessary information, in cases where the relative position of the parties warrants that one of them has a duty to inform the other. Negligently providing incorrect information can also serve as a basis for precontractual liability. Of course, liability also attaches in cases of deceit or duress, where a contracting party wrongfully causes the other party to consent to the contract.

49. Whether extracontractual liability can exist between parties to an existing contract (*concours des responsabilités—samenloop van aansprakelijkheid*), is a hotly debated issue in Belgium. This question is particularly relevant in Belgian law because of its broad concept of damage,[137] resulting in almost any contractual damage also qualifying as recoverable harm in tort. In many cases, the victim has an interest in basing his claim in tort, as that allows him to invoke certain strict liabilities not necessarily available in contract, or this makes it possible to escape a particularly short period of prescription for a contractual claim or—and this is most often the real issue—to avoid the claim being barred by an exoneration clause in the contract.

50. From the thirties to the early 1970s of the last century, the general rule was that extracontractual liability was not excluded just because the harm was caused at

---

135. (Federal) Act of 13 November 2011 on the Compensation for Personal Injury Caused by Technological Accidents.

136. Cass. 7 October 2011 (C.10.0227.F), *Pas.* 2011, 2148, *Arr.Cass.* 2011, 2032.

137. *See infra* para. 58 and Part VI, Ch. 2, §4.

the occasion of a contract between the victim and the wrongdoer.[138] In the nowadays seldom cited *EBES*-decision of 4 June 1971,[139] the Court of Cassation stated that an extracontractual claim is not possible, however, if the right of which the infringement serves as the basis for the claim only exists because of the contract, and the harm is only a result of the breach of this contract.[140] Then, on December 7, 1973, the Court issued its often-cited *stevedore*-decision,[141] which used phraseological units that are open to two distinct interpretations. On the facts, the owner of goods that were damaged during transport was denied an extracontractual claim against the stevedore, who had been contracted by the carrier to load the ship and who had wrongfully caused the damage.

The specific wording of this ruling was on the one hand interpreted to express a rule that extracontractual liability between contract parties is only available if both the fact invoked as the basis for liability and the damage for which compensation is claimed are unrelated to the content of the contract.[142] This interpretation is referred to as the "disappearance theory," as these conditions will only be present in cases where no contractual liability arises, and therefore the concurrence of both types of liabilities is in this view ontologically impossible.

However, according to another feasible reading of this decision, extracontractual liability between contract parties is available if the fact invoked as the basis for liability is not merely a breach of contract but also a fact recognized as a basis for extracontractual liability, and if the damage for which compensation is claimed does not merely consist in the loss of the advantage expected from the performance of the contract or in harm caused by the loss of this contractual advantage. This interpretation is referred to as the "refining theory," as these conditions specify how the older rulings of 1930 and 1971 can be explained by one principle, allowing contractual and extracontractual liability to concur in certain circumstances.

51. In 2006, the Court of Cassation issued a new ruling on the issue.[143] Now, the Court explicitly stated that extracontractual liability between contract parties can exist if the fact invoked as the basis for liability is *not merely* a breach of contract *but also* a fact recognized as a basis for extracontractual liability. Hence, this decision could be regarded as choosing sides with the refining theory. However, hope that this decision would have ended the debate turned out to be futile, as the Court added that extracontractual liability can only be invoked for damage that is "not the consequence of the bad performance of the contract." The proponents of the refinement theory argue that this condition merely requires that the damage does not consist of the loss of the advantage expected from the performance of the contract or consequential damage. They read the wording as referring to a type of damage, which they call purely

138. Cass. 13 February 1930, *Pas.* 1930, 115.
139. Cass. 4 June 1971, *Arr.Cass.* 1971, 989, *Pas.* 1971, 940.
140. The claim in this case was about damage consisting in not receiving the supply of electricity and harm caused by the interruption of this supply, the archetypical pure economic loss case.
141. Cass. 7 December 1973, *Arr.Cass.* 1974, 395, *Pas.* 1974, 376.
142. This interpretation seemed to be confirmed in Cass. 3 December 1975, *Pas.* 1976, 412, *Arr. Cass.* 1976, 417.
143. Cass. 29 September 2006 (C.03.0502.N), No. 447, *Arr.Cass.* 2006, 1863, *Pas.* 2006, 1911.

contractual damage.[144] The proponents of the disappearance theory, however, interpret this wording as referring to a causal requirement: extracontractual claims are only possible for harm which is not caused by a fact that constitutes a breach of contract, a type of wrong, and thus concurrence remains ontologically impossible.

52. The Court of Cassation has recognized one exception to its rule, but here debate about its exact meaning is possible as well. In its original decision on the issue, the Court stated that a particular type of harm that is a constituent element of a particular type of criminal offense—such as for instance physical injury in cases of unlawful wounding[145]—cannot be regarded as mere contractual damage just because it was caused by a breach of a contractual duty.[146] This can be understood as an application of the concurrence principle recognized by the refinement theory, allowing extracontractual claims between contract parties for the compensation of harm that is not merely the loss of the advantage expected from the contract. However, the proponents of the disappearance theory read this as a separate exception to their general rule and state that extracontractual liability can be claimed in any case where the fault invoked as its basis is not only a civil wrong but also a criminal offense, irrespective of the type of damage this offense has caused and whether the causation of this type of harm is a constituent element of the offense or not. This also seems to be the interpretation that can be found in a recent decision of the Court.[147]

§6. Interests Protected by Civil Liability: The Concept of Damage

53. For liability to attach under Belgian law, three constituent elements are required: the person claiming compensation has to have suffered (1) damage that was (2) caused by (3) a fact generating liability. This fact generating liability is a fact recognized in a specific legal rule as a basis for liability. The fact can be a fault committed by the person held liable, in which case the liability is sometimes referred to as subjective liability, or another fact that is used as the basis for a strict liability, in which case the liability is usually called objective liability in Belgian literature. These different bases for liability will be discussed later.[148] The required causal relation between this fact generating liability and the loss for which compensation is sought will also be discussed later.[149] Here, attention is focused on the first requirement, the concept of damage.

54. Civil liability requires harm—called a loss (*perte—verlies*)—that, for it to be recoverable, can legally be qualified as "damage" (*dommage—schade*). Whether harm is suffered, is a question of fact, to be determined by the courts on the basis of

144. This reading uses the clarification offered in Cass. 25 October 1990, No. 107, *Arr.Cass.* 1990–1991, 237, *Pas.* 1991, 210, on the question whether a breach of contract is a wrong resulting in liability toward third parties.

145. Article 418 PC defines this offence as the causation of this type of harm by negligence.

146. Cass. 26 October 1990, No. 110, *Arr.Cass.* 1990–1991, 244, *Pas.* 1991, 216.

147. Cass. 10 June 2015 (P.15.0419.F), No. 385, *Pas.* 2015, 1528, *Arr.Cass.* 2015, 1530.

148. *See infra* Parts I, II and III.

149. *See infra* Part V.

the evidence supplied by the parties. Whether an established harm constitutes damage, however, is an issue to be answered by the court based on the law, under the potential review by the Court of Cassation. Not all harm suffered by a person is recoverable in civil liability. However, compared to many other legal systems, Belgian civil liability law is very victim friendly in this regard.

55. Damage consists of an injury to an *interest* (*intérêt—belang*). It is not necessary for the victim to have had a *right* (*droit—recht*) to something he has lost, for him to suffer damage.[150] Already in 1939 the Court of Cassation ruled that a person who loses the support of the sibling he is living with because this sibling is killed, suffers damage, even though siblings do not have a duty to support each other and he, therefore, had not lost a right.[151]

An injury to an interest does not only suffice to constitute damage, it is also required for damage to exist. The loss or infringement of a right in itself is not recognized as damage, if the right holder's interests were in fact not hurt. For example, a person losing his right to an appeal in a lawsuit caused by the negligence of his attorney cannot claim compensation if in this particular case it is clear that the appeal could not have produced any benefit.[152] For the same reason, a child losing a parent, who under Belgian law has a general duty to support his children, does not suffer material damage if in the particular case no financial support was provided.[153] Infringing a subjective right may by itself—i.e., without injury to the interests the right protects—not be a loss, it will constitute a civil wrong if committed without ground of justification, as the act infringing the right violates a legal rule that specifically requires other persons to abstain and recognize the exclusive authority of the right holder.[154]

56. When the concept of damage is based on the infringement of a right, damage consists of a loss of something the victim had before. When an injury to a mere interest is sufficient, the harm in essence does not consist in something the victim has "lost," but in the victim not enjoying something which it would have enjoyed but for the accident. In such a counterfactual account, damage consists in the difference between the victim's *actual* interest position after the fact with the *hypothetical* position this victim would have enjoyed if the fact had not happened. Based on this line of reasoning, the Court of Cassation recently has ruled that wrongful life claims must fail in principle: according to the Court, one cannot make a comparison between a person's handicapped existence and his nonexistence.[155]

57. For harm to be recoverable, the injured interest must be legitimate (*intérêt légitime—rechtmatig belang*).[156] An interest can be illegitimate because it conflicts with the law or public policy, or because it implies an infringement of someone else's right. However, a distinction is made between on the one hand the loss of an advantage

150. *See* e.g. Cass. 24 March 1969, *Arr.Cass.* 1969, 690, *Pas.* 1969, 655; Cass. 17 June 1975, *Arr. Cass.* 1975, 1105, *Pas.* 1975, 999.
151. Cass. 16 January 1939, *Pas.* 1939, 15.
152. Cass. 21 June 1990, No. 615, *Pas.* 1990, 1204, *Arr.Cass.* 1989–1990, 1358.
153. Cass. 19 March 1991, No. 376, *Arr.Cass.* 1990–1991, 755, *Pas.* 1991, 670.
154. *See infra* para. 61.
155. Cass. 14 November 2014 (C.13.0441.N), No. 694, *Arr.Cass.* 2014, 2597, *Pas.* 2014, 2541; Cass. 21 April 2016 (C.15.0286.N).
156. Cass. 16 January 1939, *Pas.* 1939, 15.

that itself is illegitimate, which does not constitute recoverable damage,[157] and on the other hand a loss of an advantage that in itself is legitimate but which was enjoyed by a victim in an illegitimate situation or under illegitimate circumstances.[158] For example, the costs for cleaning up a pond polluted as a result of an accident caused by someone else's fault cannot be recovered by the owner if the pond was illegal under applicable urban planning rules, because the owner has no legitimate interest in having this pond at all.[159] However, the cost of repairing a trailer home damaged in an accident caused by someone else's fault can be recovered by the owner, even though he did not have valid permit for positioning the trailer where it was, because his interest in having an undamaged trailer home, which can be moved elsewhere, in itself is not illegitimate.[160] The legitimacy of the interest is judged at the time it is injured.[161]

58. Apart from the legitimacy requirement, there are no general restrictions on the type of interests that can result in legally recognized damage if injured. There is, therefore, no limited list of interests that are protected by liability law. Because of its broad concept of damage, Belgian civil liability allows claims for economic losses and contains no rule that, in principle, would exclude pure economic loss.[162]

Belgian law also does not use a system of relative wrongfulness or a theory of a *Normzweck* or *Schutznorm*, which would limit liability in case of a breach of a specific legal rule of conduct to losses the violated rule was intended or serves to prevent.[163] This means, for instance, that an accountant can be held liable for losses suffered by the investing public that relied on his incorrect account statements, irrespective of whether the rule the accountant violated was intended to protect the investing public or only the accountant's client.

59. Harm is only considered damage if the injured interest is personal to the claimant.[164] In case of injury to a public interest, the harm is considered not to be suffered by any individual person. As a result, liability law has not been an efficient instrument to protect public or collective interests in Belgium, although in areas such as the protection of the environment, progress has been made.[165]

157. Cass. 3 October 1997 (C.96.0334.F), No. 387, *Pas.* 1997, 965, *Arr.Cass.* 1997, 921.
158. Cass. 2 March 2006 (C.05.0061.N), No. 120, *Arr.Cass.* 2006, 486, *Pas.* 2006, 483; Cass. 16 June 2014 (C.12.0402.F), No. 429, *Pas.* 2014, 1556, *Arr.Cass.* 2014, 1550.
159. Cass. 27 June 2013 (C.12.0340.F), No. 402, *Pas.* 2013, 1502, *Arr.Cass.* 2013, 1644.
160. Cass. 2 April 1998 (C.94.0438.N), No. 188, *Arr.Cass.* 1998, 407, *Pas.* 1998, 431.
161. Cass. 6 June 2008 (C.06.0640.F), No. 351, *Pas.* 2008, 1430, *Arr.Cass.* 2008, 1468.
162. *See infra* paras. 231–232.
163. *See infra* para. 70, text accompanying footnotes 201–203.
164. *See* e.g. Cass. 6 January 2010 (P.09.1152.F), No. 5, *Pas.* 2010, 20, *Arr.Cass.* 2010, 19.
165. *See infra* para. 174.

Part I. Liability for One's Own Acts

Chapter 1. General Principles

§1. The Concept of Fault: Culpable Wrong

60. The basic general rules on civil liability are stated in Articles 1382 and 1383 of the Civil Code. In their present interpretation, no difference in meaning is perceived between these two articles. As a result, courts and authors nowadays refer only to Article 1382 as the statutory basis for the general liability for losses caused by one's own fault. Article 1382 of the Civil Code obliges the person who is guilty of a wrongful act that has caused damage to someone else to compensate this harm. The liability is linked to a "fault" (*faute—fout*). A fault consists of two elements.

First, the act or behavior itself has to be wrongful in the objective sense (*acte illicite—onrechtmatige daad*).[166] The traditional rendition of Belgian tort law recognizes two types of wrongful acts: on the one hand negligence and on the other hand the violation of a legal rule of conduct, which could be called illegality.[167] Both types of wrongs will be looked at below in §2 and §3.

Wrongfulness, however, is not sufficient. As opposed to French law, which considers a fault to consist only of an objectively wrongful act,[168] Belgian law requires the wrong to be attributable or imputable (*imputabilité—toerekenbaarheid*) to the free will of the person who has committed it, for him to be liable. The second element of a fault is therefore culpability (*culpabilité—schuld*).[169] This subjective element of fault will be discussed below in §4.

---

166. Article 1382 CC uses the terms *fait* in French and *daad* in Dutch for this facet of the fault. This objective element is sometimes also referred to as the "fault" (*faute—fout*) by authors and courts, which confusion does not render Belgian literature on the subject conceptually very clear.
167. Cass. 8 December 1994 (C.93.0303.F), No. 541, *Arr.Cass.* 1994, 1074, *Pas.* 1994, 1063; Cass. 5 June 2008 (C.06.0366.N), No. 347, *Arr.Cass.* 2008, 1442, *Pas.* 2008, 1411; Cass. 25 March 2010 (C.09.0403.N), No. 219, *Arr.Cass.* 2010, 920, *Pas.* 2010, 1007; Cass. 21 September 2012 (F.11.0085.N), No. 481, *Arr.Cass.* 2012, 2008, *Pas.* 2012, 1719.
168. Cour de Cassation of France 9 May 1984 (five decisions), *Dalloz jurisprudence* 1984, 525.
169. Article 1382 CC uses the terms *faute* in French and *schuld* in Dutch for this facet of the fault, adding to the confusion.

61. There has been debate in the literature whether the infringement of a subjective right in itself can be qualified as civil wrong on which Article 1382 CC liability can be based.

For a long time, the generally accepted view was that the infringement of a right constitutes damage. As causing a loss in itself cannot be considered wrongful per se,[170] the necessary conclusion was that the infringement of a right itself is not wrongful.[171] For liability to attach, the act constituting the infringement of the right has to be either negligent or illegal, distinct from the infringement of the right.

Recently, however, a growing number of authors recognize that one has to make a conceptual distinction between the interests protected by a right and the subjective right itself. For example, the interests of an owner of a good are the use he can make of this good and the needs he can satisfy using the good. If the good is damaged, the owner's interests are hurt. The right of an owner, on the other hand, consists in the legal claims he can make in relation to the good, such as his exclusive authority to decide how the good will be put to use. An act that damages the good, does not infringe on this right; an act denying the right holder his exclusive authority to use the good, however, does infringe on this right. A physical injury resulting from a traffic collision constitutes damage for the victim, but in itself, it does not constitute an infringement of the victim's right to physical integrity. Operating a patient without his permission, however, does infringe on his right to physical integrity,[172] even though it does not necessarily result in hurting his interests and therefore does not necessarily constitute a loss.

Under this newer conceptual view, the infringement of a right can cause damage if the act of negating or usurping the exclusive authority of the right holder results in hurting his interests. However, the infringement in itself does not necessarily hurt his interests, and therefore does not constitute damage.[173] On the other hand, a right holder derives his exclusive authority from the law. Someone else's act of negating or usurping this exclusive authority therefore violates a legal rule of conduct and thus constitutes an illegal act, and is by that token wrongful under Article 1382 CC. In this more modern view, the infringement of a subjective right is according to Belgian law not to be viewed as a separate, third category of wrongs next to the two already mentioned categories of negligence and illegality,[174] but merely as a subcategory of the category of unlawfulness consisting of illegal behavior.

§2. Duty of Care and Negligence

62. Negligence (*négligence—onzorgvuldigheid*) is wrong under Article 1382 of the Civil Code. Behavior is negligent is if falls short of the standard level of care. Care is effort aimed at protecting the interests of others. In the traditional formulation

---

170. *See infra* footnote 178.

171. Cass. 22 August 1940, *Pas.* 1940, 205, *Arr. Verbr.* 1940, 76.

172. *See infra* para. 184.

173. *See supra* footnotes 152 and 153.

174. In Dutch law, infringing a subjective right is mentioned as such a third, separate category of unlawfulness in Art. 6:162(2) Dutch Civil Code.

the standard level of care is the amount of care a "normally prudent person" would have taken.[175]

63. The standard level of care relates to all legitimate interests of all other persons potentially adversely affected by the wrongdoer's behavior. Under Belgian law, extracontractual fault liability is not restricted to losses suffered by victims with whom the wrongdoer has a specific relation. This does not mean that Belgian law contains a generally applicable positive duty of care. One cannot ask the courts to order another person to behave carefully. Only when a party has entered into a contract containing a duty of care or when a specific rule of law imposes a duty of care in a certain relationship, such as for instance the duty of parents to care for their children,[176] can one speak of an obligation or a real "duty" of care. At one point in history, it may have seemed as if the Court of Cassation required the lower courts to find a violation of a duty before they could qualify behavior as wrongful.[177] However, later decisions have made clear and the literature commonly agrees that no breach of a preexisting duty is required for a fault to be established. What is usually referred to as the generally "required level" or the "duty" of care, is therefore more properly qualified not as a legal duty or obligation, but merely a standard of behavior serving as the yardstick for judging whether an act is negligent or not for purposes of establishing liability.

64. Care can consist of positive action aimed at limiting the risk for others, such as taking protective measures to shield the interests of others from potential injury resulting from known risky behavior, or of abstaining from undertaking certain conduct that increases this risk to others. Thus, both action and inaction can be negligent. However, there is no requirement to commit all efforts necessary to avoid harm to others: the fact of having caused damage in itself does not amount to negligence.[178]

To judge whether behavior is negligent, it should not be compared to the "general behavior" or the habitual behavior.[179] "Normal" behavior has to be understood in the normative sense, not in the statistical sense. The amount of care a normally prudent person would have applied is the amount that is considered "reasonable." In reality, therefore, the legal test is not the comparison of the person who is alleged to have behaved wrongfully with a standard person, often called the *bonus pater familias*, the test consists of the comparison of the behavior that is alleged to be negligent with the standard of reasonableness. As in many circumstances reasonable persons can differ on the precise behavior they consider to be appropriate in the given circumstances, an act is only negligent if it falls outside the range of behavior that can be expected of normally careful persons in those circumstances. However, once the court has established these margins of reasonable behavior for the circumstances of the case, every deviation, even the slightest, outside this range of acceptable behavior is considered negligent and therefore wrongful.[180]

175. *See* e.g. Cass. 21 September 2012 (F.11.0085.N), No. 481, *Arr.Cass.* 2012, 2008, *Pas.* 2012, 1719.
176. Article 203 CC.
177. Cass. 22 August 1940, *Pas.* 1940, 205, *Arr.Verbr.* 1940, 76.
178. Cass. 4 May 2012 (C.10.0080.F), No. 276, *Pas.* 2012, 1007, *Arr.Cass.* 2012, 1178.
179. Cass. 4 September 2013 (P.13.0358.F), No. 417, *Pas.* 2013, 1550, *Arr.Cass.* 2013, 1707.
180. Cass. 14 November 2012 (P.11.1611.F), No. 612, *Pas.* 2012, 2204, *Arr.Cass.* 2012, 2541; Cass. 22 March 1957, *Pas.* 1957, 885, *Arr.Verbr.* 1957, 610.

65. What level of effort aimed at protecting the interests of others—i.e., what level of care—is reasonable, depends on the extent of the burden the effort to reduce the risk entails and on the limitation of the risk expected from such effort. Therefore, all circumstances of the case that bear on those factors are taken into account.

Thus, whether an act is negligent can depend on objective circumstances such as the time and place, the surroundings,[181] the expected behavior of others involved, the climatologic circumstances,[182] and the technical possibilities,[183] as these conditions can influence both the risk of adverse consequences to others and the availability of methods to reduce this risk, their likely effectiveness and their cost. Traditional theoretical consensus holds that these so-called external circumstances should be taken into account, by stating that the standard is the behavior of a normally prudent person "placed in the same circumstances."

However, this also means that the purpose for which an act is committed, i.e., the normally expected benefit of the act, is relevant. For instance, certain behavior such as excessive speed and risk taking when driving can be negligent in the context of normal transportation on public roads but not negligent in the context of a race, where the accepted useful purpose is to win by being the fastest.[184] Flying military jets at very high speed at very low altitude so that a ceiling in a private house collapses might be reasonable behavior in war, but during peacetime, it can be considered negligent.[185]

66. One of the most relevant circumstances to decide whether behavior is negligent is the foreseeability (*prévisibilité—voorzienbaarheid*) of the occurrence of harm.[186] Reason only requires one to take into account risks one can be aware of. Therefore, the same behavior can be negligent in one set of circumstances in which one should have realized certain third parties would be subject to the risk, and not negligent in another in which one would not have expected others to be affected. This also means that whether behavior is negligent is to be judged at the point in time when

181. A good example are two cases relating to mown grass eaten by cows or horses. Apparently, eating cut grass can be very dangerous for cows and horses. In one decision (JPC Borgworm 15 March 2001, *Journal des juges de paix* 2003, 329), the person who had left the cut grass next to the fence of a meadow was held liable, as it happened in an agrarian area where one is supposed to know the risk, while in another decision (CFI Marche-en-Famenne 12 November 1987, *RGAR* 1990, No. 11,730) the person who had actually fed the cut grass to a horse was not considered to have committed a fault, as it happened in an urban area where one is not supposed to be aware of the risk.

182. *See* e.g. CA Ghent 4 May 1965, *Jurisprudence du port d'Anvers* 1965, 406, finding industrial activity which creates smoke next to a canal in itself negligent because the misty weather conditions combined with the smoke hampered the visibility and increased the risk of collisions between ships too much; the court found that reasonable behavior in the circumstances would either be refraining from the smoke creating activity or asking the government to temporarily halt shipping traffic next to the factory.

183. *See* e.g. CA Brussels 2 December 1966, *RGAR* 1967, No. 7,873, finding the exploitation of high voltage power lines that in windy conditions generate hindering low frequency noise not wrongful, as there was no alternative technology at the time.

184. *See* e.g. CFI Kortrijk 18 December 2001, *RW* 2005–2006, 267.

185. JPC Grâce-Hollogne 3 October 1978, *Jurisprudence de Liège* 1978, 71.

186. Cass. 12 November 1951, *Pas.* 1952, 128, *Arr.Verbr.* 1952, 118.

the behavior took place, and not at a later moment, when maybe more information is known.

However, this does not mean that one is only liable for foreseeable losses under Belgian law. Negligence requires that the wrongdoer could foresee that some kind of losses could result from his behavior, it does not require him to have foreseen the specific type of accident that actually occurred.[187] As a result, liability under Belgian law also covers losses suffered by persons that the wrongdoer could not foresee as being affected by his behavior as long as his behavior is negligent, because he could foresee that some people could be hurt by his behavior and he did not take the reasonable steps to reduce this risk.[188]

67. Traditional theory states that negligence does not depend on the personal characteristics of the person acting, usually referred to as the internal circumstances. Elements such as the age of the person,[189] his education, character, intelligence, physical strength and experience[190] can in principle not be invoked to lower the applicable standard of care. Thus, anybody will be judged by the same standard. However, careful study of case law reveals that courts actually do take certain personal characteristics into account when determining whether an act is negligent. First, courts tend to lower the standard for people who have physical or mental impairments. Especially when applied to behavior by the victim contributing to the causation of its harm, the courts tend to be lenient to victims that are especially vulnerable. Second, courts tend to find a person who actually knew of the existence of a risk but chose to ignore it negligent even when a normally prudent person in the same circumstances would not have known this risk and therefore would also not have taken it into account. Actual knowledge by the person whose behavior is being judged—which is not an "external circumstance"—is always taken into account. Third, courts very often are prepared to consider certain behavior not to be negligent merely because the person acting is relatively young and therefore less educated or knowledgeable, even though the minor has reached the age of reason and therefore has the capacity to be culpable.[191] The Court of Cassation has recently refused to reverse such a decision of a court that had found a scouts volunteer not negligent because his or her behavior had not been different from the behavior to be expected from a normally careful "young volunteer."[192] As a result, the exact extent to which personal characteristics are relevant in determining whether behavior is negligent under Belgian law is at present a point of debate.

187. *See* e.g. Cass. 12 November 1951, *Arr.Verbr.* 1952, 118, *Pas.* 1952, 128.
188. Cass. 5 May 1971, *Pas.* 1971, 802, *Arr.Cass.* 1971, 869.
189. Cass. 24 October 1974, *Arr.Cass.* 1975, 259, *Pas.* 1975, 237.
190. *See* e.g. Cass. 9 December 2011 (C.11.0015.F), not published, annulling a decision of a lower court that had held there not to be any comparative negligence when a female student was electrocuted in a shower in her boyfriend's boarding room as a result of the water exhaust of a laundry machine being placed in the shower basin, because this was the young woman's first life experience outside the protected environment of her family home and she did not realize the risk.
191. *See infra* Part I, Ch. 1, §4.
192. Cass. 5 June 2003 (C.01.0252.F), No. 337, *Pas.* 2003, 1125, *Arr.Cass.* 2003, 1337.

§3. Illegality and Wrongfulness

68. As a general principle, Belgian law considers the violation of a legal rule prohibiting or requiring certain specific behavior, committed without ground of justification, to be per se wrongful.[193] This is usually referred to as the "unity theory," equating the concepts of illegality and wrongfulness.[194] Thus, even a breach of a legal behavioral rule that in circumstances could be considered as reasonable and therefore not negligent, still remains a civil wrong.[195] This means in particular that no foreseeable harm is required for such an act to result in liability if it has caused damage. As a result, every criminal offense is also a civil wrong.[196] The victim of a criminal offense can therefore always claim compensation for the damage the offense has caused based on Article 1382 of the Civil Code.

69. For the illegal act to be wrongful, it is not required that the wrongdoer realized his behavior was illegal. The fact that he was not aware of the existence of the legal rule he violated, is no excuse. In general, ignorance of the law is no valid excuse for having violated it.[197] However, if circumstances are such that *any* reasonable person would not have realized the behavior is illegal, the person that violated the legal rule can invoke an unsurmountable error, which excludes liability.[198]

While the person acting does not have to realize his action is illegal for it to be wrongful, the act that constitutes the violation of the rule has to be committed knowingly

193. Cass. 13 May 1982, No. 547, *Pas.* 1982, 1056, *Arr.Cass.* 1981–1982, 1134; more recent: Cass. 16 May 2011 (C.10.0664.N), No. 320, *Arr.Cass.* 2011, 1230, *Pas.* 2011, 1339. *See* already Cass. 22 March 1957, *Pas.* 1957, 885, *Arr. Verbr.* 1957, 610.

194. While illegal behavior is in itself wrongful, the opposite is not true. The fact that a person has behaved legally does not imply that he has not committed a wrong. The general standard of care, discussed above, can result in specific behavior which complies with all applicable legal rules to be still being wrongful when it is unreasonable under the circumstances. This means, for instance, that a company complying with all conditions in its licenses and permits can still be held liable for losses caused. It also means that the government that complied with all information duties can still be held liable for negligently not having informed citizens of their options to reclaim incorrectly collected taxes. *See* Cass. 1 June 2012 (F.11.0082.F), No. 353, *Pas.* 2012, 1260, *Arr.Cass.* 2012, 1503.

195. *See* e.g. Cass. 6 June 2011 (C.10.0095.F), No. 377, *Pas.* 2011, 1599, *Arr.Cass.* 2011, 1478, a case involving a taxi cab normally stopping to drop off a customer in a city street with tram tracks, thereby necessarily partially obstructing the tramway; Cass. 22 September 1988, No. 47, *Arr.Cass.* 1988–1989, 94, *Pas.* 1989, 83; Cass. 19 December 1980, No. 241, *Arr.Cass.* 1980–1981, 449 *Pas.* 1981, 453.

196. *See supra* para. 44.

197. This principle is very often misformulated in Belgian literature by the Latin phrase *nemo censetur ignorare legem*, as if one is supposed to know the law. This is not an adequate formulation, because the rule does not depend on one's knowledge of the law, that then would have to be presumed for the rule to apply. The principle is that it does not matter whether a person knows the law or not, and hence it is not necessary nor useful to presume the person does know all of the law.

198. *See infra* paras. 192–193.

and willingly for it to be wrongful.[199] Several grounds of justification recognized in this regard will be looked at in more detail below.[200]

70. The principle applies to rules imposed by law, irrespective of the formal source of the legal rule. The unity theory applies to constitutional rules, statutory and regulatory rules from the federal, regional and community governments, regulatory rules from provinces and municipalities, and rules imposed by a treaty or an international or supranational instrument, including EU law, if it has direct effect.

The purpose of the law that is breached is not considered relevant in this respect. Belgian liability law does not use a relative concept of unlawfulness as Dutch law does,[201] nor does it adhere to a *Normzwecktheorie* as German law does.[202] This means for example that a hospital with a revolving door at its entrance is liable for the injury suffered by an old aged man who fell because the door turned too fast for him and hit his ankles, as hospitals are strictly prohibited from having revolving doors under existing fire safety regulations, even though such doors are only prohibited because they are too slow and thereby create a risk by hindering an evacuation in case of an emergency.[203]

It also applies to an infringement of a right, such as an intellectual property right[204] or someone's privacy,[205] as such infringement necessarily implies the violation of the legal rule granting the subject this right and thereby imposing a duty on all others to respect this.[206]

71. However, the principle does not apply to behavioral rules which are not imposed by law, i.e., which are not unilaterally imposed by the government on citizens. The violation of such a behavioral rule will only be wrongful if a normal reasonable person would not have committed it in the given circumstances.

This is particularly relevant in cases involving sports injuries. The rules of the game are not imposed by the government; they are agreed among citizens in private sports associations. They are not part of the law. The violation of a rule of a sports game—a "foul"—is therefore not necessarily a "fault" in the sense of Article 1382 of the Civil Code. The victim claiming compensation for a sports injury resulting from foul play will have to show that the wrongdoer behaved negligently,[207] that his behavior

199. Cass. 3 October 1994 (C.93.0243.F), No. 412, *Pas.* 1994, 788, *Arr.Cass.* 1994, 807; Cass. 22 September 1988, No. 47, *Pas.* 1989, 83, *Arr.Cass.* 1988–1989, 94; Cass. 10 April 1970, *Pas.* 1970, 682, *Arr.Cass.* 1970, 729.

200. *See infra* Part IV, Ch. 2.

201. Article 6:163 of the Dutch Civil Code.

202. §823(2) of the German Civil Code.

203. Cass. 26 September 2002 (C.00.0086.N), No. 482, *Arr.Cass.* 2002, 1968, *Pas.* 2002, 1753; *see also supra* para. 58.

204. Cass. 3 September 2009 (C.08.0337.N), No. 476, *Arr.Cass.* 2009, 1926, *Pas.* 2009, 1782.

205. Belgian case law reveals that the infringement of the right to privacy is considered to be wrongful, even though Belgian law does not know a statutory provision like the one in Art. 9 of the French Civil Code. *See* Cass. 29 June 2000 (C.98.0530.F), No. 420, *Pas.* 2000, 1222, *Arr.Cass.* 2000, 1245. This shows that the violation of a behavioral rule of law constitutes a wrong even if this rule is not imposed by legislation.

206. *See supra* para. 61.

207. Cass. 16 June 1969, *Arr.Cass.* 1969, 1026, *Pas.* 1969, 950.

was unreasonable in these circumstances, and one cannot assume that a normal reasonable person would obey all rules of the game in all circumstances.

72. For the same reason, the violation of a contractual rule of behavior—a breach of contract—does not *ipso facto* constitute a wrong that leads to extracontractual liability.[208] The opposite view, which would make it possible for third parties to base a claim in liability on a contract they are not a party to, is considered inconsistent with the principle of privity of contract.[209] However, some breaches of contract can be wrongful and serve as the basis for extracontractual liability for losses suffered by third parties because they consist of behavior that apart from breaching the contract also violates a generally applicable legal rule or that can be considered unreasonable under the given circumstances and therefore negligent.[210] Also, in some types of contracts that are intended to result in benefits for or protection of third parties and where the contract party is aware that his performance directly affects the interests of third parties, the breach of a contractual duty can be considered as negligent and therefore wrongful.[211] The textbook example is the elevator maintenance contract,[212] but also the contract between a corporation and an accountant certifying the accounts can be interpreted this way, resulting in the possibility that third-party victims—users of the elevator in the one case, investors in securities issued by the corporation in the other—can claim damages for the harm they suffer as a consequence of sloppy performance of contractual duties by these service providers. As was mentioned earlier, the fact that a breach of contract at the same time constitutes a civil wrong does not necessarily mean that the harmed contract party can claim compensation for his loss based on extracontractual liability: the contract the parties have entered into is binding, and will limit the possibility to claim in tort.[213]

73. Because of its content, the unity theory is necessarily only operative for legal rules that either prohibit or impose specified behavior. A statutory or regulatory provision that imposes a duty of care—in the Belgian literature called an *obligation de moyen* (*middelenverbintenis*)—is only violated if the person did not spend the required level of care.[214] As this required level of care is based on reasonableness, determined by the circumstances, the foreseeability of losses is a relevant factor in deciding whether such a legal rule is actually violated. The standard of behavior under such a statutory or regulatory rule of conduct therefore substantively becomes similar

208. Belgian law differs from French law, which recognizes a breach of contract as a wrong that can serve as the basis for extracontractual claims by third parties suffering damage caused by this breach. *See* Cour de Cassation of France 6 October 2006, *Dalloz* 2006, 2825.

209. Article 1165 CC.

210. Cass. 25 October 2012 (C.12.0079.F), No. 568, *Pas.* 2012, 2039, *Arr.Cass.* 2012, 2332; Cass. 11 June 1981, *Arr.Cass.* 1980–1981, 1168, No. 583, *Pas.* 1981, 1159.

211. Cass. 22 June 2009, *NJW* 2009, 724, *RW* 2011–2012, 1003.

212. *See* e.g. CA Ghent 15 May 1995, *Tijdschrift voor Aannemingsrecht* 1996, 369; CA Brussels 4 February 1992, *RGAR* 1995, No. 12,460.

213. *See supra* General Introduction, §5.

214. *See* e.g. CFI Bruges 27 March 2000, *TMR* 2001, 495, finding that the violation of Art. 22, para. 2, of the now replaced Flemish Environmental Licence Act of 28 June 1985, which imposed a duty on the license holder to take the necessary measures to avoid damage, hindrance and accidents that can significanlty influence humans or the environment, requires the claimant to show that the license holder did not take the measures that were reasonably required.

to the general standard of negligence. In other words: the violation of such a legal behavioral rule is *ipso facto* also negligent. This, however, is not the case for statutory or regulatory rules imposing or prohibiting specified behavior. Whether such a rule is violated, does not depend on the circumstances and on the risk the behavior foreseeably entails to others. It is only for these type of legal rules that the principle of unity between illegality and unlawfulness plays any determinative role.[215]

In practice, courts sometimes struggle to determine the exact meaning of a legal rule and have trouble deciding whether the rule imposes or prohibits specific behavior, in which case any culpable violation is per se a fault, or merely imposes a duty of care, in which case the finding of a violation requires first that losses were foreseeable and second that a normal reasonable person in the same circumstances would have behaved differently. This is particularly the case for regulations imposing safety requirements. In some cases, the courts tend to decide that insufficient safety requirements were implemented and therefore the regulation was violated merely based on the finding that the losses or injury the regulation was intended to prevent did in fact occur,[216] while in other cases courts require on top of the occurrence of the loss the showing of negligence of the person held to the safety requirements for a violation of the regulation to be established.[217] In an extreme case, the same statutory provision imposing on any holder of an environmental permit a general duty to take measures to avoid environmental damage was interpreted to be a duty of care, using the same standard of behavior as the negligence standard by the Constitutional Court,[218] while the Court of Cassation decided that this rule required more specific behavior, avoiding in effect any damage even if the costs for the required safety measures was unreasonable.[219]

74. Recently, however, some doubt has appeared whether the principle that any violation of a specific legal rule of behavior is per se wrongful still stands. In cases relating to civil liability of a governmental entity, the Court of Cassation has at least issued three rulings that seem hard to reconcile with this general principle.[220] As a result, there is debate possible on the question whether a violation of a specific legal rule at present still can always be unequivocally equated to a wrong.

§4. Culpability and Capacity

75. Liability based on Article 1382 of the Civil Code requires a culpably committed wrong. Culpability (*culpabilité—schuld*) means that the person can be

---

215. *See* Cass. 21 September 2012 (F.11.0085.N), No. 481, *Arr.Cass.* 2012, 2008, *Pas.* 2012, 1719, in which the Court clarifies that the liability of a company director who caused the company not to comply with tax rules has to be based on the generally required level of care, even though the liability of the company for this violation of tax rules is wrongful based on the unity theory, because the legal behavioral rule is only applicable to the company as a legal entity.
216. *See* e.g. Cass. 14 November 2012 (P.11.1611.F), No. 612, *Pas.* 2012, 2204, *Arr.Cass.* 2012, 2541; Cass. 6 October 1972, *Arr.Cass.* 1972–1973, 136, *Pas.* 1973, 137.
217. *See* e.g. Cass. 30 November 1998, *RW* 1999–2000, 875.
218. Con.C. No. 36/2008 of 4 March 2008.
219. Cass. 17 June 2008 (P.06.1348.N), No. 375, *Arr.Cass.* 2008, 1569, *Pas.* 2008, 1536.
220. *See infra* para. 113.

blamed for his behavior, which is only possible if the wrong that was committed is imputable (*imputable—toerekenbaar*) to the person. One can only blame a person if that person is capable of guilt (*capacité de discernement—schuldbekwaamheid*). This capacity relates to three elements.

First, a person can only be blamed for the wrong he committed if he has the ability to understand what the rule or standard of behavior is. For liability to attach, it is not required that the person did in fact realize that his particular behavior was unlawful. However, a person that is at the time of the act not capable of distinguishing right from wrong cannot be culpable for the unlawful act he has committed. Culpability therefore requires a minimum level of moral or normative insight.

Second, a person can only bear guilt if he has a sufficient awareness and understanding of reality. A person that is not capable of understanding his act or the consequences of his behavior cannot be blamed for this act. This does not mean that a person must have actually realized the full consequences of his behavior for him to commit a wrong. However, the person has to be capable of understanding these consequences. Culpability thus requires a minimum level of factual insight.

Third, a person can only be responsible for the behavior he can effectively control. If a person in fact does not have the capacity to restrain his actions, he cannot steer his behavior and any wrong committed is not his doing. One cannot be blamed for a wrongful act one could not have prevented from occurring.

76. Whether a wrong is imputable to a person, is a question of fact, to be determined for each individual case. Under Belgian law, the general presumption is that a person has the required capacity, and therefore is liable for the losses caused by his wrongs. This means that lack of culpability is an affirmative defense in civil liability proceedings. It is up to the person who is alleged to be liable to prove that the wrong he has committed does not amount to a fault because he is not culpable. If incapacity of guilt is not invoked and proven by the defendant, the court cannot legally exclude liability on this basis.[221] However, this is different when the alleged wrong is a criminal offense. As a defendant in criminal proceedings enjoys the presumption of innocence and the prosecution bears the full burden of proof, the defendant can suffice with showing an element that indicates the plausibility for a ground of lack of culpability, for the claimant to have to show his culpability.[222]

77. Capability of guilt is not a fixed legal status a person has and keeps, it always is the qualification of the relationship between a specific wrongful act and a specific actor at a specific time in specific circumstances. In reality, however, there are not many disputes about culpability reaching the courts resulting in published case law. Cases involving a normally capable person to commit a wrong because of sudden momentary lack of culpability are very often treated by finding a justification for the wrongful act in force majeure.[223] The available cases about culpability mostly concern categories of persons that systematically lack the capacity for culpability.

221. Cass. 30 October 1980, *Pas.* 1981, 262, *Arr.Cass.* 1980–1981, 235, No. 136.
222. *See supra* para. 45 and footnote 123.
223. *See infra* Part IV, Ch. 2, §2.

78. As opposed to Dutch[224] and German[225] law, Belgian law does not impose a fixed age under which one does not have the capacity of incurring extracontractual liability. The age of legal majority, set at eighteen,[226] is only relevant for the competence of a person to commit legal acts (*acte juridique—rechtshandeling*),[227] such as to enter into a valid and thus binding legal transaction.[228] As a wrong is not a legal act but a material fact (*fait juridique—rechtsfeit*),[229] no legal capacity is required.

Thus, there is no categorical reason why a juvenile would not be civilly liable for the harm he has wrongfully caused.[230] Certainly the fact that parents are vicariously liable for the damage caused by their minor children,[231] does not preclude these juveniles themselves to be liable as well. However, in responding to this liability by compensating the victim, by agreeing to a settlement, or by defending against a claim in liability brought by a victim, the minor will be legally represented by his parents, who are his legal custodians.

However, very young children—often referred to as *infantes*—have not yet acquired the characteristics required to be capable of guilt. One says that they have not yet reached the "age of reason," which is an elliptic construction to state that they do not yet have sufficient moral insight, factual insight or control over their actions.[232] At which age a child obtains these characteristics, is a question of fact that has to be determined by the courts on a case-by-case basis.[233] Reviews of case law, however, have concluded that Belgian courts in general tend to find that children from the age of seven to nine onward can be held liable based on their own fault, depending on the particular development of the child but also taking into account the type of wrongful act committed.

According to the generally accepted theory, the age and development of the minor is relevant to determine his culpability (the subjective element of the fault), but should not be taken into account when judging the wrongfulness of his behavior (the objective element of the fault).[234] Therefore, to decide whether a minor has committed a wrong, his behavior has to be compared to the general standard of behavior. As was

---

224. Art. 6:164 Dutch Civil Code.
225. §828 German Civil Code.
226. Articles 388 and 488 CC.
227. A legal act is an act performed with the intent of creating the legal consequences the law attaches to it. For such act to be valid—and thus to have these consequences—the person has to have legal capacity. Art. 1124 CC.
228. Minors are therefore represented by their parents (Arts. 373–374 CC) or a custodian (Arts. 389 et seq. CC) in legal transactions.
229. A material fact is either something happening without any interference of a person but it can also be an act of a person that is not performed with the intent of creating the legal consequences the law might attach to it in the given circumstances. Such acts have consequences if they occur, without any "validity" being required.
230. Cass. 24 January 1985, No. 306, *Arr.Cass.* 1984–1985, 682, *Pas.* 1985, 603.
231. *See infra* Part II, Ch. 2, §2.
232. Cass. 30 May 1969, *Pas.* 1969, 879, *Arr.Cass.* 1969, 943; Cass. 13 October 1999 (P.99.0861.F), No. 528, *Pas.* 1999, 1308, *Arr.Cass.* 1999, 1255.
233. Cass. 3 May 1978, *Arr.Cass.* 1978, 1037, *Pas.* 1978, 1012; Cass. 30 October 1980, *Pas.* 1981, 262, *Arr.Cass.* 1980–1981, 235, No. 136.
234. *See supra* para. 67.

mentioned earlier, however, legal practice reveals that courts do in fact sometimes apply a lower standard of behavior in cases involving minors. The Court of Cassation has at least in one occasion allowed a judgment that specifically referred to the age of the alleged wrongdoer to find that no wrong was committed to stand.[235]

79. When a wrong is committed by a person with a mental illness that impairs their judgment or limits their control over their actions, the court will have to decide whether the person is capable of guilt. Again, no fixed legal status exists which implies such incapacity. As it is a question of fact, it has to be determined based on the person's specific capabilities at the time of the disputed act. If a person is considered irresponsible, the wrongs he has committed cannot be imputed to him, and he cannot be liable on the basis of a fault.

As this renders a category of persons who are more likely to behave irrationally and thereby to cause harm in effect immune from fault liability, the legislature has in 1935 decided to insert a specific rule into the Civil Code,[236] which makes it possible for mentally ill to be held fully or partially liable for the damage they wrongfully cause, even though any guilt is lacking.[237] Under the present interpretation of the Court of Cassation, this liability can only be applied to people whose loss of control is due to mental causes, and not to a person that suffers from a momentary lapse of consciousness as a consequence of a physical condition.[238] A mentally retarded person, however, can be held liable on this basis.[239]

---

235. Cass. 5 June 2003 (C.01.0252.F), No. 337, *Pas.* 2003, 1125, *Arr.Cass.* 2003, 1337. *See also supra* footnote 192 and accompanying text.
236. Article 1386*bis* CC, inserted by Art. 1 of the (federal) Act of 16 April 1935, *Moniteur belge—Belgisch Staatsblad* 18 April 1935, and recently reworded by Art. 86 of the (federal) Act of 5 May 2014 on Involuntary Commitment.
237. On the extent of this liability, *see infra* para. 255.
238. Cass. 24 April 1980, No. 542, *Pas.* 1980, 1055, *Arr.Cass.* 1979–1980, 1065; Cass. 20 June 1979, *Arr.Cass.* 1978–1979, 1258, *Pas.* 1979, 1217.
239. Cass. 6 September 2013 (C.12.0360.F), No. 428, *Pas.* 2013, 1578, *Arr.Cass.* 2013, 1744.

Chapter 2. Specific Cases

§1. Liability of Professionals

I. In General

80. While in general the personal characteristics of the alleged wrongdoer are not to be taken into account when judging whether his behavior is negligent or not,[240] the negligence of a professional's behavior is judged using the criterion of what would be reasonable for a normal person from the same profession in the given circumstances. This standard is obviously higher than what would be reasonable for a layperson. In effect, the courts apply the age-old adage *spondet peritiam artis, et imperitia culpae adnumeratur*, holding professionals to the state of the art of their profession. Thus, the rules that are considered to hold standard practices for a profession are used to specify the vague general standard of care applied in fault liability. This, however, does not mean that a professional is shielded from liability if he acted in the way that is general practice in his profession: the fact that others are also behaving unreasonably, is no excuse.[241]

81. Professionals are especially held to information duties. The unequal situation between the uninformed client and the specialized professional and the fact that the client uses the professional's services just because of the assumed and expected competence of the professional are cited as a basis for imposing a special duty of care on the professional. This means that although according to the general rules a person that has provided incorrect information would only be liable if the victim has proved that the incorrectness of the provided information is a result of his negligence, the Court of Cassation has reversed the rule by allowing courts to hold the provision of incorrect information in itself to be wrongful if the information receiver legitimately should have been able to rely on the information being correct because of the special qualification of the information provider.[242]

82. Historically, Belgian law contained several provisions prohibiting professionals such as physicians and attorneys to limit their personal liability. Full personal liability was considered to offer the client or patient the best guarantee for top quality and completely honest service. This meant also that liberal professions could not be performed by incorporated partnerships with limited liability, which in fact would

240. *See supra* para. 67.

241. Cass. 4 September 2013 (P.13.0358.F), No. 417, *Pas.* 2013, 1550, *Arr.Cass.* 2013, 1707.

242. Cass. 5 January 2012 (C.11.0125.N), No. 11, *Arr.Cass.* 2012, 44, *Pas.* 2012, 35.

shield the partners from personal liability.[243] Rules of professional ethics imposed minimum professional insurance requirements.[244] Recently, those laws have been changed, allowing liberal professionals to offer their services through corporations or incorporated partnerships with limited liability. In effect, this limits their liability to the extent the corporate entity is solvent to compensate the victims. Recent versions of rules of professional ethics also allow contractual limitation of liability versus clients.[245]

II. Medical Practitioners

83. In most cases, the relation between a patient and a medical practitioner or the hospital or other health institutions is contractual. However, as the victim in most cases involving liability of medical practitioners has suffered bodily or personal harm that allegedly was caused by a fault, the liability is based on a criminal offense,[246] and can as such be based on the extra contractual fault liability of Article 1382 of the Civil Code.[247] In practice, most court decisions in medical disputes are based on tortious liability, not on contractual liability.

84. The basic rights of patients are set out in the (federal) Patients' Rights Act of 22 August 2002. They include the right to receive qualitative treatment that is appropriate for his needs,[248] the right to freely choose the medical practitioner,[249] the right to receive complete and accurate information on his medical situation and the likely evolution of his health,[250] and the right to freely and fully informed consent to

243. Article 61, §1, Companies Code, states that corporations and incorporated partnerships act through their organs, whose powers and authority are specified in this Code, their corporate purpose and their company charter, and adds that the members of these organs are not personally bound by the obligations of the incorporated entity. Because of the immunity of subcontractors (*see infra* Part II, Ch. 1, §2), the physical person in fact performing the professional activity would not be liable.

244. *See* e.g. Art. 272 of the Codex Deontologie voor Advocaten of the Orde van Vlaamse Balies, applicable to members of the Flemish Bars Association.

245. *See* e.g. Art. 74 of the Codex Deontologie voor Advocaten of the Orde van Vlaamse Balies, which allows members of the Flemish Bars Association to limit their liability upto the amount which is covered by the professional insurance through the Bar, i.e., EUR 1,250,000.

246. Articles 398–400 PC specify the criminal offences of voluntary wounding, and according to Arts. 418–421 PC he who unintentionally by lack of care causes physical injury, commits the offence of unintentional wounding. The courts interpret this lack of care to be identical to the concept of fault as used in Art. 1382 CC, so that any civil negligence that results in personal damage *ipso facto* becomes a criminal offence. *See supra* para. 45, in particular the text accompanying footnote 124.

247. *See supra* para. 52.

248. Article 5 (federal) Patients Rights Act of 22 August 2002.

249. Article 6 (federal) Patients Rights Act of 22 August 2002.

250. Article 7 (federal) Patients Rights Act of 22 August 2002.

the treatment.[251] These rights have to be honored by the medical practitioner and by the medical institution in which the practitioner treats the patient.[252]

A violation of such a right will almost always be considered as wrongful. Apart from and additionally to the general rules relating to vicarious liability,[253] the legislation on hospitals and other institutions where medical care is provided renders the institution liable for the loss caused by a violation of a patient's rights by any professional working in the institution, irrespective of the legal qualification of the relation between the institution and this professional.[254] However, the institution can limit or exclude this vicarious liability for independent practitioners, i.e., practitioners that are not servants and thus not employees of the institution,[255] if it has informed the patient of this exclusion in a written form, clarifying the type of relation it has with the medical practitioner, before the care has been provided.[256]

85. There are no special or separate rules on civil liability for medical interventions. Based on the general principles, however, medical treatment can only be performed with the consent of the patient, for a therapeutic purpose, and with respect for a reasonable proportionality between the foreseeable risk and the expected benefit of the treatment, adhering to the state of the art practices in the relevant sector. An intervention that does not comply with any of these requirements will be considered wrongful under the general standard of Article 1382 of the Civil Code.

86. Many disputes about the liability of medical practitioners turn around alleged shortcomings in the performance of information duties or actions undertaken without properly informed consent of the patient. Information duties are considered to be *obligations de moyens*, meaning that they only require the information debtor to apply reasonable effort and care. According to standard rules of evidence as applied to a liability dispute, this means that the victim, here the patient, has to prove that the information debtor, here the medical practitioner, has not provided him with sufficient correct information and thus has committed a fault.[257] In practice, this is of course extremely difficult for the patient, as most often information is given and discusses orally and no record remains of the information given.

In an important decision of 25 June 2015, the Court of Cassation ruled that an attorney bears the burden of proof that he has complied with his duty to inform his client about his options to receive legal aid, instead of the client having to prove that the lawyer committed a fault by not giving him the necessary information.[258] The Court thus applies the general rules on the burden of proof for disputes about the performance of contractual obligations—which require the claimant to show that the obligation

251. Article 8 (federal) Patients Rights Act of 22 August 2002.
252. Article 30, para. 1, (federal) Coordinated Act of 10 July 2008 on Hospitals and Other Institutions of Care.
253. *See infra* Part II, Ch. 1, §1.
254. Article 30, para. 4, (federal) Coordinated Act of 10 July 2008 on Hospitals and Other Institutions of Care.
255. *See infra* Part II, Ch. 1, §2.
256. Article 30, para. 4, (federal) Coordinated Act of 10 July 2008 on Hospitals and Other Institutions of Care.
257. Cass. 16 December 2004 (C.03.0407.N), No. 616, *Arr.Cass.* 2004, 2081, *Pas.* 2004, 2022.
258. Cass. 25 June 2015 (C.14.0382.F), No. 445, *Pas.* 2015, 1753, *Arr.Cass.* 2015, 1763.

exists[259] and the defendant to show that he has been relieved because the obligation was already performed[260]—to disputes about the liability for not having performed an obligation, which according to these rules normally should have required the claimant (here the patient) to prove that all constituent elements of the liability—including the fault of the defendant, the medical practitioner—are present to comply with its burden to show the obligation to compensate for the loss exists.[261] This decision can be understood to be relevant for disputes between patients and medical practitioners as well, requiring the practitioner to show that he has correctly and sufficiently informed the patient and releasing the patient from the impossibly heavy burden to prove he did not receive the required information.

87. In general, patients encounter great difficulties in proving the elements required for liability to attach. In particular, it turns out to be hard to show that the medical practitioner acted negligently, and the establishment of a causal relation between an eventual fault and the physical condition the patient is in is often impossible in the light of the uncertain result of any medical treatment. To help victims of such cases, a general no-fault system of compensation for serious cases of harm resulting from medical treatment was created.[262] Within the (federal) State Institute for Health and Invalidity Insurance, that is part of the national social security system, a Fund for Medical Accidents is created, financed by the government.

This Fund fully compensates victims suffering sufficiently serious damage caused by so-called medical accidents without liability.[263] A medical accident without liability is an accident related to the supply of medical or health services that does not give rise to civil liability of the practitioner, that does not follow from the condition of the patient, and that causes abnormal damage to the patient. Abnormal damage is damage that should not have occurred taking into account the state of science, the condition of the patient and its objectively predictable evolution.[264] This system thus only covers damage that is not the result of the normal evolution of the condition of the patient. Hence, harm caused by an incorrect diagnosis or by therapeutic failure, allowing the underlying condition of the patient to deteriorate, is not covered. Only very serious cases—such as when the patient has died, suffers from permanent invalidity of 25% or more, has been unable to work for at least six months during a period of a year, or suffers from exceptionally gravely disturbed living circumstances—give a right to compensation in cases without liability.[265] This very severe restriction of the system, resulting in very few patients actually receiving such compensation, was deemed to be necessary to avoid the system, which offers full compensation, from becoming budgetary not feasible in the given circumstances.

88. The Fund for Medical Accidents also performs the function of a guarantee fund for medical practitioners and their insurers. It compensates patients that are the

259. Article 1315, para. 1, CC.
260. Article 1315, para. 2, CC.
261. Article 1315, para. 1, CC.
262. (Federal) Act of 31 March 2010 on the Compensation of Damage as a Consequence of Health Care.
263. Article 4, 1°, Act of 31 March 2010.
264. Article 2, 7°, Act of 31 March 2010.
265. Article 5, Act of 31 March 2010.

victim of harm caused by a medical treatment that gives rise to the civil liability of the practitioner when that practitioner is not or not sufficiently insured[266] or the insurer is not prepared to offer sufficient compensation.[267] For sufficiently serious cases, the Fund also compensates the victim if the practitioner or his insurer dispute the liability.[268] After compensating the victim, the Fund is subrogated in the patient's rights based on civil liability, so it can recover the paid compensation from the practitioner or his insurer. The patient, therefore, cannot combine this type of compensation by the Fund and compensation based on civil liability by the liable practitioner.[269]

III. Legal Practitioners

89. Authors and courts agree that the relation between an attorney and his client is contractual. Because of the very limited possibilities to invoke extracontractual liability between contract parties,[270] the potential liability of the lawyer for losses suffered by his client is almost exclusively contractual. As this monograph does not treat Belgian contractual liability, this will not be discussed here.

90. Extracontractual liability is in principle only applicable if the attorney's fault is a criminal offense,[271] or if his action or inaction caused losses to a third party.[272] As most instances of professional liability of legal practitioners deal with losses suffered by the lawyer's client, not many published court decisions deal with extracontractual liability of legal practitioners. However, there is no reason to assume that the normal general rules would not apply to an attorney's liability to any third party that suffers a loss caused by his professional action. To decide whether a legal practitioner's behavior is negligent, his action or inaction will be compared with the behavior of a normal reasonable legal practitioner in the same circumstances. A violation of a legal rule imposing or prohibiting specified behavior will per se constitute a wrong if no ground of justification is present.[273] Specifically, a lawyer that violates a rule of professional ethics and thereby causes damage to the opposing party in a litigation can be held to compensate that opposing party for its loss.[274]

266. Article 4, 2°, Act of 31 March 2010.
267. Article 4, 4°, Act of 31 March 2010.
268. Article 4, 3°, Act of 31 March 2010.
269. Article 3, §3, Act of 31 March 2010.
270. *See supra* General Introduction, §5.
271. *See supra* para. 52.
272. *See supra* para. 72.
273. On the grounds of justification, *see* Part IV, Ch. 2.
274. *See* e.g. CA Brussels 24 February 2009, *JLMB* 2009, 1430.

IV. Builders and Architects

91. The liability of construction companies and architects for harm suffered by their client is based in contract.[275] As this monograph only covers extracontractual liability, this liability will not be discussed here. It should be noted, however, that while the general liability for defects that are visible at the time of formal delivery of the construction ends by the acceptance of the construction by the client, there is a special mandatory rule[276] rendering the construction company and the architect liable for a fixed period of ten years after this acceptance for damage resulting from serious defects in the stability of the construction.[277] The architect and construction company are required to have third-party insurance covering this liability.[278]

92. The civil liability of construction companies and architects for losses suffered by third parties is governed by the general rules.

The special third-party liability that exist in relation to constructed immovable goods, Article 1386 of the Civil Code, only imposes a strict liability on the owner of the construction.[279] The other provision invoked for losses caused by things, Article 1384, paragraph 1, of the Civil Code, which can also be invoked for damage caused by a defective immovable good,[280] places the strict liability on the custodian of the defective thing,[281] so can neither be invoked against the architect or construction company, unless the damage is caused during the works when the construction has not yet been delivered and the construction company can be considered to be the custodian,[282] and the damage is not caused by a partial or total collapse of the building, as in that case the special rule of Article 1386 of the Civil Code is understood to exclude the application of the general rule of Article 1384, paragraph 1, of the Civil Code.[283]

This means that the liability of architects and construction companies will most often have to be based on Article 1382 of the Civil Code, requiring a fault according to the general rules.[284] This fault can consist in a violation of specific legal or regulatory rules relating to the workplace or a lack of care in keeping the workplace safe, also for third parties that might gain access to the grounds, and in a violation of specific legal or regulatory rules or negligence in the way the construction is designed or the plans have been executed.

275. On the very limited possibilities to invoke liability in tort between contract parties, *see supra* General Introduction, §5.
276. This liability cannot be excluded or limited by contract. *See* Cass. 10 May 1984, No. 519, *Pas.* 1984, 1106, *Arr.Cass.* 1983–1984, 1177.
277. Article 1792 CC.
278. (Federal) Act of 31 May 2017 on the Mandatory Insurance of the Ten Year Liability of Construction Companies and Architects.
279. *See infra* para. 150.
280. Cass. 12 July 1945, *Pas.* 1945, 202, *Arr.Verbr.* 1945, 188; Cass. 24 May 1945, *Pas.* 1945, 172, *Arr.Verbr.* 1945, 161; Cass. 25 March 1943, *Pas.* 1943, 110, *Arr.Verbr.* 1943, 68.
281. *See infra* para. 148.
282. *See* e.g. CA Brussels 8 November 2011, *RDC* 2012, 91.
283. *See* Cass. 28 November 2016 (C.15.0521.F), *JT* 2017, 210, *RDC* 2017, 317, *Forum de l'assurance* 2017.
284. Cass. 4 October 1973, *Pas.* 1974, 124, *Arr.Cass.* 1974, 135; Cass. 18 May 1961, *Pas.* 1961, 1006.

93. Neither the construction company nor the architect is subject to the no-fault liability based on nuisance, which only rests on persons holding an attribute of the property right on the premises from which the hindrance originates.[285] However, if the excessive hindrance a neighbor suffers from construction works is caused by an act of the constructor or the architect which is part of the work that the owner has assigned them to undertake, the owner is liable based on nuisance, as this act can then be considered to be part of the performance of the property right on the hindering premises.[286] This is not the case if the construction company causes damage to a neighbor by an act that cannot be considered part of its task demanded by the owner.[287]

V. Others

94. Belgium knows a so-called Latin notary system, which was introduced at the start of the nineteenth century when the territories that now constitute the country were annexed by France.[288] This system is very different from the Anglo-American notary system, where the notarial function is largely limited to certification. Here, an intervention of a notary is required for many types of transactions to be either valid or opposable to third parties. The notary is exercising a liberal profession. He is working as an independent or as a partner in a partnership with other notaries. However, the notary has received an official mandate, and can be considered to be a public officer when performing acts that are part of this mandate. On the other hand, the notary also acts in a private capacity, for instance, by advising clients or helping them draft transactions for which no authentic deed is required.

Traditionally, the liability of a notary when supplying services as a liberal professional has been treated as contractual,[289] while the liability of the notary when intervening as a public official is considered to be extracontractual. This difference is mainly relevant for the length of the statutory prescription period, which is ten years for contractual liability but only five years after the discovery of the harm and the identity of the person liable for extra contractual liability.[290] The Court of Cassation had implicitly decided in 2004 that the notary's liability is based on Article 1382 of the Civil Code when it causes damage while performing its public role.[291] However, the Constitutional Court has later decided that an interpretation of Article 2262*bis* of the Civil Code, that would result in a prescription period of ten years for the liability

285. *See infra* para. 110.
286. Cass. 24 April 2003 (C.01.0371.F), No. 262, *Pas.* 2003, 870, *Arr.Cass.* 2003, 1035; Cass. 13 March 1987, No. 416, *Arr.Cass.* 1986–1987, 920, *Pas.* 1987, 834.
287. *See* e.g. Cass.25 June 2009 (C.07.0354.F), No. 438, *Pas.* 2009, 1665, *Arr.Cass.* 2009, 1821, involving a case of fire caused by a worker that was careless with a cigarette.
288. Act of 25 venôse year XI (i.e., 16 March 1803) on the Office of the Notary, which after several amendments is still part of Belgian statutory law.
289. Cass. 23 October 2008 (C.06.0158.F – C.06.0478.F), No. 576, *Pas.* 2008, 2336, *Arr.Cass.* 2008, 2340.
290. Article 2262*bis*, §1, CC, which is applicable to notaries according to Art. 2276*quinquies* CC. *See infra* Part IV, Ch. 1.
291. Cass. 29 September 2004, *Revue du notariat belge* 2009, 214; *cf.* Cass. 24 September 2009 (C.08.0617.N), No. 525, *Arr.Cass.* 2009, 2104, *Pas.* 2009, 1985.

of a notary when helping parties to draft and execute a contract and a prescription period of five years for that same liability if the contract happens to be executed in an authentic deed, would constitute an unconstitutional discrimination.[292] In a later decision, the Court of Cassation has allowed a lower court to qualify as contractual the relation between a bank and a notary that was drafting an authentic deed for a credit contract, to the extent the bank had asked the notary to verify the identity of borrowers, so that the longer prescription period could be applied even though the notary was drafting an authentic deed, which is part of its official role.[293] In a later decision, the Court has ruled that the notary's liability is based in contract every time he performs his function at the request of a client, even if the acts he performs are part of his official duties.[294] The only instance in which the notary's liability will be extracontractual is therefore limited to the cases in which the notary has been appointed and instructed by a court and is not acting at the request of a client.

When a notary would in the performance of his function cause damage not to one or more of his clients but to third parties, his liability is purely extracontractual.[295]

95. Company auditors perform a liberal profession. They perform tasks that are required by law, most of them enumerated in the Companies Code. These tasks include the verification of the company accounts and other particular certifications. Apart from these statutory tasks, they can also perform functions their clients demand.

Company auditors are liable according to the general rules of civil liability. This means that the liability of the auditor toward the company or its client is contractual,[296] while his liability toward third parties is extracontractual, based on Article 1382 of the Civil Code. Their liability when performing tasks required by law, however, is limited to an amount of EUR 12 million for assignments for a corporation quoted on the stock exchange (regulated market) and EUR 3 million if related to assignments for other persons if the fault is not intentional.[297] This liability is mandatory, so it cannot be limited or excluded by contract.[298] For tasks an auditor performs that are not imposed by statute but are purely contractual services provided to the client, however, the parties are free to limit or exclude liability consistent with the general rules.[299]

96. A fault committed by an auditor can of course consist in a violation of a legal rule requiring specific behavior or imposing a specific duty on the auditor. For company auditors appointed as *commissaires* in a corporation, the Companies Code specifically states that they are liable toward the company and toward third parties for all damage that is caused by a violation of the provisions of that Code or of clauses in the company charter. For violations in which they did not take part, they can escape

---

292. Con.C. No. 150/2012 of 13 December 2012.
293. Cass. 6 June 2013 (C.12.0224.F), *JT* 2013, 629, *Revue du notariat belge* 2014, 268.
294. Cass. 29 June 2017 (C.12.0590.F), *NJW* 2017, 796.
295. Cass. 15 October 1891, *Pas.* 1891, 254.
296. This liability can only be based in tort when the fault committed by the auditor is a criminal offence. *See supra* para. 52.
297. Article 9*bis*, para. 1, (federal) Act of 22 July 1953 on the Institute of Company Auditors and Organizing Public Supervision on the Profession of Company Auditor, delegating power to the King (i.e., the federal executive) to change these amounts.
298. Article 9*bis*, para. 2, (federal) Act of 22 July 1953 on the Institute of Company Auditors and Organizing Public Supervision on the Profession of Company Auditor.
299. *See infra* Part IV, Ch. 5.

this liability if they show that they have correctly fulfilled their duties and they, as soon as they became aware of the violation, have complained about it with the board of directors and if this board did not react to their complaint to the general meeting of shareholders.[300]

Auditors, however, are also subject to rules of professional ethics and disciplinary supervision by their professional organization.[301] Violation of such rules can also constitute a wrong, which can be invoked as a basis for liability by third parties suffering damage.

Finally, Belgian law does not require a preexisting duty to be breached for a wrong to be committed, and neither are violations of rules and duties understood to constitute only relative wrongs, depending on the purpose or function of the rule.[302] As the tasks of an auditor are generally known to be not only aimed at the interests of the client but also at the (investing) public at large, an auditor that performs his functions carelessly will not only be contractually liable toward his client but will also risk extracontractual liability for all losses suffered by third parties, in particular investors.[303]

97. External independent accountants and tax consultants are liable based on the general rules.[304] They cannot limit or exclude this liability for faults committed when performing statutorily required tasks or for intentional acts.[305] They are required to have professional third-party insurance, approved by the Council of the Institute for Accountants and Tax Consultants.[306]

98. Banks are subject to the general rules of civil liability. Their liability toward clients will most often be based in contract. Extracontractual liability will only apply toward third parties,[307] or between contract parties if the fault committed by the bank is a criminal offense.[308] Belgian courts have generally been very open to the idea that, while the function of banks may not be a public service in the strict sense of the concept, their role is so important for the fabric of interconnecting relationships in modern society, that a lack of care by a bank in the performance of its functions constitutes a wrong that can be invoked as a fault for liability toward third parties. For instance in the area of liability for providing credit to an economically unhealthy debtor, thus artificially creating an unwarranted public perception of solvency and creditworthiness on which third parties rely to subsequently suffer losses when the debtor eventually defaults, Belgian law is pretty strict, relatively easily convicting banks to compensate third parties for their losses. Also withdrawing credit in a careless manner, without

300. Article 140, para. 2, Companies Code.
301. (Federal) Act of 22 July 1953 on the Institute of Company Auditors and Organizing Public Supervision on the Profession of Company Auditor.
302. *See supra* para. 70.
303. *See* e.g. CA Brussels 2 January 1986, *RDC* 1987, 425.
304. Article 33, para. 1, (federal) Act of 22 April 1999 on Bookkeeping and Taxation Professions.
305. Article 33, para. 2, (federal) Act of 22 April 1999 on Bookkeeping and Taxation Professions.
306. Article 33, para. 3, (federal) Act of 22 April 1999 on Bookkeeping and Taxation Professions.
307. The fact that the fault which caused damage to a third party at the same time also constitutes a beach of contract to the other contract party does not preclude the person who has committed the act—or the one who is vicariously liable for this person—to be liable in tort toward this third party. *See* 25 October 2012 (C.12.0079.F), No. 568, *Pas.* 2012, 2039, *Arr.Cass.* 2012, 2332; Cass. 11 June 1981, *Arr.Cass.* 1980–1981, 1168, No. 583, *Pas.* 1981, 1159.
308. *See supra* para. 52.

taking the proper interests of the debtor into account, is comparably easily recognized as a fault leading to liability.

§2. Abuse of Rights

99. [309]Having the right to do something does not mean that one is shielded from any liability for the losses one imposes on others by acting this way. Under Belgian law, a particular way of exercising a subjective right can be considered wrongful in certain circumstances. Of course, the fact that a person has a right means that he has a certain leeway in deciding how to act. If one exercises a right outside this margin of discretion, however, this is considered to be an abuse of right (*abus de droit—rechtsmisbruik*), which constitutes a civil wrong and thus leads to liability based on Article 1382 of the Civil Code if it has caused damage.

100. An abuse of power is a wrong, leading to liability to restore the resulting damage. Thus, if a person has an authority to act which is granted for a specific purpose, he abuses his right if he uses this power for another purpose. Some authors consider this abuse of authority not to be a type of abuse of rights but a separate legal phenomenon. On the other hand, one can say that there are good reasons to consider using a right with another motive than furthering the protection of one's legitimate interests as an analogous problem. Rights are a form of legal protection the law offers persons to allow them to protect their own interests. If they exercise a right without legitimate interest in doing so, one can consider this a deviation of the right from its purpose.[310]

101. Within this narrower concept of abuse of right, as distinguished from abuse of power or authority, four categories of cases have developed.

The first category of cases recognized by the courts involve the exercise of a right with the intent to cause damage.[311]

The second category contains cases in which the right holder exercises his right in a harmful manner without having any interest in doing so.[312] The typical example

309. Another remedy against an abuse of right is the forfeiture of the option of the right holder to exercise his right in this particular abusive way. *See* Cass. 6 January 2011 (C.09.0624.F), No. 12, *Pas.* 2011, 44, *Arr.Cass.* 2011, 41.

310. *Cf.* Cass. 24 September 1992, No. 626, *Pas.* 1992, 1049, *Arr.Cass.* 1991–1992, 1129.

311. Although the possibility of limiting the exercise of property rights in case of intent to harm another was already hinted at in CA Ghent 19 April 1834, *Pas.* 1834, II, 95, the first court decisions in which an abuse of right was actually found to exist according to the court, occurred in France: CA Colmar 2 May 1855, *Dalloz* 1856, 9 (involving a case where a person had built a chimney only to ruin his neighbor's view); Cour de Cassation of France 3 August 1915, *Dalloz* 1917, I, 79, *Sirey* 1920, 300 (a case involving a farmer having built a high metal fence with sharp peaks to hinder hot air balloons landing and departing from a neighboring field). Later, Belgian courts ruled in the same way. *See* for more recent examples, Cass. 19 February 2010 (C.09.0118.F – C.09.0132.F – C.09.0134.F), No. 114, *Pas.* 2010, 510, *Arr.Cass.* 2010, 489; Cass. 14 February 1992, No. 311, *Arr.Cass.* 1991–1992, 557, *Pas.* 1992, 528; Cass. 18 February 1965, *Pas.* 1965, 621; Cass. 29 November 1962, *Pas.* 1963, 406; Cass. 11 April 1958, *Arr. Verbr.* 1958, 595, *Pas.* 1958, 867.

312. Cass. 30 January 2003 (C.00.0632.F), No. 69, *Pas.* 2003, 227, *Arr.Cass.* 2003, 270; Cass. 6 January 2006 (C.04.0358.F), No. 18, *Pas.* 2006, 71, *Arr.Cass.* 2006, 71.

is an unsecured creditor (or a creditor holding a lower rank mortgage on a property) that forecloses on a property of his debtor that is (also) mortgaged to another creditor (with a higher rank) while the potential proceeds are not sufficient to fully repay the (higher ranked) mortgage(s). This foreclosure cannot benefit the foreclosing creditor, but in some circumstances—such as during depressed market conditions—might harm the debtor and/or the other higher ranked secured creditors, who would prefer to wait with the forced sale until the market value of the mortgaged property has risen back to a normal level.[313]

Then, the doctrine was expanded to a third category of cases where the right holder can choose between two equally advantageous alternatives to exercise his right and he chooses the manner in which he causes more damage.[314] The textbook example is a case where a department store could freely choose to place its neon sign at its façade at different places but chose exactly this spot that made its sign block the view to the sign of another store further down the street.[315]

The fourth category contains cases where the court finds that the harm created for another person is completely disproportionate to the relative advantage the right holder gains from exercising his right in this particular way.[316] The typical example is the case where a person has not knowingly built a garage half a building brick over the line that separates his lot from his neighbor's, and this neighbor invokes his property right to demand the demolition of this building after more than twenty years.[317]

102. Based on the criterion used in this last category of cases, the Court of Cassation nowadays uses one general criterion to define an abuse of right. In this general rule, exercising a right is abusive and therefore wrongful if the right holder has chosen to exercise his right in a particular manner that "obviously" falls outside of the margin of ways in which a normal reasonable person would exercise this right in these circumstances.[318] Thus, the Court in effect has introduced an efficiency

---

313. *Cf.* Cass. 27 October 1950, *Pas.* 1951, 101, *Arr.Verbr.* 1951, 82, a case where the Court approved a decision that had held the foreclosure of a pledge or property lien wrongful because it could not benefit the creditor in the given circumstances.

314. *See* Cass. 16 November 1961, *Pas.* 1962, 332.

315. Cass. 12 July 1917, *Pas.* 1918, 65, One can wonder why precisely this case is used as the textbook example for this category, while one can imagine that it was in the context of competition of course in the interest of the department store to focus the attention of potential customers only on itself and to try to avoid them realizing there are alternative stores.

316. Cass. 17 February 2012 (C.10.0651.F), No. 118, *Pas.* 2012, 369, *Arr.Cass.* 2012, 403; Cass. 6 January 2011 (C.09.0624.F), No. 12, *Pas.* 2011, 44, *Arr.Cass.* 2011, 41; Cass. 17 May 2002 (C.01.0101.F), No. 302, *Pas.* 2002, 1169, *Arr.Cass.* 2002, 1306; Cass. 19 November 1987, No. 168, *Pas.* 1988, 332, *Arr.Cass.* 1987–1988, 354.

317. Cass. 10 September 1971, *Arr.Cass.* 1972, 31, *Pas.* 1972, 28.

318. *See* originally Cass. 10 September 1971, *Arr.Cass.* 1972, 31, *Pas.* 1972, 28. More recent: Cass. 6 January 2011 (C.09.0624.F), No. 12, *Pas.* 2011, 44, *Arr.Cass.* 2011, 41; Cass. 14 October 2010 (C.09.0608.F), No. 603, *Pas.* 2010, 2643, *Arr.Cass.* 2010, 2507; Cass. 1 October 2010 (C.09.0565.N), No. 571, *Arr.Cass.* 2010, 2385, *Pas.* 2010, 2470; Cass. 8 February 2010 (C.09.0416.F), No. 89, *Pas.* 2010, 402, *Arr.Cass.* 2010, 383; Cass. 9 March 2009 (C.08.0331.F), No. 182, *Pas.* 2009, 689, *Arr.Cass.* 2010, 762.

requirement into the legitimate exercise of rights.[319] The words used by the Court do not seem to be different from the general standard of care applied in negligence, although it is argued that the use of the word "obviously" (*manifestement—kennelijk*) means that an abuse of right requires some form of "gross" negligence, whatever that may mean.

§3. Injury to Reputation and Privacy

103. Personality rights (*droits de la personalité—persoonlijkheidsrechten*) give the holder legal control and authority over the use and protection of the intrinsic elements or expressions of his personality. Examples are the right to one's portrait or image, voice sound, name, and the general right to privacy. Although personality rights are not statutorily defined or protected in Belgium,[320] they are generally recognized as being part of existing positive law, as they are routinely invoked to serve as a basis for court decisions.[321] The Court of Cassation recognizes these rights to be based on the general principle of law that prohibits the intrusion into someone else's personality.[322]

104. Restoration in case of an infringement of a personality right in Belgium often takes the form of damages. Analysis of the case law shows that, although plenty of judgments continue to apply the general principles of civil liability—requiring the showing of a specific loss caused by a proven fault for liability to attach, and imposing an obligation to pay damages equal to the losses actually suffered—some systematic deviation from this pattern can be discerned.

105. First, in many cases the infringement of the personality right is in itself considered a sufficient basis for liability. As discussed earlier, this can be explained to be in conformity to the general theory of Belgian civil liability law, as the infringement of a subjective right violates specific behavioral legal rules that are part of existing positive law, on which this subjective right is based.[323] For instance, a surgeon operating on a patient without his consent commits a wrongful act if there is no emergency that

319. Cass. 6 January 2006 (C.04.0358.F), No. 18, *Pas.* 2006, 71, *Arr.Cass.* 2006, 71, in which the Court stated that an abuse entails the invocation of a right without "reasonable and *sufficient* interest"; Cass. 6 January 2011 (C.09.0624.F), No. 12, *Pas.* 2011, 44, *Arr.Cass.* 2011, 41, stating that a right is exercised in a way which obviously goes beyond the normal exercise if the caused harm is not in proportion to the benefit the rightholder was pursuing.

320. Belgian law does not know a provision like the one found in Art. 9 of the French Civil Code, protecting the privacy of persons. There is, however, an indirect recognition of the portrait right in Article XI.174 CEL (formerly Art. 10 of the now replaced Belgian Author Rights Act of 1994), which limits the intellectual property right with respect to photographs by stating that the photographer or owner of a portrait or any other person possessing a portrait does not have the right to reproduce it or to make it public without the permission of the portrayed person or, during twenty years after his death, without permission of his heirs.

321. The first court decisions mentioning such rights date from the 1970s, the first doctrinal studies of personality rights date from the 1980s of the last century.

322. Cass. 17 December 1998 (C.96.0182.N), No. 525–526, *Pas.* 1998, 1233, *Arr.Cass.* 1998, 1141.

323. *See supra* para. 61.

can serve as a ground of justification for the infringement of the exclusive authority of the patient over his physical integrity.[324]

This legal basis also explains why courts mostly do require the showing that the act harming someone's reputation—which is not a subjective right but is a mere legitimate interest, and is therefore only protected by civil liability—was unlawful in itself, distinct from the fact that it resulted in harming the person's good name, for liability to attach,[325] while they do not require the showing of an unlawful act distinct from the infringement in cases of invaded privacy,[326] or cases involving the exploitation without permission of a person's name,[327] image,[328] or voice.[329]

While the traditional view remains that the private law protection of infringed personality rights is limited to the remedies offered by civil liability, some authors have argued that the personality right itself can serve as a basis for a claim of damages, independent of Articles 1382–1383 CC, and some courts seem to be prepared to follow this route.[330] Under this theory, damages can be awarded without the requirements of civil liability having been met. And indeed, while some courts explicitly state that the infringement of the personality right is a wrong on which civil liability is based, there are plenty of court decisions that go straight from the establishment of the infringement to the conclusion that damages are due, without explicitly referring to civil liability and without mentioning Article 1382 CC.

106. Second, one can notice that in many cases, if not most, a substantial part of the damages awarded for the infringement of a personality right are allegedly intended to compensate the right holder for moral losses. Under general principles of civil liability, moral losses consist of psychological suffering or discomfort, physical pain or emotional distress.[331] In the past, it has been argued that the infringement of a personality right in itself constitutes a moral loss, irrespective of any actual interests of the right holder being injured. The Court of Cassation, however, has firmly ruled that the infringement of a right in itself does not constitute a loss, so that no liability attaches if the claimant is not able to show that his actual interests were injured, separately from but as a consequence of the violation of his right.[332] If one wants to

324. *See* e.g. Corr. Liège 25 April 1947, *RGAR* 1948, No. 4,306; CA Liège 23 October 1964, *Pas.* 1964, II 242.
325. *See* e.g. CFI Tournai 22 November 2010, *AM* 2011, 109; CFI Brussels 20 September 2001, *AM* 2002, 77.
326. *See* e.g. CFI Tournai 22 November 2010, *AM* 2011, 109.
327. CFI Hasselt 19 December 2003, *AM* 2004, 388 and CFI Ghent 19 November 2003, *AM* 2004, 384 (use of famous tennis player Kim Clijsters' name for commercial purposes); CFI Dendermonde 26 October 2001, *RW* 2002–2003, 1068 (use of the name of an aristocratic family for a restaurant).
328. CFI Brussels 28 September 2010, *AM* 2011, 334 (use of portrait without permission is an infringement and in itself unlawful, even if person was acting in good faith); *see also* Court of Appeal Ghent 21 February 2008, *AM* 2008, 318 (use of pictures of Kim Clijsters for commercial purposes without permission); CFI Brussels 20 September 2001, *AM* 2002, 77.
329. CFI Brussels 19 January 2001, *AM* 2002, 450, *RW* 2001–2002, 207 (imitation of voice of singer Rocco Granata in commercial).
330. *See* e.g. CFI Ghent 24 June 2002, *AM* 2003, 143.
331. Cass. 3 February 1987, No. 322, *Pas.* 1987, 646, *Arr.Cass.* 1986–1987, 724.
332. Cass. 21 June 1990, No. 615, *Pas.* 1990, 1204, *Arr.Cass.* 1989–1990, 1358 ; Cass. 19 March 1991, No. 376, *Arr.Cass.* 1990–1991, 755, *Pas.* 1991, 670.

reconcile these decisions with general principles of civil liability, requiring the finding of an effective loss for liability to attach, one has to conclude that the courts at least implicitly consider the infringement of a personality right to constitute a (moral) loss.[333] Some authors and courts do criticize this automatism and protest against this conflation of the concepts of unlawfulness and loss.[334]

While up to the 1970s of the last century, the awards for moral losses tended to be very low, resulting in the courts doing not much more than symbolically acknowledging the claimant's status as a victim, analysis has shown that since the 1980s and more clearly since the mid-1990s, Belgian courts have become more willing to award higher amounts of moral damages in cases of infringements of personality rights.[335] For example, these awards are regularly higher than the amounts these same courts award for the loss of a loved one or a next-of-kin. As it is hard to accept that the actual moral loss that a person suffers from the infringement of a personality right is much graver than the grievance and emotional distress one suffers when losing a partner or a young child, one cannot help but feel that the courts in fact base the amounts of damages in cases of infringements of personality rights also on other elements than the extent of the actual loss.[336]

§4. Third-Party Interference in Contractual Relations

107. In the nineteenth century, the principle of the privity of contract[337] was considered to preclude the possibility that a third party could be liable for the losses a contract party suffers as a consequence of the breach of contract by the other contract party. At the beginning of the twentieth century, the Court of Cassation accepted the distinction between the internal legal effects or the obligatory effects of a contract, which only exist between the parties to the contract, and the existence of the contract or the existence of the legal consequences that follow from the contract, which can be relied upon or invoked by third parties against contract parties or *vice versa*.[338] This has opened the route to allow the party that suffers a loss because of the breach of contract to claim compensation from a third party that wrongfully was an accomplice in the violation of the contract (*tierce complicité à la violation d'une obligation contractuelle—derde-medeplichtigheid aan contractbreuk*). The existence of the contract is a circumstance that has to be taken into account when judging whether a

333. *See* e.g. CA Ghent 20 September 2006, *AM* 2007, 386; CA Antwerp 11 October 2005, *AM* 2006, 202; CFI Antwerp 12 June 2008, *AM* 2008, 321, *Rechtspraak Antwerpen Brussel Gent* 2008, vol. 6, 1267; CFI Liège 12 December 1997, *JLMB* 1998, vol. 105, 819 (1998).

334. *See* e.g. CFI Brussels 17 April 2004, *AM* 2005, 81 CA Antwerp 5 May 2003, *RW* 2004–2005, vol. 68, 1145, *AM* 2004, 67, *NJW* 2003, vol. 2, 1193; CFI Kortrijk 17 November 1989, *Tijdschrift voor Gentse Rechtspraak* 1990, vol. 6, 116; CFI Brussels 20 February 1996, *AM* 1998, 259.

335. *See* e.g. CFI Brussels 11 January 2011, *AM* 2013, 263; CFI Antwerp 12 June 2008, *AM* 2008, 321, *Rechtspraak Antwerpen Brussel Gent* 2008, vol. 6, 1267; CFI Brussels 30 April 2006, *AM* 2007, 390; CA Antwerp 5 May 2003, *RW* 2004–2005, vol. 68, 1145, *AM* 2004, 67, *NJW* 2003, vol. 2, 1193.

336. *See supra* para. 43 and *infra* para. 287.

337. Article 1165 CC.

338. Cass. 27 May 1909, *Pas.* 1909, 275.

wrong was committed by the third party, even if that third party is not bound to performance under the contract.

108. For a long time, there was significant disagreement in Belgian literature and case law about what criterion is to be used to decide whether the third party acted wrongfully when participating in a contract party breaching its contractual duties. In one view, liability for third-party complicity to contract breach is restricted to cases where the third party intentionally wanted to hurt the harmed contract party or intended to help the breaching contract party to violate its contractual duty.[339] Since the 1980s of the last century, however, it is clear that a third party acts wrongfully when he knowingly participates in someone else's breach of contract.[340]

This means that on the one hand the third party is only liable if he actually participates in the contract breach, but on the other hand that this liability attaches irrespective of the motive behind this participation. However, the third party is only liable if he knew or should have known that the contract existed and that by his action he participated in the violation of a right the harmed party derived from the contract.[341] While the remedy in most cases will consist of monetary damages, the court can by way of restoration in kind annul the contract the liable third party entered into with the contract party, by which this contract party violated its preexisting contract with the harmed party.[342]

§5. Nuisance

109. Historically, cases of nuisance were dealt with under Article 1382 of the Civil Code, interpreting the act that imposes excessive hindrance on a neighbor as a fault. Since 1960, the Court of Cassation recognizes nuisance (*troubles de voisinage—burenhinder* or *evenwichtsleer*) as a separate tort, directly based on the property rights on the neighboring premises and on the general principle of law that underpins the constitutional protection of property, and therefore no longer requiring the courts to qualify the hindrance as wrongful.[343]

In the present day interpretation, a case of nuisance involves a person exercising an attribute of the property right to a premise without violating any rules or being negligent. The hindrance consists in the limitation of the enjoyment of the property right on another parcel of land or piece of real estate. For this liability to attach, the claimant must have suffered excessive hindrance, which means that the nuisance is significantly more serious than one is normally expected to accept among neighbors living together in that specific area.

339. Cass. 24 November 1932, *Pas.* 1933, 19.

340. Cass. 22 April 1983, No. 462, *Arr.Cass.* 1982–1983, 1022, *Pas.* 1983, 944; recently Cass. 12 October 2012 (C.11.0692.N), No. 527, *Arr.Cass.* 2012, 2168, *Pas.* 2012, 1898.

341. Cass. 28 November 2002 (C.01.0532.F), No. 642, *Pas.* 2002, 2293, *Arr.Cass.* 2002, 2613.

342. Cass. 27 April 2006 (C.04.0591.F), No. 246, *Pas.* 2006, 976, *Arr.Cass.* 2006, 993; Cass. 30 January 1965, *Pas.* 1965, 538, *RW* 1964–1965, 1553.

343. Cass. 6 April 1960 (two decisions), *Pas.* 1960, 920, *Arr.Verbr.* 1960, 722.

110. This hindrance has to be caused by the neighbor.[344] More specific, the hindrance has to be attributable to a form of exploitation of the property right on the premise, which can consist in an act or a specific inaction of the person held liable, without this having to constitute a fault.[345] Thus, the liability can only rest on a person who is exercising an attribute of the property right on the neighboring premise.[346] This can be the owner, but it also can be a tenant. A construction company working in or on the premises, however, does not itself exercise an attribute of the property right, and is thus not subject to this liability.[347] If his activities cause damage to a neighbor, he will only be liable if the harm was caused by a fault for which the construction company is responsible. The owner will only be liable based on nuisance if the actions of the construction company that caused the hindrance were part of its specific task and thus constituted an exercise of his property right by the owner himself.[348]

Nuisance can only be invoked by a victim that is hampered in the exercise of an attribute of the property right on the premise suffering the hindrance. Thus, not only the owner of the neighboring premise is protected, but also, for instance, a tenant renting those premises.[349]

111. Nuisance results in an obligation to restore the balance between the enjoyment of the property rights. This means that only the fraction of the hindrance that is considered "excessive" has to be removed.[350] This can result in the court awarding an injunction forcing one neighbor to limit his use of his property, as long as the court order does not completely preclude the liable neighbor from using his property,[351] as that would only reverse the imbalance between the exercise of the rights involved.[352]

§6. Liability of Public Authorities

112. Belgian law has been one of the first to afford citizens the protection of civil liability against actions of the government. Already in 1852, the Court of Cassation

344. Cass. 15 November 2013 (C.11.0656.F), No. 605, *Pas.* 2013, 2222, *Arr.Cass.* 2013, 2407.
345. Cass. 3 April 1998 (C.97.0088.F), No. 192, *Pas.*1998, 440, *Arr.Cass.* 1998, 417; Cass. 4 May 2012 (C.10.0080.F), No. 276, *Pas.* 2012, 1007, *Arr.Cass.* 2012, 1178.
346. Cass. 10 January 1974, *Pas.* 1974, 488, *Arr.Cass.* 1974, 520; Cass. 9 June 1983, No. 561, *Arr. Cass.* 1982–1983, 1256, *Pas.* 1983, 1145.
347. Cass. 13 March 1987, No. 416, *Arr.Cass.* 1986–1987, 920, *Pas.* 1987, 834.
348. Cass. 25 June 2009 (C.07.0354.F), No. 438, *Pas.* 2009, 1665, *Arr.Cass.* 2009, 1821. The neighbor from whose premises the hindrance originates cannot escape this liability because the hindrance was caused by a fault of a third party. Cass. 24 April 2003 (C.01.0371.F), No. 262, *Pas.* 2003, 870, *Arr.Cass.* 2003, 1035.
349. Nuisance can be invoked by a tenant of an apartment against the tenant of another apartment in the same building. *See* Cass. 4 June 2012 (C.10.0672.N), No. 357, *Arr.Cass.* 2012, 1519, *Pas.* 2012, 1269.
350. Cass. 20 April 2012 (C.10.0103.F), No. 243, *Pas.* 2012, 844, *Arr.Cass.* 2012, 1008; Cass. 23 November 2000 (C.99.0104.F), No. 639, *Pas.* 2000, 1789, *Arr.Cass.* 2000, 1828.
351. *See* e.g. Cass. 8 February 2010 (C.09.0196.F), No. 87, *Pas.* 2010, 388, *Arr.Cass.* 2010, 372; Cass. 27 April 1962, *RW* 1962–1963, 57, *Pas.* 1962, 938; Cass. 26 November 1974, *RW* 1974–1975, 1768.
352. Cass. 14 December 1995 (C.93.0354.N), No. 550, *Arr.Cass.* 1995, 1125, *Pas.* 1995, 1163.

ruled that the civil liability provisions of the Civil Code are also applicable to the State and that a governmental agency is only free from such liability if its act is excluded from the province of civil law by a statutory provision or by its political character (*acta jure imperii*).[353] In its landmark decision in the *Flandria* case in 1920, the Court decided that the principle of the separation of powers, as it must be understood in Belgian constitutional law, does not preclude the judiciary from judging whether the executive has committed a fault, even in the performance of its political function.[354] As a result, even *acta jure imperii* can lead to government liability under Belgian law.

113. While the earliest cases involved the liability for damage caused by material acts of the executive,[355] the courts have gradually expanded this liability to harm caused by a regulatory intervention of the executive[356] or by their wrongful neglect to regulate.[357]

Executive behavior is wrongful if it violates a specific legal rule of conduct or if it constitutes negligence, using a reasonable executive placed in the same circumstances as the standard.[358] In judging whether governmental behavior is negligent, the courts respect the constitutional margin of discretion of the executive, which leads commentators to call the review of executive action by the courts to be "marginal," only sanctioning "obviously" unreasonable executive behavior.[359] It was in cases involving the executive that the Court of Cassation formulated the principle that the violation of a legal rule *ipso facto* constitutes a wrong.[360] In recent years, however, the Court has used some reasoning which has created doubt whether there might be a slight diversion from this general principle when the government is concerned. In the first of these decisions, the Court seems to recognize that the executive enjoys some margin of leeway in applying statutes, so that a later finding by a court that the executive did not take the legally required decision does not *ipso facto* mean this decision is wrongful.[361] In the second, most recent decision, the Court has ruled that in deciding whether the violation of a specific statutory rule for which the legislature has not provided a sanction constitutes a wrong, the court has to take the purpose of the violated rule into account.[362] It is not clear whether these decisions are signs of a new development or mere accidental deviations from the rule the traditional doctrine has read into the Court's case law.

114. While the Court of Cassation seems to be looking for ways to restrict the liability of the government for violations of statutory or constitutional rules by the

353. Cass. 27 May 1852, *Pas.* 1852, 370; *see also supra* para. 26. The distinction between *acta jure imperii* and *acta jure gestionis* is under Belgian law made on the basis of the nature of the act, and not based on the purpose of the government. *See* Cass. 11 June 1903, *Pas.* 1903, 301.
354. Cass. 5 November 1920, *Pas.* 1920, 193.
355. *See* e.g., the *Flandria*-decision, *supra* footnote 354; *see also* Cass. 7 March 1963, *Pas.* 1963, 744, *RW* 1963–1964, 1115.
356. Cass. 26 April 1963, *Pas.* 1963, 905, *RW* 1963–1964, 287, a case about mandatory vaccination.
357. Cass. 23 April 1971, *Arr.Cass.* 1971, 786, *Pas.* 1971, 752.
358. *See* e.g. Cass. 7 March 1963, *Pas.* 1963, 744, *RW* 1963–1964, 1115.
359. Cass. 4 March 2004 (C.03.0346.N – C.03.0448.N – C.03.0449.N), No. 124, *Arr.Cass.* 2004, 392, *Pas.* 2004, 374; Cass. 27 October 2006 (C.03.0584.N), No. 518, *Arr.Cass.* 2006, 2132, *Pas.* 2006, 270.
360. Cass. 19 December 1980, No. 241, *Arr.Cass.* 1980–1981, 449, *Pas.* 1981, 453; Cass. 13 May 1982, No. 547, *Pas.* 1982, 1056, *Arr.Cass.* 1981–1982, 1134. *See supra* Part I, Ch. 1, §3.
361. Cass. 25 October 2004 (S.03.0072.F), No. 507, *Pas.* 2004, 1667, *Arr.Cass.* 2004, 1688.
362. Cass. 10 April 2014 (C.11.0796.N), No. 282, *Arr.Cass.* 2014, 962, *Pas.* 2014, 949.

executive, the legislature has recently done the opposite. As part of the reorganization of the administrative proceedings before the Council of State, the legislature has now given the Council jurisdiction over claims for compensation.[363] If the Council has found a decision or regulation of the executive to be illegal, the person who has asked the Council to nullify it has the choice between bringing a claim in civil liability before the civil court, invoking the illegality as the fault, and asking for compensation in the proceedings before the Council. Remarkable features of this new basis for compensation are that: (1) no wrong has to be invoked, as the established illegality itself is sufficient; and (2) the Council is not bound to award full compensation but can determine the amount awarded taking into account all circumstances of private and public interest.[364]

115. Near the end of the twentieth century, the Court of Cassation has recognized that there are no objections to the State being liable for damage caused by faults committed by the judiciary.[365] To avoid such liability claims to render nugatory the procedural system of appeals against court decisions, a limitation was introduced: a liability claim against the State is only admissible if the disputed court decision has been reversed by an appellate court.[366]

116. In principle, the criterion of a wrongful act committed by the government in performing its judicial function, is identical to the general concept of a civil wrong, including on the one hand negligence and on the other hand illegality.[367] However, the so-called unity theory, which states that any violation of a legal rule imposing particular behavior is wrongful, has to be applied taking into account the intrinsic characteristics of a judicial act. Therefore, the Court of Cassation has clarified that the fact that a higher court has reversed a decision of a lower court because in its opinion, the lower court erred in law—and thus violated the law in the interpretation of this higher court—does not imply this lower court committed a wrong. The explanation is that the legal rule a court has to interpret and apply to the case can contain a specific rule of conduct from the perspective of the parties to the dispute, but it is not to be understood as a rule of behavior for the court.[368] Therefore, a fault of the government in the performance of its judicial function will in almost all cases have to involve negligence, requiring the claimant to show that the judge or court acted in a way that is unreasonable, a way in which a normal reasonable court placed in the same circumstances would not act. Violation of law will be restricted to those legal rules that specifically pertain to the behavior of a judge or a court, i.e., mostly procedural rules or rules regulating how the judicial function is performed.

363. Article 6 (federal) Act of 6 January 2014 on the Sixth Reform of the State in matters under Art. 77 of the Constitution. *See supra* para. 23.
364. Article 11*bis* (federal) Coordinated Act of 12 January 1973 on the Council of State.
365. Cass. 19 December 1991, No. 215, *Pas.* 1992, 316, *Arr.Cass.* 1991–1992, 364; Cass. 8 December 1994 (C.93.0303.F), No. 541, *Arr.Cass.* 1994, 1074, *Pas.* 1994, 1063.
366. This requirement is fulfilled if no appeal is possible just because the victim lacks procedural interest (Cass. 5 June 2008 (C.06.0366.N), No. 347, *Arr.Cass.* 2008, 1442, *Pas.* 2008, 1411), and if the decision has been ruled to be in violation of the ECHR by the ECtHR (Cass. 25 March 2010 (C.09.0403.N), No. 219, *Pas.* 2010, 1007, *Arr.Cass.* 2010, 920).
367. Cass. 25 March 2010 (C.09.0403.N), No. 219, *Arr.Cass.* 2010, 920, *Pas.* 2010, 1007. *See supra* para. 60.
368. Cass. 26 June 1998 (C.97.0236.F), No. 343, *Pas.* 1998, 812, *Arr.Cass.* 1998, 762.

117. If no appeal is available because the alleged wrong was committed by a supreme court such as the Court of Cassation or the Council of State, the Constitutional Court has ruled that liability has to be possible if the court has committed a "sufficiently qualified breach," transplanting a concept from EU state liability law for violations of EU law.[369] Under EU law, state liability in general has to be available in case of a sufficiently qualified breach.[370] The ECJ has ruled that a Member State cannot restrict state liability for violations of EU law committed by the judiciary to those instances where the judicial decision containing the wrong is withdrawn, reversed or undone in some other way.[371] While EU law requires Member States to provide the same remedies against violation of EU law as it offers against a violation of national law,[372] the Constitutional Court now apparently has turned this rule around to make sure Belgian law offers the same liability protection against a violation of national law as Belgium according to EU law has to offer against a violation of EU law. However, by doing so, the Constitutional Court has removed an unconstitutional unequal treatment in a procedural requirement by substituting an unequal treatment in the applicable rule of material law, the standard of wrongfulness, as the Court of Cassation in the past has specifically ruled that limiting wrongs to qualified breaches of law violates Article 1382 of the Civil Code.[373] How this new rule will be interpreted and implemented, remains to be seen.

118. More recently, the Court of Cassation has allowed courts to find the State liable for damage caused by wrongs committed by Parliament, the legislative branch of government,[374] even if the allegedly wrongful act was part of the legislative function of the government.[375] The Court has decided, however, that a ruling by the Constitutional Court holding a statute unconstitutional and thus establishing the violation of a rule of law does not imply that the legislature has acted wrongfully. The civil court deciding on liability will have to determine for itself whether the legislature's act constitutes a

369. Con.C. No. 99/2014 of 30 June 2014.

370. ECJ, *Francovich and Others v. Italian Republic*, Case Nos. C-6/90 and C-9/90, ECLI:EU:C:1991:428, decision of 19 November 1991; ECJ, *Brasseñe du Pêcheur and Factortame*, Case Nos. C-46/93 and C-48/93, ECLI:EU:C:1996:79, decision of 5 March 1996.

371. ECJ, *João Filipe Ferreire da Silva e Brito*, Case No. C-160/14, ECLI:EU:C:2015:565, decision of 9 September 2015; ECJ, *Köbler*, Case No. C-224/01, ECLI:EU:C:2003:513, decision of 30 September 2003.

372. ECJ, *Francovich and Others v. Italian Republic*, Case Nos. C-6/90 and C-9/90, ECLI:EU:C:1991:428, decision of 19 November 1991; ECJ, *Norbrook Laboratories Limited*, Case No. C-127/95, ECLI:EU:C:1998:151, decision of 2 April 1998; ECJ, *Köbler*, Case No. C-224/01, ECLI:EU:C:2003:513, decision of 30 September 2003.

373. Cass. 14 January 2000 (C.98.0477.F), No. 33, *Pas.* 2000, 102, *Arr.Cass.* 2000, 104.

374. Cass. 1 June 2006 (C.05.0494.N), No. 306, *Arr.Cass.* 2006, 1267, *Pas.* 2006, 1274, involving libel allegedly committed in a report of a parliamentary investigation commission on religious sects.

375. Cass. 28 September 2006 (C.02.0570.F), No. 445, *Pas.* 2006, 1870, *Arr.Cass.* 2006, 1848. Before this decision, the ruling precedent was Cass. 27 June 1845, *Pas.* 1845, 392, which held Arts. 1382 et seq. CC not applicable to statutes.

wrong.[376] Also, the Court of Cassation has decided that the finding that a Belgian statute violates superior law, such as a constitutional rule or a rule of EU law, does not in itself imply that a wrong was committed, as a violation of a rule of law is only wrongful if it was not the consequence of an invincible error and there was no other ground of justification.[377]

119. The courts have been willing to apply the rules of nuisance in cases where neighboring citizens suffer excessive hindrance from activities on public premises, in practice mostly from road construction works.[378] However, instead of judging whether the normal balance between the enjoyment by the respective parties of their property rights on the neighboring premises has been disturbed—the criterion in nuisance cases between private parties—the courts verify whether the hindrance suffered by this particular neighbor significantly exceeds the amount of hindrance a citizen in general can be required to accept from activities in the public interest.[379]

This case law is not so much based on the idea underlying the private tort of nuisance, but forms an application of a general principle that all citizens should equally (or better: proportionally, i.e., without discrimination) share the burdens required by living in society. Recently, the Court of Cassation has ruled that the government is liable to compensate a citizen for the disproportional burden it suffers from an in itself not wrongful act of government, as the burden of such acts in the general interest has to be spread equally over society.[380] This general principle of equal sharing of public burdens has also been recognized as a constitutional principle by the Constitutional Court.[381]

120. Government civil liability in most cases results in the obligation for the government to compensate the victim for its loss by paying damages. However, in some cases the victim might prefer the actual or physical reparation of the damage it has suffered to monetary compensation. In general, Belgian civil liability results in a duty to restore the loss.[382] Only in cases where restoration is physically impossible or extremely unreasonable, so insisting on reparation in kind amounts to an abuse of

376. Cass. 10 September 2010 (F.09.0042.N), No. 508, *Arr.Cass.* 2010, 2135, *Pas.* 2010, 2228. This decision seems to be at odds with the reasoning in an earlier decision, holding that a finding by the Council of State of a violation of a statutory or constitutional rule by the executive *ipso facto* established the wrongfulness of the behavior. *See* Cass. 13 May 1982, No. 547, *Pas.* 1982, 1056, *Arr.Cass.* 1981–1982, 1134; Cass. 21 December 2001 (C.99.0528.F), No. 719, *Pas.* 2001, 2204, *Arr.Cass.* 2001, 2273. At present, it is not clear on what basis the Court of Cassation uses a different rule for the legislature than for the executive, as the Court has not explained its reasoning.

377. Cass. 30 April 2015 (C.12.0637.F), No. 285, *Pas.* 2015, 1077, *Arr.Cass.* 2015, 1114. *See also supra* para. 69 and *infra* Part IV, Ch. 2.

378. Cass. 6 April 1960 (second decision), *Pas.* 1960, 932, *Arr.Verbr.* 1960, 724.

379. Cass. 28 January 1991, No. 281, *Pas.* 1991, 509, *Arr.Cass.* 1990–1991, 572; Cass. 23 May 1991, No. 488, *Pas.* 1991, 827, *Arr.Cass.* 1990–1991, 943; Cass. 4 December 2008 (C.04.0582.F), No. 696, *Pas.* 2008, 2753, *Arr.Cass.* 2008, 2831.

380. Cass. 24 June 2010 (C.06.0415.N), No. 453, *Arr.Cass.* 2010, 1903, *Pas.* 2010, 2004, a case about damage to an apartment in which the police had held a perfectly legal search.

381. Con.C. No. 55/2012 of 19 April 2012; Con.C. No. 132/2015 of 1 October 2015.

382. *See infra* paras. 217–218.

right,[383] liability results in a duty to restore by equivalent, i.e., by paying damages.[384] Already in 1980, the Court of Cassation ruled that a court that orders the government to undertake specific actions to restore the damage or that issues an injunction ordering the government to cease the violation of a citizen's rights does not violate the constitutional separation of powers.[385] More recently, the Court has even allowed the courts to give a private citizen the permission to undertake the acts required to restore the damage itself if the government refuses to do so, on the condition that such action by the private citizen does not jeopardize the continuity of the public service, i.e., that would not hinder the government in permanently performing its public function.[386]

383. *See infra* Part I, Ch. 2, §2.
384. *See infra* para. 219.
385. Cass. 26 June 1980, No. 686, *Pas.* 1980, 1341, *Arr.Cass.* 1979–1980, 1365, approving a lower courts decision ordering the government to remove constructions in an army barrack which violated the property rights of a neighbor.
386. Cass. 24 April 1998 (C.97.0252.F – C.97.0253.F), No. 210, *Pas.* 1998, 488, *Arr.Cass.* 1998, 462, on allowing a victim to undertake the construction works necessary to avoid flooding.

Part II. Liability for Acts of Others

Chapter 1. Vicarious Liability

§1. Liability of Masters (Including Employers) for Damage Caused by Servants (Including Employees)

121. According to Article 1384, paragraph 3, of the Civil Code, "masters" (*maîtres et commettants—meesters en aanstellers*) are liable for the damage their "servants" (*domestiques et préposés—dienstboden en aangestelden*) cause in their function. The victim claiming damages based on this liability does not have to prove any fault of the master, nor does he have to show the master actually caused the damage to occur. As the master cannot escape this liability by showing that he did not commit any fault,[387] this is a strict liability.

122. The concepts of master and servant, used in this provision, are mere factual concepts, not requiring a particular type of legal relationship between the two. For the purposes of this liability, a master-servant relationship is only characterized by subordination. This means that this liability applies to anybody who uses the efforts of another person in circumstances where he can supervise and direct the activities of this other person.[388] The subordination does not have to be legally sanctioned: if one person in fact directs the activities of another person, the first will be liable for the damage caused by the latter.[389] Thus, this vicarious liability is not restricted to employers for damage caused by their employees.[390] On the other hand, the legal possibility of supervision and direction can suffice to make one person vicariously liable for damage caused by another, even though he has not exercised this authority in fact.[391]

387. Cass. 27 March 1944, *Pas.* 1944, 275, *Arr.Verbr.* 1944, 127.
388. Cass. 16 October 1972, *Pas.* 1973, 165, *Arr.Cass.* 1973, 165; more recent: Cass. 22 January 2007 (C.04.0343.N), No. 35, *Arr.Cass.* 2007, 136, *Pas.* 2007, 122.
389. Cass. 23 January 1964, *Pas.* 1964, 548.
390. Cass. 29 June 2009 (C.07.0611.F), No. 445, *Pas.* 2009, 1698, *Arr.Cass.* 2009, 1846. Employer and employee are terms of art in Belgian law. Only when work is done as the performance of an employment contract, the parties are called employer and employee. An employment contract, specifically regulated by the ECA, is an agreement in which one party, the employee, commits himself to the other party, the employer, to carry out wowrk in return for pay, as a subordinate or under the authority of the employer.
391. Cass. 24 December 1951, *Arr.Verbr.* 1952, 196, *Pas.* 1952, 213; Cass. 16 October 1972, *Pas.* 1973, 165, *Arr.Cass.* 1973, 165.

In practice, most employers will qualify as masters of their employees so that Article 1384, paragraph 3, of the Civil Code is applicable to them. However, it is possible that an employee is in fact working under the supervision and direction of a client of his employer, in which case this client could be his master.[392] This is often the case with temporary agency work. Only a person acting for his own account can be vicariously liable as a master.[393] Thus, an employee who supervises and directs other employees—a foreman, for instance—cannot be held liable on this basis.

123. Article 1384, paragraph 3, of the Civil Code covers the damage the servant has caused through his fault, even if it is presumed. Thus, the school can as a master be vicariously liable for the damage that is caused by a student, as its servant, the teacher, is liable for this damage on the basis of Article 1384, paragraph 4, of the Civil Code,[394] a liability based on the presumed fault of the teacher.[395] This vicarious liability of the master also covers the harm for which the servant according to civil liability law bears a strict liability, for instance as custodian of a defective object[396] or as the user of an animal.[397] Whether or not the servant himself is liable or enjoys immunity[398] is not relevant.[399]

124. For Article 1384, paragraph 3, of the Civil Code to apply, the event causing the damage has to have occurred in the performance of the servant's function. The courts interpret this very broadly, requiring only that the event occurred during the time the servant is working for the master and is related to the performance of this function, even if the connection is indirect or coincidental.[400] This means that the master is not only liable in case of a wrongful performance of the function, but also in case of intentional neglect or even in case of an abuse by the servant of its position.[401] Thus, employers have been held liable for the damage caused by a criminal offense committed by an employee during his work and at the workplace,[402] and banks have been held liable for the harm suffered by clients who were misled to place savings in a Ponzi scheme organized by an agent of the bank.[403] The fact that the victim knew or should have known that the servant was acting outside of his function does not preclude

---

392. Cass. 3 January 2002 (C.98.0280.N), No. 2, *Arr.Cass.* 2002, 8, *Pas.* 2002, 5; Cass. 21 April 1971, *Arr.Cass.* 1971, 778, *Pas.* 1971, 745.
393. Cass. 22 January 2007 (C.04.0343.N), No. 35, *Arr.Cass.* 2007, 136, *Pas.* 2007, 122.
394. Cass. 28 October 1994 (C.93.0114.N), No. 461, *Arr.Cass.* 1994, 895, *Pas.* 1994, 877.
395. *See infra* Part II, Ch. 2, §3.
396. *See infra* Part III, Ch. 1.
397. *See infra* Part III, Ch. 4.
398. *See infra* Part IV, Ch. 4.
399. Cass. 18 November 1981, *RGAR* 1982, No. 10,459.
400. Cass. 27 March 1944, *Pas.* 1944, 275, *Arr.Verbr.* 1944, 127; more recent: Cass. 21 March 2013 (C.11.0476.F), No. 202, *Pas.* 2013, 744, *Arr.Cass.* 2013, 791.
401. Cass. 19 September 2008 (C.07.0317.N), No. 486, *Arr.Cass.* 2008, 1983, *Pas.* 2008, 1978; Cass. 10 February 1958, *Arr.Verbr.* 1958, 400, *Pas.* 1958, 635.
402. *See* e.g. Cass. 30 September 2015 (P.14.0474.F), No. 568, *Pas.* 2015, 2229, *Arr.Cass.* 2015, 2234, stating that a master is not only liable for the damage caused by the intentional fault of his employee, but because this was a fraudulent act of the employee, also cannot invoke the involuntary fault of the victim (contributory negligence) which allowed the fraud to be possible.
403. *See* e.g. Cass. 26 October 1989, No. 123, *Arr.Cass.* 1989–1990, 274, *Pas.* 1990, 241.

the vicarious liability of the master; it can merely result in a reduction of the liability of the master based on comparative negligence by the victim.[404]

125. This vicarious liability does not preclude the personal liability of the servant. If the constituent elements are present, both liabilities can coexist, in which case both the servant and the master are held *in solidum* to compensate the victim for its entire damage.[405] The master who has compensated the victim can have recourse against the servant that is liable for the damage. However, if the servant enjoys immunity,[406] such recourse will fail.

This vicarious liability can only be invoked by third parties suffering harm. A master cannot rely on its own vicarious liability to claim compensation from his liability insurer for losses he suffers caused by his own servants.[407] Neither can a servant invoke this liability against his own master for damage he caused to himself.

126. In principle, there is no reason why the vicarious liability of Article 1384, paragraph 3, of the Civil Code could not be applicable to the government or a public entity.[408] However, traditionally the courts consider public servants who in their function exercise a part of the governmental or public power (*puissance publique—openbare macht*), however small, not as servants in the sense of Article 1384, paragraph 3, of the Civil Code, but as organs of the public legal entity. As a result, the public legal entity was only liable for damage caused by members of its personnel within the performance of their function, which concept is construed more narrowly.[409] To correct this unequal treatment, the legislature has enacted a separate statutory basis for vicarious liability for damage caused by members of personnel of entities in the public sector, irrespective of whether they qualify as servants in the sense of Article 1384, paragraph 3, of the Civil Code.[410]

127. When the legislature in 2005 introduced a special liability regime for volunteers,[411] it imposed a strict vicarious liability on organizations for the damage caused by their volunteers when these volunteers themselves enjoy an immunity from liability.[412] Thus—significantly different from the general vicarious liability of Article 1384, paragraph 3, of the Civil Code—this liability is restricted to damage caused by a fault of a volunteer that is not an intentional fault, a gross fault, or a regularly occurring

---

404. Cass. 21 March 2013 (C.11.0476.F), No. 202, *Pas.* 2013, 744, *Arr.Cass.* 2013, 791; Cass. 11 March 1994, No. 116, *Arr.Cass.* 1994, 247, *Pas.* 1994, 244. On comparative negligence, *see infra* Part IV, Ch. 3.
405. On *in solidum* liability, *see infra* para. 214.
406. For this immunity, *see infra* Part IV, Ch. 4.
407. Cass. 20 June 2008 (C.06.0210.F), No. 385, *Pas.* 2008, 1572, *Arr.Cass.* 2008, 1603.
408. *See* already Cass. 27 May 1852, *Pas.* 1852, 370; *see also supra* para. 26. For a recent example, *see* Cass. 2 March 2016 (P.15.0929.F), *JT* 2017, 400, *RGAR* 2016, No. 15,336.
409. *See infra* para. 132.
410. Article 3 of the (federal) Act of 10 February 2003 on the Liability of Personnel of Public Legal Entities and on the Liability of Public Legal Entities for their Personnel states that public legal entities are liable for damage caused by their personnel in the same way as masters are liable for damage caused by their servants, and this also if the members of personnel are public servants and not employees and also if they have acted in the performance of governmental or public power.
411. (Federal) Act of 3 July 2005 on the Rights of Volunteers.
412. For the extent of this immunity, *see infra* Part IV, Ch. 4.

light fault.[413] Also, this vicarious liability is not restricted to subordinated volunteers,[414] but also applies to volunteers in leading functions within the organization. The organization is required to have liability insurance covering this liability.[415]

This vicarious liability is only applicable to organizations that are incorporated and to organizations that have at least one employee or that are connected to such an organization.[416] This limitation was included to avoid the strict liability and the connected mandatory insurance being applicable to people that together engage in some kind of activity without even realizing that they, by doing so, legally become an unincorporated organization.[417]

§2. Independent Contractors

128. Contractual liability covers damage a contract party suffers because of a breach of contract. A contract party is contractually liable for such damage if it has breached the contract himself but also if it has used other persons to perform its contractual obligations.[418] Whether these persons are employees, other subordinates or independent contractors, is not relevant in the contractual context. A client that suffers damage because his contract was breached by subcontractor of his contractor can only rely on contractual liability to claim compensation for so-called contractual damage. The rule precluding extracontractual liability between contract parties also excludes the option to claim compensation from the subcontractor.[419] This results in a quasi-immunity of the subcontractor toward the client of the contractor, as this client can also not invoke contractual liability against the subcontractor, who is not a party to his contract with the main contractor.

129. Outside of contract, however, the rules are different. Belgian law does not know a general rule holding a principal or client liable for damage his independent contractor causes to third parties while performing on their contract. Nor is there a general rule holding a contractor vicariously liable for the losses an independent subcontractor may cause to third parties.[420] As was mentioned above, there is one general rule for vicarious liability for persons working in a subordinated position, Article 1384, paragraph 3, of the Civil Code, which is applicable irrespective of the

413. Article 5 (federal) Act of 3 July 2005 on the Rights of Volunteers.
414. Article 3, 1° and 2°, (federal) Act of 3 July 2005 on the Rights of Volunteers.
415. Article 6 (federal) Act of 3 July 2005 on the Rights of Volunteers.
416. Article 3, 3° *juncto* Art. 5 (federal) Act of 3 July 2005 on the Rights of Volunteers.
417. This unequal treatment of organizations with and without an employee was held to be constitutional. Con.C. No. 158/2007 of 19 December 2007.
418. The Civil Code states this principle explicitly only for the contract of independent work in Art. 1797.
419. *See supra* General Introduction, §5. The famous *Stevedore*-decision (Cass. 7 December 1973, *Arr.Cass.* 1974, 395, *Pas.* 1974, 376), in which the Court of Cassation formulated its categorical rule on concurrence of contractual and extracontractual liability, involved a dispute in which the owner of goods that were damaged during transport was denied an extracontractual claim against the stevedore, who had been contracted by the carrier to load the ship and who had wrongfully caused the damage.
420. *See* e.g. CA Liège 20 June 1996, *JLMB* 1997, 382.

legal qualification of the relation between the worker and the principal.[421] This means that a third party suffering damage caused by an independent contractor performing on his contract with his client can only claim compensation from this client or principal if he in fact was the master of the contractor. If the contractor committed a fault in the performance of his contract, a third party can invoke the standard fault liability to claim compensation from the contractor.[422]

§3. Liability of Legal Entities

130. Legal entities such as corporations, incorporated partnerships or associations, and incorporated governmental or public agencies or companies, can only act through their personnel, employees and agents. If harm to a third party is caused by a member of personnel working in a subordinated position, the legal entity will be vicariously liable as the master of this servant.[423] If, however, the damage was caused by a person that is not working in a subordinated position, such as a member of the management team or a director, Article 1384, paragraph 3, of the Civil Code is not applicable.

131. Invoking a reasoning that is borrowed from the law of agency, usually referred to as the "organ theory," the courts attribute the fault committed by the director or the higher officer to the legal person, so as to hold legal persons liable based on Article 1382 of the Civil Code for the damage caused by its own fault.[424] However, the theory is not applied in all of its logical consequences, as the courts allow the victim also to claim compensation based on fault liability from the higher officer himself. The fault attributed to the legal entity is thus also viewed as a fault attributable to the officer of the legal entity.

132. This principle is only applied for damage caused by members of the personnel of the legal entity that are called organs (*organe—orgaan*). In private legal entities, these are the nonsubordinated legal representatives of the legal entity, identified by law or by the articles of association. For public law entities, the courts have traditionally not limited this qualification to legal representatives but have also included civil servants that in their function exercise a part of the governmental or public power, however small.[425]

The legal entity will only be liable if the organ has acted within its function, i.e., if the action, if performed correctly, would have been within its authority. A legal person is therefore not liable for damage caused by an action of an organ outside its authority, except if this act from the point of view of *every* prudent and reasonable

421. *See supra* para. 122.
422. *See supra* para. 123.
423. *See supra* paras. 122–123.
424. Cass. 13 December 1923, *Pas.* 1924, 82; Cass. 15 January 1946, *Pas.* 1946, 25, *Arr. Verbr.* 1946, 23. *See* H. De Wulf, "Company Law" in M. Kruithof & W. De Bondt (ed.), *Introduction to Belgian Law*, 2d ed., Alphen aan den Rijn: Kluwer Law International, 2017, 309–351, at pp. 344–346.
425. *See supra* para. 126.

observer would have been perceived as within its authority.[426] The liability of a legal entity for its organs is therefore applicable to a more restricted category of acts than the vicarious liability of a master for its servant.[427]

426. Cass. 29 May 1947, *Arr.Verbr.* 1947, 170, *Pas.* 1947, 216; Cass. 19 December 1991, No. 215, *Pas.* 1992, 316, *Arr.Cass.* 1991–1992, 364.

427. *See supra* para. 124.

Chapter 2. Liability of Parents for Minors and Teachers for Students

§1. Shared Characteristics

133. The specific parent and teacher liability rules discussed in this chapter, based on Article 1384 of the Civil Code, share a number of characteristics.

134. First, this liability only covers damage that is caused either by a civil wrong committed by the child or the student, or for which the child or student has to bear strict liability.[428] The fact that no fault of the minor or pupil is required but an objectively wrongful act—i.e., negligence or an illegal act[429]—is sufficient, means that this liability applies even if the juvenile or pupil is not personally liable because of lacking culpability,[430] such as will be the case with very young children,[431] but also with mentally ill children or pupils.[432]

135. Second, the liability of the parent or of the teacher does not preclude any personal liability of the juvenile or pupil. If the constituent elements are present, both liabilities can coexist, in which case both parties are held *in solidum*.[433] The parent or teacher that has compensated the victim can exercise recourse against the child or the student, if the conditions for this personal liability are fulfilled.

136. Third, this liability of parents or teachers can only be invoked by third parties suffering harm. Parents or teachers cannot rely on their own vicarious liability to claim compensation from their liability insurer for losses they suffer caused by their own children or students.[434] Juveniles and students also are precluded from invoking this liability against their parents or teacher, to claim compensation for harm they caused to themselves, or to (partially) fend off a recourse from a parent or teacher that has compensated the victim. If the minor child or the pupil wants to claim compensation from its parent or teacher for damage it caused, it will have to base its claim on Article 1382 of the Civil Code, and thus will have to prove that its behavior that created the damage was caused by a fault committed by the parent or the teacher. A third party

428. There is hardly any case law to be found on the issue, but no author doubts that the parents can also be liable on this basis for damage caused by an animal or a defective good of which their minor child is the owner or keeper.

429. As opposed to a fault of the child or the pupil. *See* Cass. 28 October 1971, *Arr.Cass.* 1972, 219, *Pas.* 1972, 200; Cass. 3 May 1978, *Arr.Cass.* 1978, 1037, *Pas.* 1978, 1012; Cass. 11 December 2009 (C.09.0301.F), No. 739, *Pas.* 2009, 2977, *Arr.Cass.* 2009, 2996; Cass. 4 June 2012 (C.10.0734.N – C.11.0177.N – C.12.0070.N), No. 358, *Arr.Cass.* 2012, 1527, *Pas.* 2012, 1271.

430. *See* on this requirement of culpability, *supra* Part I, Ch. 1, §4.

431. Cass. 7 March 1957, *Arr.Verbr.* 1957, 546, *Pas.* 1957, 806; more recent: Cass. 4 June 2012 (C.10.0734.N), No. 358, *Arr.Cass.* 2012, 1527, *Pas.* 2012, 1271.

432. Cass. 18 October 1990, No. 90, *Arr.Cass.* 1990–1991, 193, *Pas.* 1991, 171.

433. On *in solidum* liability, *see infra* para. 214.

434. Cass. 20 June 2008 (C.06.0210.F), No. 385, *Pas.* 2008, 1572, *Arr.Cass.* 2008, 1603.

that together with the minor or the student—or the parents or teacher—was held liable *in solidum* for the loss caused by the minor or student,[435] cannot invoke Article 1384 of the Civil Code as a basis for recovering its own loss consisting of the damages it had to pay to the victim from the parents or the teacher. However, if that third party was subrogated in the rights of the original victim by paying damages,[436] it can exercise the rights of that victim, and these rights include a claim against the parents or teacher based on Article 1384 of the Civil Code. The rule thus means that a jointly liable third party will not derive any more rights from the special liability of parents or teachers than the original victim of the damage caused by the minor or the student.

137. Fourth, the victim that suffered the damage and that claims compensation from the parent or the teacher does not have to prove that the parent or teacher caused the damage.[437] Thus, the only evidence required has to show that the minor or student wrongfully caused the damage or is strict liable for the damage, and that the defendant is the parent of this minor or was the teacher at the time the student caused the damage.

138. Finally, the vicarious liability imposed by Article 1384 of the Civil Code is limited to the three categories of persons specifically mentioned in the second, third and fourth paragraph: parents for their minor children, masters for their servants,[438] and teachers and artisans for their students, pupils and apprentices. The highest court of France has ruled that the originally identical provision of Article 1242 of the French Civil Code has to be interpreted as containing a more general principle of vicarious liability, on the basis of which institutions can be held liable for losses caused by the minors or mentally handicapped persons they are responsible for, without a fault of the institution being required.[439] The Belgian Court of Cassation has explicitly refused to read such a general principle in the first paragraph of Article 1384 of the Belgian Civil Code.[440] Thus, only parents and teachers can be held vicariously liable for losses caused by their children or pupils, and there is no vicarious liability for institutions, schools, sports clubs, or other organizations that have responsibilities to supervise children or handicapped persons.

§2. Liability of Parents

139. According to Article 1384, paragraph 2, of the Civil Code, parents are liable for the damage caused by their minor children. A minor is a person who has not reached the age of majority,[441] which in Belgium is set at eighteen years.[442] However, the liability is not based on this age, but on the legal status of minority. Parents are

---

435. On *in solidum* liability, *see infra* para. 214.
436. Such subrogation would be based on Art. 1251, 3°, CC.
437. Cass. 20 October 1999 (P.99.0652.F), No. 549, *Arr.Cass.* 1999, 1305, *Pas.* 1999, 1360.
438. *See supra* Part II, Ch. 1, §1.
439. Cour de Cassation of France 29 March 1991, 1991 *Dalloz jurisprudence* 324, 1992 *Gazette du Palais—Jurisprudence* 513, *RGAR* 1991, No. 11,857.
440. Cass. 19 June 1997 (C.96.0254.F – C.96.0258.F), No. 284, *Pas.* 1997, 700, *Arr.Cass.* 1997, 670.
441. Article 388 CC.
442. Article 488 CC.

thus not liable on this basis for losses caused by their child who is less than eighteen but who is married.[443]

The liability of both parents is cumulative, so the victim can claim compensation from both parents. The parents are liable *in solidum*,[444] which means that the victim can also claim full restoration from one of the parents.

140. The basis for this liability is the legally recognized affiliation. Whether this legal relationship is based on a (real or presumed) biological affiliation or on adoption is irrelevant. As recently the law was changed to allow the same sex partner of a biological mother of a child to be legally recognized as its second mother,[445] one can expect the courts to interpret this liability to be applicable to both mothers. Article 1384, paragraph 2, Civil Code only mentions the father and the mother, so grandparents, older siblings or other caretakers of minor children, such as educators in institutions that take care of children, cannot be held liable on this basis. Foster parents are not subject to this liability. Not only is there no legally recognized affiliation between a foster child and its foster parents, but also it is feared that the risk of such liability would make it even harder to find people prepared to become foster parents for children with a problematic background that might influence their behavior.

The liability is not dependent on there being any parental authority. Before the amendment of this provision in 1977,[446] the father—and the mother after the death of the father—was only liable if he or she lived together with the minor. This limitation was removed, so now both parents are liable, irrespective of the residence of the child. Even if the parents are separated and one of them has only a restricted right to personal contact, he or she is still subject to Article 1384, paragraph 2, of the Civil Code.[447]

141. Article 1384, paragraph 5, of the Civil Code allows a parent to escape liability by proving that he could not have prevented the minor causing the damage.

Over the last decades, some courts—including the important Brussels Court of Appeal[448]—had begun to adopt a strict interpretation of this provision, allowing parents only to escape if they prove force majeure. Recently, however, the Court of Cassation has rejected this interpretation. In its view, the parental liability is based on a double presumption. First, the law apparently assumes that if a minor wrongfully causes any damage, his or her parents are presumed to have committed a fault.[449] Second, the law assumes that this presumed fault of the parents was the cause of the behavior of the minor that caused the damage.[450] Therefore, the Court remains of the opinion that a

443. Cass. 11 February 1946, *Pas.* 1946, 62, *Arr. Verbr.* 1946, 54; Cass. 6 March 1950, *Pas.* 1950, 447, *Arr. Verbr.* 1950, 449. According to Art. 476 CC, a minor that marries is automatically emancipated.

444. On *in solidum* liability, *see infra* para. 214.

445. *See* Arts. 325/1–325/10 CC.

446. Act of 6 July 1977, *Moniteur belge—Belgisch Staatsblad* 2 August 1977.

447. Cass. 12 November 2002 (P.02.0095.N), No. 598, *Arr.Cass.* 2002, 2454, *Pas.* 2002, 2157; Cass. 30 May 1984, No. 561, *Arr.Cass.* 1983–1984, 1286, *Pas.* 1984, 1200.

448. *See* e.g. CA Brussels 4 October 2010, *Journal des juges de paix (et de police)* 2012, 593/225; CA Brussels 24 June 2009, *RGAR* 2009, No. 14,554; CA Brussels 23 October 2007, *RGAR* 2010, No. 14,652; CA Brussels 25 October 2007, *NJW* 2008, 128.

449. Cass. 20 April 1982, No. 484, *Arr.Cass.* 1981–1982, 1003, *Pas.* 1982, 944; Cass. 5 April 1995 (P.94.1363.N), No. 185, *Arr.Cass.* 1995, 377, *Pas.* 1995, 390.

450. Cass. 20 October 1999 (P.99.0652.F), No. 549, *Arr.Cass.* 1999, 1305, *Pas.* 1999, 1360.

parent is not liable if he or she shows not to have committed any fault in supervision and education.[451]

The case law of the lower courts shows a varying attitude of judges in accepting such rebutting evidence. Some allow parents to escape as soon as they have shown that they provided a normal education and appropriate supervision.[452] Others seem to consider the wrongful behavior of the juvenile in itself sufficient evidence of a shortcoming in education (*res ipsa loquitur*),[453] thus in effect excluding all possibilities of rebutting the presumption of fault except by proving force majeure. Some courts tend to allow parents to escape liability in case of serious offenses committed by their minor child if they can prove that they took specific measures trying to cope with their child's problems, such as getting professional help.[454]

142. This interpretation by the Court of Cassation also means that a parent remains liable even if the damage was caused by the minor child while it was under supervision of someone else, even if the damage was caused while the child was at school. Thus, a victim of a loss wrongly caused by a minor child while being under the supervision of a teacher, can claim compensation from the teacher based on Article 1384, paragraph 4, of the Civil Code[455] and from the parents based on Article 1384, paragraph 2, of the Civil Code.[456]

§3. Liability of Teachers and Artisans

143. According to Article 1384, paragraph 4, of the Civil Code, teachers and artisans are liable for the damage caused by their pupils or apprentices during the time they are under their supervision. This liability applies to losses caused by students, pupils or apprentices irrespective of their age, so also persons who are teaching adults are subject to this liability.

---

451. Cass. 4 March 2015 (P.14.1873.F), No. 159, *Pas.* 2015, 558, *Arr.Cass.* 2015, 585; previously: Cass. 23 February 1989, No. 356, *Arr.Cass.* 1988–1989, 721, *Pas.* 1989, 649.

452. *See* e.g. CA Ghent 13 May 2004, *NJW* 2004, 1279; Corr. Tongeren 25 November 1987, *RW* 1989–1990, 755. The Court of Cassation has approved such decision. *See* e.g. Cass. 12 January 1971, *Arr.Cass.* 1971, 452, *Pas.* 1971, 434.

453. All courts of appeal have issued such decisions. *See* e.g. CA Antwerp 27 March 2002, *RW* 2005–2006, 106; CA Ghent 13 February 2004, *RGAR* 2005, No. 13,963; CA Mons 23 April 2009, *CRA* 2009/4, 278; CA Liège 28 May 2003, *Bull.Ass.* 2004, 772; CA Brussels 30 March 2004, *RGAR* 2007, No. 14,256. The Court of Cassation has also approved these types of decisions. *See* Cass. 15 April 1971, *Pas.* 1971, 725, *Arr.Cass.* 1971, 758; Cass. 21 December 1989, No. 257, *Pas.* 1990, 501, *Arr.Cass.* 1989–1990, 560.

454. *See* e.g. Corr. Mons 31 May 2000, *RGAR* 2002, No. 13,589; Corr. Brussels 21 February 1992, *Revue de droit pénal* 1992, 909; JCt Brussels. 3 May 2002, *Tijdschrift voor Jeugdrecht en Kinderrechten* 2002, 196; Pol. Verviers 5 mei 2008, *CRA* 2008/4, 294.

455. *See infra* Part II, Ch. 2, §3.

456. Cass. 23 February 1989, No. 356, *Arr.Cass.* 1988–1989, 721, *Pas.* 1989, 649; Cass. 21 December 1989, No. 257, *Pas.* 1990, 501, *Arr.Cass.* 1989–1990, 560.

Only physical persons are subject to this liability. A school, as an institution, cannot be held liable on this basis, as it is not a physical person.[457] However, as in many cases the teacher can be legally qualified as a (civil) servant of the school, the school will be vicariously liable as the master or the public entity for damage (presumably) wrongfully caused by its servant.[458]

144. For this liability to apply, an educational relationship has to exist between the person who has caused the damage and the person held liable. Education in this regard does not only include the transfer of technical and intellectual knowledge in organized courses, but also contains other forms of education of a scientific, artistic, professional, moral and social type.[459] Hence, artisans are considered teachers, and apprentices are pupils. No professional status nor structured organization is required. A person teaching someone to drive a car is subject to this liability as well.

Teachers are subject to this liability during the whole time the pupils are under their supervision, even if they escape this supervision. Thus, a teacher can be held liable for losses caused by a student during time when no actual teaching is taking place, such as on a school trip or during a lunch break at school. According to the dominant line of case law, however, a person whose function is limited to supervision or an administrator of a school cannot be held liable on this basis, as he is not a teacher. This produces the awkward result that if kids playing in a school yard are simultaneously supervised by a teacher and a supervisor, the teacher will be held vicariously liable for the losses caused by a student but the supervisor not.

145. According to the fifth paragraph of Article 1384 of the Civil Code, teachers and artisans can escape this liability by proving that they could not have prevented the act that led to the liability, i.e., the unlawful act of the student, pupil of apprentice or the event on which the strict liability of the student, pupil or apprentice is based. In its current interpretation, this means that the teacher can escape if he proves that he did not commit any fault by showing he applied sufficient and appropriate supervision,[460] or that his (presumed) fault did not cause the actual harm-creating event.

As many teachers in practice are employees or civil servants, enjoying an extensive immunity from civil liability,[461] most teachers can escape this liability by showing that they did not intend to cause harm and did not commit a gross fault or customary—i.e., regularly reoccurring—light fault.[462]

457. Cass. 19 June 1997 (C.96.0254.F – C.96.0258.F), No. 284, *Pas.* 1997, 700, *Arr.Cass.* 1997, 670.
458. *See supra* Part II, Ch. 1, §1.
459. Cass. 3 December 1986, No. 201, *Arr.Cass.* 1986–1987, 442, *Pas.* 1987, 410.
460. Cass. 10 October 2003 (C.02.0628.F), No. 490, *Pas.* 2003, 1583, *Arr.Cass.* 2003, 1845.
461. *See infra* Part IV, Ch. 4.
462. Cass. 25 January 1993, No. 47, *Pas.* 1993, 91, *Arr.Cass.* 1993, 98.

Part III. Forms of Strict Liability

Chapter 1. Liability for Things

146. Since the end of the nineteenth century, the Belgian courts read a strict liability of the custodian for damage caused by a defective thing (*chose vicieuse—gebrekkige zaak*) in the first paragraph of Article 1384 of the Civil Code, and the Court of Cassation has approved this reading at the beginning of the twentieth century.[463] According to the standard interpretation, this liability only applies to material things,[464] but it can also apply to objects that are composed of several parts, including software to make the object function. Software itself, however, is not considered a thing by most authors.[465]

147. The fact that a thing has caused damage, is not sufficient for this liability to attach,[466] and neither is the fact that the thing is dangerous, i.e., likely to cause harm. Belgian law does not impose a general strict liability for damage caused by dangerous objects. The liability attached to Article 1384, paragraph 1, of the Civil Code is only applicable if the thing caused the harm because it is defective.[467] A defect is defined as an abnormal characteristic or state—i.e., the object deviates from the normal "model"—that causes the object to be capable of causing harm—i.e., increasing the risk for damage—in certain circumstances.[468] The circumstances in which the increased risk exists have to be those present for a normal, foreseeable use of the object.[469] As

463. Cass. 26 May 1904, *Pas.* 1904, 246; Cass. 25 March 1920, *Pas.* 1920, 110.
464. In Cass. 21 April 1972, *Arr.Cass.* 1972, 789, *Pas.* 1972, 773, the Court ruled that a hospital, consisting of an organization involving people and their behavior, is not a thing in the sense of Art. 1384, para. 1, CC.
465. Recently, the issue is becoming very important in the context of the introduction of self-driving or autonomous cars in traffic, so the question whether software can be a thing in the context of Art. 1384, para. 1, CC, is receiving new attention in the literature. There is no case law on the question yet.
466. Cass. 24 February 2006 (C.05.0112.F), No. 109, *Pas.* 2006, 442, *Arr.Cass.* 2006, 443.
467. The Court based this requirement on an analogy with other liabilities in the Civil Code: a person is liable when the damage is caused by his "defective" (i.e., wrongful) behavior (Art. 1382, *supra* Part I, Ch. 1, §1), the "defective" behavior of a person for whom he is responsible (Art. 1384, paras. 2–4, *see supra* para. 134), or a defect of a his building (Art. 1386, *see infra* para. 150). Cass. 26 May 1904, *Pas.* 1904, 246.
468. Cass. 23 September 1971, *Arr.Cass.* 1972, 88, *Pas.* 1972, 80; recent: Cass. 4 January 2016 (C.15.0191.F), *RGAR* 2016, No. 15,334, *NJW* 2016, 917; Cass. 17 January 2014 (C.12.0510.F), No. 39, *Pas.* 2014, 143, *Arr.Cass.* 2014, 161.
469. Cass. 30 January 2003 (C.00.0726.F), No. 70, *Pas.* 2003, 235, *Arr.Cass.* 2003, 278.

a result of this requirement, Article 1384, paragraph 1, of the Civil Code has not played the role in traffic accidents that it has had in France, where this liability can be invoked when the behavior of a thing caused the damage.

The defect does not have to be "intrinsic" to the object in the sense that it is not caused by an external factor, nor needs the "structure" of the object to be affected.[470] In fact, the courts often rule an object to be defective if it does not conform to the reasonable expectations one would have and this unexpected condition is what caused the damage.[471] The fact that the specific victim may have been aware of the deviant condition of the thing, however, does not mean that the object is no longer defective,[472] resulting in case law that is hard to reconcile with one single explanatory theoretical concept of a defect.

The courts tend to be lenient toward the victim if it faces difficulty providing positive evidence of the defect that caused the abnormal behavior of the object that caused the damage. In general, the courts allow a negative proof, showing that all other reasonably possible causes for the deviant behavior can be excluded in the particular case.[473]

148. Liability for damage caused by a defective object attaches to the person who has the thing under his guard. Although this person is referred to as the "custodian" (*gardien—bewaarder*), this term should not be understood in its legal sense, in which it refers to the party to a contract of custodianship or deposit (*depot—bewaargeving*) who has the obligation to safekeep an object (*depositaire—bewaarnemer*). The custodian, as the term is used in the context of Article 1384, paragraph 1, of the Civil Code, is most often the owner of the thing, but it can also be someone else, such as a lessee or a borrower. The liability attaches to the person who had the thing under his detention or used it, and who had factual control over the object.[474] Thus, a thief will be strict liable for the harm caused by defective stolen goods.

149. The custodian is liable, irrespective of whether he has committed any fault. He is subject to the liability even if he was not aware or could not have been aware of the defect.[475] The cause of the defect is irrelevant. However, if the custodian has compensated the victim, he can have recourse against the person liable for having caused the thing to become defective.[476]

470. Cass. 13 March 2015 (C.14.0284.N), No. 193, *Arr.Cass.* 2015, 737, *Pas.* 2015, 721; Cass. 2 January 2009 (C.08.0074.N), No. 2, *Arr.Cass.* 2009, 3, *Pas.* 2009, 2.
471. Cass. 4 January 2016 (C.15.0191.F), *RGAR* 2016, No. 15,334, *NJW* 2016, 917; Cass. 11 March 2010 (C.09.0186.N), No. 171, *Arr.Cass.* 2010, 715, *Pas.* 2010, 777.
472. Cass. 17 January 2014 (C.12.0510.F), No. 39, *Pas.* 2014, 143, *Arr.Cass.* 2014, 161; Cass. 21 November 2003 (C.02.0619.F), No. 590, *Pas.* 2003, 1878, *Arr.Cass.* 2003, 2183.
473. Cass. 11 September 2008 (C.07.0200.F), No. 646, *Pas.* 2008, 1916, *Arr.Cass.* 2008, 1917; *see* already Cass. 25 March 1943, *Arr. Verbr.* 1943, 68, *Pas.* 1943, 110.
474. Cass. 13 September 2012 (C.10.0226.F), No. 463, *Pas.* 2012, 1647, *Arr.Cass.* 2012, 1923; Cass. 25 March 1999 (C.96.0404.N), No. 183, *Arr.Cass.* 1999, 442, *Pas.* 1999, 453.
475. Cass. 3 May 1974, *Arr.Cass.* 1974, 989, *Pas.* 1974, 914; Cass. 26 April 2013 (C.12.0286.N), No. 260, *Arr.Cass.* 2013, 1010, *Pas.* 2013, 985.
476. Cass. 4 February 2011 (C.10.0236.N), No. 104, *Arr.Cass.* 2011, 401, *Pas.* 2011, 429; Cass. 14 February 2013 (C.11.0793.F), No. 109, *Pas.* 2013, 429, *Arr.Cass.* 2013, 443.

150. The courts do apply Article 1384, paragraph 1, of the Civil Code also to damage caused by defective immovable goods.[477] However, Article 1386 of the Civil Code contains a special rule for damage caused by collapsing buildings. This liability only applies to man-made constructions that are durably connected to the ground.[478] According to this rule, the owner is liable for all damage caused by the total or partial[479] collapse of the building that itself is a consequence of either a construction defect or a lack of proper maintenance. A collapse itself is therefore not sufficient to trigger this liability, as it can also be caused by force majeure.[480] The Court of Cassation has recently decided that the general liability for defective things based on Article 1384, paragraph 1, of the Civil Code cannot be invoked for damage that is caused by a total or partial collapse of a building as a consequence of a construction defect of a lack of proper maintenance: for such damage, only the owner bears a strict liability, based on Article 1386 of the Civil Code.[481]

This rule contains a strict liability, as it is irrelevant what caused the defect in the construction or who is responsible for the maintenance.[482] The owner of the building remains liable if the construction defect that caused the collapse was the consequence of an error made by the architect or of sloppy work by the construction company,[483] and the owner is also liable if the collapse was the consequence of insufficient maintenance when a tenant was responsible for the maintenance.

The owner who has compensated the victim, however, will be able to have recourse against the person liable for the cause of the collapse.[484]

---

477. Cass. 12 July 1945, *Pas.* 1945, 202, *Arr.Verbr.* 1945, 188; Cass. 24 May 1945, *Pas.* 1945, 202, *Arr.Verbr.* 1945, 161; Cass. 25 March 1943, *Pas.* 1943, 110, *Arr.Verbr.* 1943, 68.

478. The liability is also applicable to damage caused during construction. Cass. 3 February 1955, *Pas.* 1955, 578, *Arr.Verbr.* 1955, 436; Cass. 16 June 1995 (C.93.0319.N), No. 305, *Arr.Cass.* 1995, 621, *Pas.* 1995, 643.

479. A collapse of an "important part" of the building is sufficient. Cass. 17 December 1992, No. 802, *Pas.* 1992, 1390, *Arr.Cass.* 1991–1992, 1445; Cass. 18 April 1975, *Arr.Cass.* 1975, 917, *Pas.* 1975, 828. Whether the part is "important," is a question of fact.

480. Cass. 8 January 1982, No. 280, *Arr.Cass.* 1981–1982, 586, *Pas.* 1982, 573.

481. Cass. 28 November 2016 (C.15.0521.F), *JT* 2017, 210, *RDC* 2017, 317, *Forum de l'assurance* 2017.

482. Cass. 17 December 1992, No. 802, *Pas.* 1992, 1390, *Arr.Cass.* 1991–1992, 1445.

483. Cass. 16 June 1995 (C.93.0319.N), No. 305, *Arr.Cass.* 1995, 621, *Pas.* 1995, 643.

484. Cass. 23 October 1970, *Arr.Cass.* 1971, 176, *Pas.* 1971, 169.

Chapter 2. Product Liability

151. The Belgian regime for product liability, which can be found in the Act of 25 February 1991 on the Liability for Defective Products (hereafter referred to as the "Product Liability Act"), is the implementation of the EU Product Liability Directive.[485]

152. Before the introduction of this statutory regime, the Belgian courts found ways to gradually introduce a system of product liability based on an expanding interpretation of existing liabilities.

On the one hand, Article 1645 of the Civil Code provides that a seller is liable for the damage a buyer suffers because a sold good has a hidden defect if the seller knew of the defect but did not tell the buyer. The courts used this statutory provision to impose the traditional rule *spondet peritiam artis, et imperitia culpae adnumeratur*, holding a professional or specialized seller, which includes a producer, to an *obligation de resultat*, in effect placing a strict liability on the shoulders of a producer or specialized seller that can only be avoided in cases where discovery of the hidden defect was objectively impossible.[486] This liability was not only applied in the relation between the producer or the specialized seller and the buyer, but through the technique of considering this claim in liability to be an accessory good to the sold product, the courts allow the final recipient of the defective good to invoke this contractual liability against any earlier seller of the good, including the original seller, i.e., the producer.[487]

On the other hand, the courts tended to consider that bringing a defective product onto the market in itself constitutes a wrongful act, rendering the producer liable based on Article 1382 of the Civil Code for any damage suffered by third parties.[488]

One could have expected these two developments, which stretched certain legal concepts to the point of irrationality, to be reversed once the legislature had introduced a separate statutory basis for product liability claims, irrespective of whether they are brought by contract parties or by third parties. However, this has not happened, and in Belgian case law, one can still find more cases applying these general liability bases to cases involving defective products than decisions in which the courts invoke the Act of 25 February 1991. Most courts and authors consider this no problem, as they interpret Article 13 of the EU Product Liability Directive to mean that product liability as it is specified in that legislation is an additional basis for liability, not in any way restricting or modifying any other possible basis for liability in national law. That this

485. Council Directive 85/374/EEC of 25 July 1985 on the Approximation of the Laws, Regulations and Administrative Provisions of the Member States concerning Liability for Defective Products, *Official Journal* L210/29 of 7 August 1985, as amended.

486. Cass. 4 May 1939, *Pas.* 1939, 223; Cass. 13 November 1959, *Arr. Verbr.* 1960, 225, *Pas.* 1960, 313; Cass. 18 oktober 2001, No. 556, *Arr.Cass.* 2001, 1721, *Pas.* 2001, 1659.

487. Cass. 5 December 1980, No. 212, *Arr.Cass.* 1980–1981, 382, *Pas.* 1981, 398; Cass. 18 mei 2006 (C.05.0097.N), No. 297, *Arr.Cass.* 2006, 1118, *Pas.* 2006, 1154; Cass. 15 December 2006, *RW* 2008–2009, 230; Cass. 23 April 2007 (C.04.0137.N), No. 200, *Arr.Cass.* 2007, 852, *Pas.* 2007, 753; Cass. 15 September 2011 (C.10.0456.N – C.10.0464.N), No. 474, *Arr.Cass.* 2011, 1816, *Pas.* 2011, 1962.

488. *See* e.g. CA Liège 7 November 2005, *Revue générale de droit civil belge* 2006, 620; CA Brussel 28 November 2005, *RGAR* 2008, No. 13,341; *see also* Cass. 23 April 2012 (C.10.0737.N – C.11.0639.N), not published.

is not consistent with what the ECJ has ruled,[489] has not found its way into Belgian case law yet.

153. Under the statutory regime based on the EU Directive, a mandatory[490] strict liability is imposed for damage caused by a defective product. Products are all "tangible" movables,[491] even when they are incorporated into another movable or into an immovable.[492] Electricity is explicitly included.[493] A product is defective when it does not provide the safety that a person is entitled to expect, taking all circumstances into account, including the presentation of the product, the use to which it could reasonably be expected that the product would be put, and the time when the product was put into circulation.[494] The criterion for defectiveness is thus the so-called consumer expectation test.

154. The liability rests with the producer of the product.[495] This is the manufacturer of a finished product, the producer of any raw material or the manufacturer of a component part, but also includes any person who, by putting his name, trademark or other distinguishing feature on the product presents himself as its producer.[496] The importer of a product into the EU in the course of his business also bears this liability.[497] If the producer (or importer) cannot be identified, each supplier of the product will bear this liability unless he informs the victim within a reasonable time of the identity of the producer (or importer) or of the person who supplied him with the product.[498]

155. The victim that wants to recover damages only has to prove that the harm he suffered was caused by a defect of the product.[499] The producer can escape this liability if he proves that he did not put the product into circulation, that it is probable that the defect did not exist at the time he put the product into circulation, that the product was not manufactured by him for sale or any form of distribution for economic purpose nor manufactured or distributed by him in the course of his business, that the

489. *See* ECJ, *Commission v. French Republic*, Case No. C-52/00, ECLI:EU:C:2002:252, decision of 25 April 2002, ECR 2002, I-3827; ECJ, *Commission v. Hellenic Republic*, Case No. C-154/00, ECLI:EU:C:2002:254, decision of 25 April 2002, ECR 2002, I-3879; ECJ, *María Victoria Gonzales Sánchez & Medicina Asturiana SA*, Case No. C-183/00, ECLI:EU:C:2002:255, decision of 25 April 2002, ECR 2002, I-3901; ECJ, *Skov Æg v. Bilka Lavprisvarehus A/S and Bilka Lavprisvarehus A/S v. Jette Mikkelsen and Michael Due Nielsen*, Case No. C-402/03, ECLI:EU:C:2006:6, decision of 10 January 2006, ECR 2006, I-199; ECJ, *Commission v. Kingdom of Denmark*, Case No. C-327/05, ECLI:EU:C:2007:409, decision of 5 July 2007, ECR 2007, I-93.

490. This liability cannot be reduced or excluded by agreement, Art. 10, §1, PLA.

491. The Belgian statute limits product liability to tangible products, but this is not explicitly so stated in the EU Directive, which only mentions "movables." There is a discussion in the literature whether software can be considered as a product under this statutory regime and the EU Directive. As of yet, the highest courts—the Belgian Court of Cassation and the ECJ—have not ruled on the matter yet.

492. Article 2, para. 1, PLA.

493. Article 2, para. 2, PLA.

494. Article 5, PLA.

495. Article 1, PLA.

496. Article 3, PLA.

497. Article 4, §1, PLA.

498. Article 4, §2, PLA.

499. Article 7, PLA.

defect is due to compliance of the product with mandatory regulations issued by public authorities or in the cases of a component instructions given by the manufacturer of the product, or that the state of scientific and technical knowledge at the time when the product was placed into circulation did not allow for the existence of the defect to be discovered.[500]

156. If the damage is caused both by a defect in a product and by a fact attributable to a third party, the producer remains liable for the full damage suffered by the victim. However, the producer that compensates the victim may have recourse against the other liable party based on the general rules of liability. If the damage is caused by a defect in a product and by the fault of the victim or of a person for whom the victim is responsible, the court can reduce or exclude the liability of the producer.[501]

157. The statutory product liability covers all damage caused by death or by personal injury, including moral damage.[502] Damage to goods is only covered for goods other than the defective product itself and if the damaged goods are of a type ordinarily intended for private use or consumption and they were in fact used by the injured person mainly for his own private use or consumption.[503] The Belgian statute interprets the lower threshold of EUR 500, mentioned in Article 9(b) of the EU Directive, as if it were a deductible as is often used in insurance, allowing the victim only to recover any damage to the extent it exceeds that amount,[504] following the French language version of the Directive and not the English one. That the ECJ has in the meantime already indicated that the Directive should be understood to include a threshold and not a deductible[505] has not yet been invoked by Belgian courts to ignore the literal text of the Belgian statute.

500. Article 8, PLA.
501. Article 10, §2, PLA.
502. Article 11, §1, PLA.
503. Article 11, §2, PLA.
504. Article 11, §2, *in fine*, PLA.
505. ECJ, *Commission v. Hellenic Republic*, Case No. C-154/00, ECLI:EU:C:2002:254, decision of 25 April 2002, ECR 2002, I-3879, paras. 23 and 30; ECJ, *Commission v. French Republic*, Case No. C-52/00, ECLI:EU:C:2002:252, decision of 25 April 2002, ECR 2002, I-3827, para. 30.

Chapter 3. Liability for Services

158. Belgian law contains no general rule imposing a strict liability on service providers. As professionals, however, their behavior has to be judged based on the more strict standard based on the traditional principle *spondet peritiam artis, et imperitia culpae adnumeratur* when applying the general fault liability of Article 1382 of the Civil Code and the contractual duty of care.[506] As the once proposed EU Council Directive on the Liability of Suppliers of Services[507] was officially withdrawn because the Commission came to the conclusion that its proposal stood no chance of being adopted without sweeping changes which would risk voiding it of much of its substance and the measure might not stand the test of subsidiarity,[508] it is not expected that a general system of no-fault liability for service providers will be introduced any time soon.

159. The EU Product Liability Directive and the Belgian Product Liability Act impose a strict liability on the producer of a defective product. A supplier of a defective product is only liable if the producer cannot be identified.[509] Given the context and global idea of this strict liability, one is to presume that a service supplier that has done maintenance work on a product or that has done repairs, even replacing some components or parts, is not to be considered a producer.[510] One can expect, however, that a service provider that in rendering a service which makes important changes to a product aiming to modify its original performance, purpose or type, may be considered as a producer and therefore under strict liability for defects his service causes, as the product in that case will be considered to be a new product under EU harmonization legislation.[511] In this context, software updates or repairs could be assimilated to maintenance operations provided that they do not modify a product already placed on the market in such a way that compliance with the applicable requirements may be affected.[512]

506. *See supra* para. 80.
507. Proposal for a Council Directive on the Liability of Suppliers of Services, COM(90) 482 final, 9 November 1990, *Official Journal* C12/8 of 18 January 1991.
508. Communication from the Commission on New Directions on the Liability of Suppliers of Services, COM (94) 260 final, 23 June 1994.
509. *See supra* para. 154.
510. *See* CA Liège 7 November 2005, *Revue générale de droit civil belge* 2006, 620, holding a bike shop, assembling together the frame and the sadle and other parts of a bicycle before actually delivering it to the buyer, is not liable based on product liability if the actual producer is known.
511. Commission Notice, The "Blue Guide" on the Implementation of EU Products Rules 2016, *Official Journal* C 272/01 of 26 July 2016, para. 2.1, pp. 15–17.
512. Commission Notice, The "Blue Guide" on the Implementation of EU Products Rules 2016, *Official Journal* C 272/01 of 26 July 2016, para. 2.1, p. 17.

Chapter 4. Liability for Animals

160. Article 1385 of the Civil Code contains a general strict liability for damage caused by an animal. For this liability to apply, no deviant behavior or "defect" of the animal is required. It is sufficient that the damage was caused by the animal. However, the fact that an animal was merely "involved" in an event causing damage that would not have happened if the animal was not present, apparently does not imply that the event was caused by the animal.[513]

161. The liability rests on the owner or on the person who uses the animal, provided he has in fact the power of control over the animal in the same way an owner has.[514] A person using the animal while performing a task in a subordinate position, who therefore can be qualified as a "servant," can still have the power of control over an animal and can therefore be held liable for damage caused by this animal on the basis of Article 1385 of the Civil Code. Thus, a victim suffering damage caused by an animal used by a servant in the performance of his assignment can invoke the vicarious liability of the master of Article 1384, paragraph 3, of the Civil Code to recover damages.[515]

162. Article 1385 of the Civil Code is understood to contain a strict liability. The victim therefore does not have to prove that the owner or the person using the animal has committed a fault. More even, it is generally accepted that the owner or person using the animal cannot escape this liability by showing he has not committed any fault.[516] However, case law reveals that if the harm has been caused by a normal reaction of the animal to a wrongful provocation by the victim[517] or by a third party,[518] the liability is not applied. Moreover, courts also tend to refuse to allow a victim that unnecessarily, knowingly and wrongfully exposed itself to the known risk posed by the normal behavior of an animal compensation on the basis of this liability.[519]

513. Cass. 26 February 1987, No. 383, *Pas.* 1987, 772, *Arr.Cass.* 1986–1987, 852.
514. Cass. 18 November 1993 (C.93.01154.F), No. 472, *Pas.* 1993, 970, *Arr.Cass.* 1993, 966; Cass. 19 November 2012 (C.09.0379.F), No. 620, *Pas.* 2012, 2253, *Arr.Cass.* 2012, 2595.
515. Cass. 5 November 1981, *Pas.* 1982, 316, *Arr.Cass.* 1981–1982, 328, No. 159; Cass. 19 November 2012 (C.09.0379.F), No. 620, *Pas.* 2012, 2253, *Arr.Cass.* 2012, 2595.
516. *See* already Cass. 23 June 1932, *Pas.* 1932, 200.
517. Cass. 20 May 1983, No. 526, *Pas.* 1983, 1061, *Arr.Cass.* 1982–1983, 1165.
518. Cass. 19 January 1996 (C.95.0193.F), No. 41, *Pas.* 1996, 85, *Arr.Cass.* 1996, 78.
519. *See* e.g. Cass. 12 October 1984, No. 119, *Arr.Cass.* 1984–1985, 254, *Pas.* 1985, 220; Cass. 6 January 2012 (C.11.0025.F), No. 15, *Pas.* 2012, 49, *Arr.Cass.* 2012, 60. In both these cases the behavior of the animal was not provoked by the victim, but still the Court allowed the fact-finding court to exclude all liability based on Art. 1385 CC, even though the harm was clearly also caused by the normal behavior of the animal.

Chapter 5. Road and Traffic Accidents

163. Belgian law does not contain a general strict liability regime for traffic accidents. In general, liability for damage caused by traffic accidents is based on the fault liability of Article 1382 of the Civil Code, with the Road Code[520] to a large extent determining what behavior is wrongful.[521] However, if conditions for their application are met, other basis of liability such as the liability for damage caused by a defective thing[522] or product liability[523] can also be used.

164. This liability regime is strengthened by a system of mandatory third-party motor vehicle insurance.[524] This insurance covers the civil liability of the owner, any holder and any driver of the insured vehicle, and also the liability of any passenger and of any person who is vicariously liable for any of the mentioned persons, except for the civil liability of a person who has obtained control over the vehicle by theft, violence or fencing.[525] The victim of a traffic accident has a direct right of compensation against the liability insurer of the insured person who is liable for the accident,[526] so that he will not bear the risk of the insolvency of the person that is liable.

165. In accidents involving two or more motor vehicles for which it is not possible to establish who is liable, the damage suffered by innocent victims—i.e., any victim who definitely is not liable for the accident—which is not covered by the general compensation system for personal injuries in traffic accidents[527] and the damage to vehicles that definitely have not wrongfully caused the accident is to be compensated by the insurers of all vehicles involved that have not been excluded as a possibly liable party.[528] A victim can demand full compensation from any of those insurers, who after compensating the victim can have recourse on all insurers involved, each contributing an equal share.[529] This duty to compensate is statutorily imposed on the insurer, not on the insured person who may have wrongfully caused the accident, but who cannot be held liable as the conditions for such liability have not been proven.

520. Royal Decree of 1 December 1975 holding the General Regulation on Policing Road Traffic and the Use of Public Roads, in short referred to as the "Road Code" (*Code de la route—Wegcode*). *See* www.code-de-la-route.be.
521. As any violation of a statutory or regulatory behavioral rule is in itself wrongful if not excused by a ground of justification (*see supra* Part I, Ch. 1, §3 and *infra* Part IV, Ch. 2), an imputable violation of the traffic code is a fault.
522. *See supra* Part III, Ch. 1.
523. *See supra* Part III, Ch. 2.
524. (Federal) Mandatory Motor Vehicle Insurance Act of 21 November 1989, here in short "MVIA."
525. Article 3, §1, MVIA.
526. This direct right of the victim originally was introduced by the (federal) Mandatory Motor Vehicle Insurance Act of 1 July 1956, and kept in the (federal) Mandatory Motor Vehicle Insurance Act of 21 November 1989. It was subsequently generalized to all types of liability insurance by Art. 96 of the (federal) Land Insurance Contracts Act of 25 June 1992, which is now replaced by Art. 150 of the (federal) Insurance Act of 4 April 2014.
527. *See infra* para. 167.
528. Article 29*ter*, §1–2, MVIA.
529. Article 29*ter*, §3, MVIA.

166. A Common Guarantee Fund (*Fonds Commun de Garantie Belge, FCGB—Belgisch Gemeenschappelijk Waarborgfonds, BGWF*), which is funded by all insurance companies active in the Belgian market, covers special cases in which the victim cannot effectively obtain compensation from an insurer. The most important ones are the case where the vehicle that caused the accident was not insured,[530] the insurance company that has to compensate the victim is insolvent,[531] accidents for which the person who caused it is not liable—and hence his insurer is also not bound to compensate the victim—only because of a fortuitous event (force majeure),[532] accidents that are not covered by the insurance because the vehicle was stolen or taken by violence,[533] and accidents wrongfully caused by a driver whose care—and hence its insurance status and the identity of the insurance company—could not be identified, the hit-and-run cases.[534]

167. Near the end of the twentieth century, the general liability system was complemented by a special compensation regime for some damage caused by a traffic accident involving a motor vehicle.[535]

Only damage resulting from bodily harm or death is covered. This includes medical costs but also loss of income, i.e., consequential economic loss.[536] Harm to goods or property is not compensated, with the exception of clothes the victim was wearing and functional prosthetic devices, i.e., devices used by the victim to compensate physical deficiencies.[537]

However, not all direct victims of bodily injury are protected. The regime explicitly excludes the drivers of the motor vehicles involved in the accident.[538] This means that coverage is limited to damage caused by bodily harm to persons that were participating in traffic without driving—such as pedestrians, bicyclists and passengers of (motor) vehicles—or to persons that were not participating in traffic—such as for instance a person enjoying a drink on a terrace on the sidewalk or a person sitting in his couch in front of his television set when a truck enters into the house. The person claiming the compensation has the burden of proof that the direct victim of the physical

530. Article 19*bis*-11, §1, 8°, MVIA.
531. Article 19*bis*-11, §1, 1°, MVIA.
532. Article 19*bis*-11, §1, 3°, MVIA.
533. Article 19*bis*-11, §1, 4°, MVIA.
534. Article 19*bis*-11, §1, 7°, MVIA.
535. Article 29*bis* MVIA, inserted by the (federal) Act of 30 March 1994 and immediately amended by the (federal) Act of 13 April 1995.
536. The original political intent of the government introducing this compensation regime in 1994 was to relieve the budgetary problems in order to comply with the so-called Maastricht norms imposed on the EU Member States to be allowed to join the euro when it was going to be introduced, by creating a mechanism to allow the social security system to recover the cost of traffic accidents it effectively bears from the motor insurance companies, thereby indirectly avoiding increases in taxes or social security premiums by forcing the insurance companies to increase their insurance rates. This explains the restriction in the type of damage covered by the regime to harm which causes medical expenses or the expenditure of social security benefits.
537. Article 29*bis*, §1, para. 1 and 3, MVIA.
538. Article 29*bis*, §1 *juncto* §2, MVIA.

injury was not the driver of a motor vehicle involved in the accident.[539] On the other hand, the compensation is not limited to the damage suffered by the person that was physically injured: damage suffered by repercussion by other people is covered as well.[540]

The regime grants the victim a direct claim for compensation against the liability insurer of any motor vehicle that is involved in the accident. If the vehicle is connected to rails, the compensation is owed by the owner of the vehicle.

This compensation regime is not based on any liability. The insurer has a statutory duty to compensate the victim, even though the insured person has not committed any fault. What is more, the vehicle involved in the accident does not have to have caused the accident: it is sufficient that it played a role in the totality of the accident.[541] If there was contact between the victim and the vehicle, this vehicle is obviously involved.[542] However, also without any contact, a vehicle can be involved in an accident, such as when it is the destination of a pedestrian who is hit by another participant in traffic.[543]

The victim has a right to compensation even if it has wrongfully caused the accident itself. The only exception is the case of a victim over 14 years old that intentionally caused the injury, i.e., cases of suicide or self-mutilation.[544]

After compensating the victim, the insurer can have recourse against the insurers of all other cars involved, and the total burden of this statutory obligation to compensate the victim will be shared equally between them.[545] If the conditions for liability are present, however, the insurer, who by compensating the victim is subrogated in its rights, can have full recourse against the person who is liable for the accident or against

539. Cass. 26 October 2007 (C.06.0341.F), No. 507, *Pas.* 2007, 1866, *Arr.Cass.* 2007, 2017; Cass. 20 December 2007 (C.06.0301.N), No. 650, *Arr.Cass.* 2007, 2528, *Pas.* 2007, 2401; Cass. 24 April 2009 (C.07.0120.N), No. 275, *Arr.Cass.* 2009, 1090, *Pas.* 2009, 1003.

540. Thus, the driver of one of the motor vehicles involved in the accident does not have a right to compensation of his or her own bodily harm, but can claim compensation of the damage he or she suffers by repercussion from the bodily harm suffered by a passenger in the car, for instance his or her spouse, except for when he or she has intentionally caused the harm to this passenger (Article 29*bis*, §2, MVIA).

541. Cass. 3 October 2008 (C.07.0130.N), No. 524, *Arr.Cass.* 2008, 2138, *Pas.* 2008, 2131; Cass. 15 November 2012 (C.11.0523.F), No. 615, *Pas.* 2012, 2229, *Arr.Cass.* 2012, 2568.

542. Cass. 28 April 2011 (C.10.0492.F), No. 286, *Pas.* 2011, 1195, *Arr.Cass.* 2011, 1107.

543. *See* e.g. Cass. 12 September 2014 (C.13.0567.N), No. 519, *Arr.Cass.* 2014, 1880, *Pas.* 2014, 1870, where a tram was considered to be involved in the accident while its role was limited to having been the destination of a pedestrian that was victim of an accident while crossing a street on its way to catch a ride; Cass. 22 October 2009 (C.08.0420.N), No. 604, *Arr.Cass.* 2009, 2431, *Pas.* 2009, 2374, a case where a pedestrian was hit when crossing a street on his way to deposit the trash in a garbage truck at the other side of the road.

544. In such a case, also the persons suffering harm by repercussion cannot claim compensation under this regime. Cass. 26 June 2008 (C.07.0494.N), No. 407, *Arr.Cass.* 2008, 1709, *Pas.* 2008, 1698.

545. This recourse will be based on the general provision on subrogation in Art. 1251, 3°, CC. Cass. 4 October 2007, *Bull.Ass.* 2008, 150; Cass. 28 September 2012 (C.11.0404.N), No. 501, *Arr. Cass.* 2012, 2081, *Pas.* 2012, 1787; Cass. 30 June 2016 (C.15.0447.N), *CRA* 2016/5, 17.

this person's liability insurer.[546] Recourse against the person whose damage was compensated, however, is not possible.[547]

168. When accidents are caused by the condition of the road, victims often try to invoke the liability of the government. Several bases are available.

First, the government can be liable if the condition of the road that has caused the accident can be traced back to its fault. Already in the 1930s of the last century, the Court of Cassation ruled that a government that opens a road giving the public the impression that it is safe while in fact it is not, is liable on the basis of Article 1382 of the Civil Code,[548] and in the 1960s the Court ruled that the government that opens a road that is not sufficiently safe commits a fault.[549] Nowadays, this fault liability can be used invoking a violation of the municipal government's statutory duty to maintain safe traffic on the public roads, streets and squares on its territory.[550] The Court of Cassation has ruled that, while this statutory rule does not require the municipality to reach the result of safety at any cost, which would result in a quasi-strict liability of the municipality for traffic accidents caused by unsafe road conditions, but only imposes a duty of care on the government to take all reasonable measures to maintain safety,[551] the government is presumed to be aware of all unsafe conditions on the roads on its territory, resulting in a very victim-friendly system in which the government in effect can only escape this supposedly fault based liability by proving that it was impossible for it to be aware of the unsafe condition that caused the accident in time to take the required measures.[552]

Second, the government can be liable as the custodian of a road that is held to be defective in the sense of Article 1384, paragraph 1, of the Civil Code.[553] Here, one can notice a very victim-friendly attitude of many courts, which are willing to consider a road defective not only when its material structure or surface is changed or damaged or abnormal, but also when an object lying on top of the road was causing an obstruction. The Court of Cassation seems to be of the opinion that the concept of defect, as it has to be applied in Article 1383, paragraph 1, of the Civil Code, can be stretched so that in effect the government bears a strict liability for accidents caused by objects left on a road which a normal user would not expect, so that the risk for an accident is increased.[554] This goes so far that the Court allows courts to hold the government liable

546. Article 29*bis*, §4, MVIA. Cass. 6 October 2005 (C.03.0377.N), No. 489, *Arr.Cass.* 2005, 1853, *Pas.* 2005, 1852; Cass. 23 January 2012 (C.09.0228.F), No. 62, *Pas.* 2012, 180, *Arr.Cass.* 2012, 202.
547. Cass. 30 June 2016 (C.15.0447.N), *CRA* 2016/5, 17.
548. Cass. 19 April 1934, *Pas.* 1934, 249.
549. Cass. 7 March 1963, *Pas.* 1963, 744, *RW* 1963–1964, 1115.
550. Article 135, §2, of the Federal Municipalities Act of 24 June 1988.
551. Cass. 28 January 2005 (C.02.0272.N), No. 55, *Arr.Cass.* 2005, 219, *Pas.* 2005, 217.
552. Cass. 17 April 2008 (C.06.0575.N), No. 230, *Arr.Cass.* 2008, 942, *Pas.* 2008, 921.
553. *See supra* Part III, Ch. 1.
554. *See* e.g. Cass. 13 March 2015 (C.14.0284.N), No. 193, *Arr.Cass.* 2015, 737, *Pas.* 2015, 721; Cass. 31 October 2013 (C.12.0628.N), No. 570, *Arr.Cass.* 2013, 2281, *Pas.* 2013, 2115; Cass. 29 September 2006 (C.04.0427.N – C.05.0192.N), No. 449, *Arr.Cass.* 2006, 1869, *Pas.* 2006, 1917.

for an accident caused by a stone lying on a road, even when a traffic sign warning road users for falling or fallen rocks was present.[555]

555. Cass. 17 January 2014 (C.12.0510.F), No. 39, *Pas.* 2014, 143, *Arr.Cass.* 2014, 161.

Chapter 6. Environmental Liability

169. Anyone suffering environmental damage can in principle claim compensation based on the general rules of civil liability.

This means that full compensation can be claimed from anyone who through committing a fault has caused such damage. As according to the so-called unity theory the violation of a specific behavioral rule of law *ipso facto* constitutes a civil wrong,[556] liability based on Article 1382 of the Civil Code will be a readily available remedy in cases of violations of specific environmental regulations. Noncompliance with the conditions imposed in an operating license, for instance, can be invoked as a fault by any third party that suffers harm as a consequence of the action that violated those conditions.[557] Compliance with the conditions imposed by a license does not provide a safe harbor for the polluter: the courts can still find environmentally damaging behavior still negligent, even though all specific regulatory provisions were complied with.[558] However, engaging in an activity based on an environmental or urbanological license that later turns out to be null and void is not necessarily wrongful.[559]

The constitutional right to the protection of a healthy environment,[560] however, is not interpreted to give every individual a subjective right to a healthy environment so that any environmental harm would become a civil wrong. This constitutional provision is interpreted as a guideline for government policy, so that it can only be invoked against the government and, which is more important, cannot be invoked to claim compensation without showing that the government wrongfully, i.e., negligently, did not sufficiently protect the environment.[561]

Nuisance can also be used as a basis to claim compensation for environmental damage.[562] The advantage of this basis for liability is that no fault has to be shown. However, the disadvantage is that only excessive hindrance will be compensated and only hindrance that is the consequence of the exercise of an attribute of the property right on the premises from which the hindrance originates is covered.

When the environmental damage was caused by a defect of a thing, such as malfunctioning machinery or leaking containers or tanks, the strict liability based on Article 1384, paragraph 1, of the Civil Code can be invoked.[563]

170. To overcome some of the problems the application of traditional fault liability poses in cases of environmental damage, the legislature has introduced a number of strict liabilities. In these cases, liability attaches as soon as the victim proves that his damage is caused by the regulated activity of the defendant, without any showing of wrongfulness being required. In several of these instances, the legislature

556. *See supra* Part I, Ch. 1, §3.
557. *See* e.g. CA Ghent 18 April 2013, *TMR* 2014, 60, a case involving the construction of a mobile telecom antenna to close next to a roof terrace.
558. *See* e.g. CA Antwerp 27 September 1996, *TMR* 1996, 291.
559. *See* e.g. CFI Brussels 18 January 2008, *TMR* 2008, 692.
560. Article 23, 4°, Con.
561. CA Antwerp 28 June 2005, *TMR* 2006, 349.
562. *See supra* Part I, Ch. 2, §5.
563. *See supra* Part III, Ch. 1.

has introduced at the same time additional measures aimed at securing actual compensation of the harm.

A first example is the nuclear sector, which creates such high risks, that imposing a strict liability is the only manner in which the operator will have the incentive to take it into account when deciding the extent to which he wants to engage in these activities. The operator of a nuclear installation is liable for all damage caused by a nuclear accident in the installation itself or during the transport of nuclear material originating from the installation.[564] The operator of a nuclear ship is liable for all damage caused by a nuclear accident caused by the ship.[565]

The owner of a sea ship is liable for all damage caused by oil originating from the ship.[566] This regime is not only applicable in case of shipwreck, but also in case of any accident or voluntary discharge of oil, such as while cleaning the tanks. More generally, anyone who causes damage or environmental disruption to the marine environment in the seawaters under Belgian jurisdiction is liable.[567] This liability applies in case of a breach of a legal rule, but also in case of an accident, even if no fault was committed.

In the Capital Region of Brussels and in Wallonia, the producer of toxic waste is liable for all damage caused during transportation, neutralization, removal, or destruction of this waste.[568]

The operator of groundwater extraction facilities and any principal of public or private works, whose activity causes the groundwater levels to drop, are liable for any damage caused to real estate, cultivation and crops.[569] Anyone who by emitting a substance pollutes the soil is liable for the resulting damage. If the emission was caused by the operation of a licensed facility, the operator of the facility is liable and not its employees.[570]

Other examples of strict liability exist for damage caused by underground activities, such as the exploration for or extraction of hydrocarbons,[571] the storage of carbon dioxides,[572] or the exploitation of geothermal heat.[573]

171. If the harm takes the form of damage to the personal goods of an individual or personal injury, the general requirement of personal damage that is applicable in

564. Convention on Third Party Liability in the Field of Nuclear Energy of 29 July 1960, ratified by (federal) Act of 1 August 1966, and implemented by Act of 22 July 1985.
565. (Federal) Act of 9 August 1963 on the Liability of the Operator of a Nuclear Ship.
566. International Convention on Civil Liability for Oil Pollution Damage, Brussels, 29 November 1969, ratified by (federal) Act of 20 July 1976.
567. Article 37 of the (federal) Act of 20 January 1999 on the Protection of the Marine Environment.
568. Article 7 of the (federal) Act of 22 July 1974 on Toxic Waste; this provision is abolished in Flanders by Art. 81 of the Flemish Act of 23 December 2011 on Sustainable Management of Material Cycles and Waste.
569. Flemish Act of 24 January 1984 on the Management of Groundwater; Walloon Act of 24 May 2004 introducing a Book II into the Walloon Environmental Code, called the Water Code.
570. Flemish Act of 27 October 2006 on Soil Protection and Remediation.
571. Article 33, §1, Flemish Act of 8 May 2009 on the Deep Underground; Art. 42, Walloon Mines Act of 7 July 1988.
572. Article 62, §1, Flemish Act of 8 May 2009 on the Deep Underground.
573. Article 63/25, Flemish Act of 8 May 2009 on the Deep Underground.

liability law will be easily met.[574] Environmental damage, however, very often consists in harm to the collective environment, to elements which are not privatized and do not belong to any particular person. As in that case nobody's private interests are harmed, there is no person who can claim to have suffered any damage, as this concept is understood in Belgian liability law.[575]

A finer distinction can be made between the harm consisting in the actual pollution of the environment itself, which through the lens of private law is perceived to be nobody's damage, and the harm consisting in the injury to the personal interests of a person as a consequence of the pollution, which in the eyes of the law is personal damage to this person. Hence, a fishing club cannot claim compensation for the pollution of collective fishing water in itself, but it can claim compensation for the loss of enjoyment of its members fishing activities that results from this pollution.[576]

172. The government has a statutory duty to control pollution and the release of dangerous substances, including radioactive materials and ionizing radiation.[577] The costs made in such interventions have to be recovered from the operator of the economic activity that caused the damage or the owner of the materials or products.[578] This operator can only escape from liability if he proves that the environmental damage or the immediate threat for such damage was caused by a third party even though appropriate safety measures were taken or was the consequence of complying with mandatory instructions from a governmental entity which is not an instruction at the occasion of an emission or incident caused by the activities of the operator.

173. To implement EU Directive 2004/35/CE on Environmental Liability,[579] which is based on the Pigovian polluter pays principle, a strict liability was introduced for environmental damage caused by transportation of dangerous or polluting goods or substances by road, train, over inland waterways, sea or through the air,[580] as well as for damage caused by genetically modified organisms[581] at the federal level. In the two main regions, the Directive was implemented by the introduction of a separate title or chapter on environmental damage into their general statutory code on environmental

574. *See* on this requirement *supra* para. 59.

575. *See also supra* para. 59 *infra* paras. 222–223.

576. *See* e.g. CFI Ypres 6 July 1963 and CFI Ghent 21 December 1963, *L'entreprise et le droit* 1973, 230; CFI Verviers 24 December 1968, *Jurisprudence commerciale de Belgique* 1970, 16,535; Corr. Hasselt 18 April 1972, *RW* 1972–1973, 776.

577. Article 11, §1, 4°, (federal) Act of 15 May 2007 on Civil Safety.

578. Article 179, §2, (federal) Act of 15 May 2007 on Civil Safety.

579. Directive 2004/35/CE of the European Parliament and of the Council of 21 April 2004 on Environmental Liability with regard to the Prevention and Remedying of Environmental Damage, *Official Journal* L143/56 of 30 April 2004.

580. Royal Decree of 8 November 2007, based on power delegated to the King by Art. 224 of the (federal) Act of 25 April 2007 holding Diverse Provisions (IV).

581. Royal Decree of 3 August 2007, based on power delegated to the King by Art. 132 of the (federal) Act of 20 July 1991 holding Social and Diverse Provisions.

policy.[582] In the Capital Region of Brussels, a separate Code of Inspection, Prevention, Finding and Punishment of Environmental Offences and of Environmental Liability was introduced.[583] Here, the concept of environmental damage is relatively limited,[584] but as the government has the duty to restore pollution irrespective of whether the environmental interests that were harmed were private or collective, and subsequently can recover the cost of these measures or cleanup operations from the enterprise that caused the pollution, these rules allow for the attribution of the costs of environmental damage to collective goods to be internalized by the polluter.

174. Environmental organizations or NGO's have only limited possibilities in invoking civil liability as a basis to use judicial proceedings against environmental damage. Based on the Aarhus Convention,[585] the Court of Cassation has recognized that environmental organizations have standing to bring a civil claim against environmental wrongs.[586] As harm to collective environmental goods is not personal damage for such organizations, they cannot claim compensation for the actual environmental harm itself.[587] However, they can claim compensation for moral damage they suffer, as their work to protect the environment has been undone by the wrong and they will need to increase their efforts to compensate for the environmental damage the wrong has caused.[588]

Recently, the Constitutional Court has ruled that a legal entity whose stated purpose is the protection of a collective interest, must be able to recover more than symbolic compensation for the moral damage it suffers because of injury to this collective interest.[589] The Court suggested that in estimating the extent of this harm,

582. In Flanders Title XV in the Flemish Act of 5 April 1995 holding General Provisions on Environmental Policy, in Flemish referred to as "DABM" (*Decreet houdende Algemene Bepalingen inzake Milieubeleid*), inserted by Flemish Act of 21 December 2007; in Wallonia Part III in Book I of the Walloon Environmental Code, introduced by Walloon Act of 22 November 2007.
583. Introduced by Brussels Ordonnance of 8 May 2014.
584. Environmental damage for this Directive only includes: (a) damage to protected species and natural habitats, which is damage that has significant adverse effects on reaching or maintaining the favorable conservation status of such habitats or species; (b) water damage, which is damage that significantly adversely affects the ecological, chemical or quantitative status or econological potential of the waters; and (c) land damage, which is land contamination that creates a significant risk of human health being adversely affected. *See* Art. 2(1) of Directive 2004/35/CE on Environmental Liability.
585. Convention on Access to Information, Public Participation in Decision-Making and Access to Justice in Environmental Matters, done at Aarhus, Denmark, on 25 June 1998.
586. Cass. 11 June 2013 (P.12.1389.N), No. 361, *Arr.Cass.* 2013, 1469, *Pas.* 2013, 1326. With this decision, the Court changed its earlier reasoning which held that an organization cannot claim to have standing based on nothing more than that its stated purpose in its articles of association is to protect interests that were hurt, if the harmed interests are not the personal interests of the entity: Cass. 19 November 1982, No. 172, *Arr.Cass.* 1982–1983, 372, *Pas.* 1983, 338; Cass. 19 September 1996 (C.95.0386.F), No. 319, *Pas.* 1996, 830, *Arr.Cass.* 1996, 775.
587. *See supra* para. 59.
588. *See* e.g. CA Antwerp 7 March 2012, *TMR* 2012, 566.
589. Con.C. No. 7/2016 of 21 January 2016.

courts can take into account the legal person's purpose, the extent of its activities and efforts it makes, and the gravity of the injury to the collective interest.[590]

590. For recent examples applying these criteria, *see* e.g. Corr. Ghent 12 April 2016, *TMR* 2016, 514; CA Ghent 18 March 2016, *TMR* 2016, 546.

Chapter 7. Liability for Fire or Explosion in Establishments Open to the Public

175. Of course, there may be several other strict liabilities imposed by statute for specific instances, but this is not the place to review them all. There is one, however, that is important enough to be mentioned.

176. A separate statute imposes a liability on the operator of a public establishment for damage caused by fire or explosion.[591] The cause of the fire or explosion is not relevant: even if the fire started in a neighboring building and spread into the public establishment, the operator remains liable. This liability can be invoked by any victim: visitors, but also neighbors and even the members of the staff of the operator, except for the arsonist or the person who willfully caused the explosion.[592]

The operator is legally required to have liability insurance covering this liability.[593] This liability is capped per incident at approximately EUR 24.5 million for bodily harm and EUR 1.25 million for property damage.[594] After compensating the victim, the insurer can have recourse against the person liable for the fire or explosion.[595]

As this statute does not only impose a strict liability but also significant measures aimed at preventing fires, this regime is only applicable to those types of establishments for which the government estimates the risks significant enough to justify the extra cost it imposes on the operators. The list includes among others discotheques, larger restaurants, hotels, larger stores, movie theatres, sports halls and stadiums, amusement parks, hospitals, schools, larger office buildings, train stations and airports, churches and court buildings.[596]

591. Article 8, para. 1, (federal) Act of 30 July 1979 on the Prevention of and Liability for Fire and Explosions.
592. Article 8, para. 7, (federal) Act of 30 July 1979 on the Prevention of and Liability for Fire and Explosions.
593. Article 8, para. 3, (federal) Act of 30 July 1979 on the Prevention of and Liability for Fire and Explosions.
594. Article 1 Royal Decree of 5 August 1991 implementing the (federal) Act of 30 July 1979. These amounts are adjusted yearly based on the index of consumer prices. The amounts mentioned here were calculated based on the index of August 2017.
595. Article 8, para. 6, (federal) Act of 30 July 1979 on the Prevention of and Liability for Fire and Explosions.
596. Royal Decree of 28 February 1991.

Part IV. Defenses and Exception Clauses

Chapter 1. Limitation of Action

177. In Belgian civil law, an action in rem has to be brought within a time period of thirty years.[597] Since the major reform of the statutory provisions on limitation in 1998, this long period no longer applies to actions in personam: here, a period of ten years is applied.[598] This general rule applies to contractual claims, but not for claims based on extracontractual liability. For such claims, the Civil Code provides two periods of limitation, one referred to as a relative period, and one referred to as an absolute period.

178. The relative period is the shorter one. It means that the claimant has to bring his action within five years from the moment the victim obtained knowledge of the existence of the damage and of the identity of the person who is liable (discovery rule).[599] This period of limitation starts running as soon as the victim knows he will suffer damage, even if this damage has not occurred yet, as will for instance be the case with loss of income. Actual knowledge is required, so the fact that the victim is legally presumed to have particular knowledge is not sufficient for the relative period of limitation to start running.[600] Generalizing this idea, the fact that a normal person would have known of the existence of the damage or the identity of the person who is liable does not start the five-year period of limitation. The exact extent of the damage does not have to be known, the awareness that damage exists or will occur is sufficient.[601] As the statutory provision requires knowledge of the identity of the person who is liable, one can conclude that some knowledge of the cause of the damage has to exist, as it is causation that links the loss to the person who is liable.[602]

179. The absolute period is longer. It means that any action in extracontractual liability is time-barred if it is brought more than twenty years after the day on which

597. Article 2262 CC.
598. Article 2262*bis*, §1, para. 1, CC.
599. Article 2262*bis*, §1, para. 2, CC.
600. Cass. 26 April 2012 (C.11.0143.N), No. 260, *Arr.Cass.* 2012, 1090, *Pas.* 2012, 922, stating that the legal rule that publication of a real estate transaction in the public Mortgage Register makes it opposable to all third parties, who cannot invoke their ignorance of the transaction anymore, does not imply that actual knowledge in the sense of Art. 2262*bis*, §1, para. 2, CC, is present.
601. Cass. 9 December 2010 (C.10.0306.F), No. 725, *Pas.* 2010, 3171, *Arr.Cass.* 2010, 2936.
602. *Cf.* Cass. 13 January 1994, No. 16, *Pas.* 1994, 23, *Arr.Cass.* 1994, 27, where the Court approved a decision by a lower court holding that the "damage" only occurred at the time the victim realized his physical injury was the consequence of a medical fault.

the fact that has caused the damage occurred.[603] This period starts running irrespective of any knowledge of loss or the cause of this loss. It is intended to allow for the insurance of liability risks, which would be very difficult if the insurer could not know in advance for what time period he has to provide cover for the risk.

180. The general rules on interruption and suspension of limitation periods apply.[604] This means that the time period does not run against a person who has not reached the age of majority and a person who is subject to a specific regime of legal incapacity.[605] The prescription period also does not run between spouses.[606] After these reasons for suspension have disappeared, the time period starts running again, with the time lapsed before and after the reason of suspension counting for the period needed for prescription. Certain events result in the time already lapsed to be lost, so that a new time period starts running. Examples are the start of formal legal proceedings by the creditor, in which case a new period of limitation starts running when a final court decision is issued,[607] and the recognition of the debt by the debtor.[608]

181. Apart from these general rules on prescription, applicable to all claims based on civil liability for which there are no exceptions, separate statutes imposing specific liabilities can also contain different prescription periods.

Claims based on product liability, for instance, have to be brought within a period of three years from the day on which the plaintiff became aware, or should reasonably have become aware, of the damage, the defect and the identity of the producer,[609] and no later than ten years to be counted from the day on which the product was put on the market.[610] Claims brought against the State expire after a period of five years, starting from January 1st of the budgetary year during which they originate.[611] This means that liability claims against the government can expire before the victim has become aware of the loss or has not discovered yet what has caused the damage.

As was mentioned earlier, the civil proceedings for liability based on a criminal offense are suspended until the criminal court has reached a final judgment on the criminal charges.[612] This means that according to the civil rules on time limitation, the victim's claim for compensation could be time-barred by the time he is legally able to bring it. To avoid this problem, there is a specific statutory provision stating that the civil claim based on a criminal offense can never be time-barred before the prescription of the criminal prosecution.[613]

182. The exception of prescription does not as such relate to the public policy of the forum. Therefore, the exception is an affirmative defense, which has to be invoked by the defendant. The court will not ex officio refuse a claim because the time

603. Article 2262*bis*, §1, para. 3, CC.
604. Articles 2242–2259 CC.
605. Article 2252 CC.
606. Article 2253 CC.
607. Article 2244, §1, CC.
608. Article 2248 CC.
609. Article 12, §2, PLA.
610. Article 12, §1, PLA.
611. Article 100, para. 1, 1°, Coordinated (federal) Acts of 17 July 1991 on State Comptability.
612. *See supra* para. 47.
613. Article 26, Preceding Title to Crim.Pro.

limitation has lapsed.[614] This also means that, although a defendant cannot in advance agree that his debt will not be time-barred or that the limitation period will be longer than prescribed by law, he can renounce his right to invoke the prescription once it has been acquired, i.e., once the statutorily set period of limitation has lapsed.[615] If, however, the time limitation relates to a matter that does touch the public policy of the forum, an exception is made to these rules. In such a case, the court will have to invoke the prescription ex officio,[616] and must refuse to recognize a voluntary renunciation of prescription by the debtor.[617]

A debtor, who voluntarily pays a debt after the time limitation on the creditor's claim has lapsed, cannot recover the sums paid based on undue payment. A claim based on undue payment is only possible if the *solvens* has paid without having a debt. The prescription, however, does not touch upon the existence of the legal duty of the debtor. It only extinguishes the right of the creditor to claim performance.[618]

614. Article 2223 CC.
615. Article 2220 CC.
616. Cass. 31 January 1980, *Pas.* 1980, 623, *Arr.Cass.* 1979–1980, 643, holding—under now old law—that a civil claim based on a criminal offence cannot be brought after the prescription of the criminal offence.
617. Cass. 3 February 1950, *Arr.Verbr.* 1950, 357, *Pas.* 1950, 382, in a case on taxation, for which the rules on time limitation belong to the public policy.
618. Article 1376 CC.

Chapter 2. Grounds of Justification

183. Several grounds of justification (*cause de justification—rechtvaardigingsgrond*) are recognized by Belgian civil liability law. In an attempt to classify these grounds systematically, one can recognize four categories:

- force majeure, meaning the person could physically not have behaved differently;[619]
- *fait du prince* or orders from the government, meaning the person was not allowed to behave differently;[620]
- state of necessity, i.e., self-defense or the defense of others, meaning the person psychologically and morally could not have behaved differently;[621] and
- unavoidable and unescapable error, meaning the person could not have known he had to behave differently.[622]

Consent of the victim or the person suffering the loss is generally not recognized as a ground of justification in Belgian tort theory, even though in in some cases it can play a role.[623]

§1. Consent

184. Consent of the victim can turn an act that would be wrongful without consent into lawful behavior. Of course, a victim cannot consent to a violation of a rule of law, i.e., a behavioral rule unilaterally imposed by the government, mandatorily applicable to the wrongdoer. However, when the wrongfulness of an act consists in the violation of a subjective right,[624] the holder of this right can by consenting to the act render it lawful, as in that case this act does not violate the subjective right anymore. Thus, an owner who consents to the destruction of his property cannot claim compensation for the loss he suffers because of this destruction. Someone who enters the house of someone else with his consent does not commit a wrong, while entering without such consent would constitute a criminal offense.[625] When a patient has consented to medical treatment,[626] one cannot subsequently claim that the fact that he was treated constitutes a fault.[627] However, the Court of Cassation has ruled in its famous *SM*-decision that

619. *See infra* Part IV, Ch. 2, §2.
620. *See infra* Part IV, Ch. 2, §4.
621. *See infra* Part IV, Ch. 2, §3.
622. *See infra* Part IV, Ch. 2, §4.
623. *See infra* Part IV, Ch. 2, §1.
624. *See supra* para. 61.
625. Article 439 PC.
626. On the principle right of patients to give or withhold consent to medical treatment, *see* Art. 8 of the (federal) Patients Rights Act of 22 August 2002.
627. *See* e.g. Cass. 14 December 2001 (C.98.0469.F), No. 705, *Pas.* 2001, 2129, *Arr.Cass.* 2001, 2200.

the consent of the victim of the criminal offense of voluntary wounding does not preclude culpability, as prohibiting voluntary wounding touches public policy.[628]

185. Voluntary assumption of risk by the victim is not recognized as a separate legal basis for denying liability in Belgian legal literature. The dominating opinion interprets the law to only allow for a diminished liability of the third party if the victim's acceptance of the risk can be judged careless or negligent.[629] In that case, the application of the general principle of comparative negligence is by itself capable of serving as a basis for limiting the liability of the third party.[630]

However, in some cases where the assumption of the risk by the victim cannot be considered wrongful, such as in most sports injury disputes, the courts and authors tend to see the voluntary assumption of risk by the victim as a circumstance which has to be taken into account to judge whether the behavior of the other player is negligent.[631] The loss causing behavior is considered not to be wrongful because it is a realization of the risk the victim has accepted by participating in the sport.[632]

In cases involving damage caused by animals, the Court of Cassation allows the fact-finding courts to exclude the liability of the owner or the person using the animal if the damage resulted from the normal and foreseeable behavior of the animal and the victim knowingly, willingly and wrongfully subjected itself to this risk, based on the reason that in such a case the accident would not be caused by the presumed fault of the custodian of the animal.[633] It is remarkable that the Court is not willing to apply the same reasoning in cases of harm caused by defective things: even if the victim specifically knew of the defect and easily could avoid it but chose not to do so, the custodian of the defective thing remains liable.[634]

§2. Force Majeure

186. Force majeure is a generally recognized concept in Belgian contract law. It is the situation in which it is impossible for the debtor to perform an obligation because of a compelling circumstance that is not attributable to him. In that case, one cannot blame a contractual debtor for a breach of contract, so no contractual liability will attach.[635] In the same way, Belgian law recognizes force majeure as a basis to

---

628. Cass. 6 January 1998 (P.97.1353.N), No. 3, *Arr.Cass.* 1998, 10, *Pas.* 1998, 11. *See* on this case also the decision of the ECtHR in the case *K.A. and A.D. v. Belgium*, Nos. 42758/98 and 45558/99, 17 February 2005.
629. *See* e.g. Cass. 1 February 2008 (C.06.0179.F – C.06.0387.F), No. 78, *Pas.* 2008, 315, *Arr.Cass.* 2008, 299, stating very explicitly the principle that assumption or acceptance of a risk can only justify a reduction of liability if it is wrongful.
630. *See infra* Part IV, Ch. 3.
631. *See supra* Part I, Ch. 1, §2.
632. *See* e.g. CA Brussels 18 April 1994, *Bull.Ass.* 1995, 442.
633. *See* e.g. Cass. 12 October 1984, No. 119, *Arr.Cass.* 1984–1985, 254, *Pas.* 1985, 220; Cass. 6 January 2012 (C.11.0025.F), No. 15, *Pas.* 2012, 49, *Arr.Cass.* 2012, 60.
634. Cass. 4 January 2016 (C.15.0191.F), *RGAR* 2016, No. 15,334, *NJW* 2016, 917; Cass. 17 December 2010 (C.10.0193.F), No. 754, *Pas.* 2010, 3275, *Arr.Cass.* 2010, 3060.
635. Articles 1147–1148 CC.

deny any wrongdoing when a specific behavioral rule of law has been violated.[636] Such force majeure is present when an event which was not caused by the defendant and which he could not reasonably avoid,[637] made it impossible to comply with the legal rule.

187. Strict liability attaches the duty to compensate the victim to the fact that the damage resulted from the realization of the risk the law attributes to the person bearing the liability. For such liability to attach, it is not required that the person held liable has through his behavior caused the loss occurrence. Hence, force majeure—which in essence means that the person whose behavior is being judged could not but act this way because of a stronger force determining his actions which he could not resist—conceptually has no role to play to exonerate this person for such strict liability. Although courts often write that strict liability does not attach because of force majeure, they in fact mean that in that particular case the loss was a consequence of a cause quite separate from the risk covered by the strict liability. In fact, force majeure is here invoked as a misnomer for a lack of causality.

188. Courts sometimes also invoke force majeure to exclude fault liability in cases involving alleged negligence. This also seems to be the consequence of imprecise use of concepts. In cases based on negligence, no behavioral rule of law was violated. Therefore, there is no need for any justification of the behavior. As the defendant's behavior, taking all circumstances including those legally qualified as force majeure into account, was reasonable in such cases, no negligence occurred either, and hence there was no wrong that can serve as a basis for liability.

§3. Necessity, Self-Help and Self-Defense

189. A state of necessity exists if a person is placed before an immediate threat of a danger that gives him the effective choice between committing a wrong or accepting a substantial greater loss. In such circumstances, the behavior is not negligent, based on the concept of negligence itself. Under Belgian law, a violation of a specific behavioral rule of law is not wrongful if it was required in the specific circumstances of the case to protect an effectively threatened interest that is generally valued higher than the interest that the violated rule protects.[638]

The violation of a legal rule is only justified if there was no reasonable alternative way to avoid the greater harm.[639] For this justification to apply, the fact that the person finds himself in this predicament cannot be the consequence of his own fault.[640] Self-defense can be seen as a subcategory of this ground of justification. However, a state

636. Cass. 13 May 1982, *Pas.* 1982, 1056, *Arr.Cass.* 1981–1982, 1134, No. 547; more recently Cass. 16 May 2011 (C.10.0664.N), No. 320, *Arr.Cass.* 2011, 1230, *Pas.* 2011, 1339.
637. There is no force majeure if the defendant could avoid the circumstances through sufficient and useful precautions. Cass. 7 May 2002 (P.01.0272.N), *RW* 2005–2006, 257.
638. Cass. 15 May 1930, *Pas.* 1930, 223; Cass. 20 March 1978, *Arr.Cass.* 1978–1979, 837, *Pas.* 1979, 842; Cass. 5 April 1996 (A.94.0002.F), No. 111, *Pas.* 1996, 283, *Arr.Cass.* 1996, 247.
639. Cass. 19 April 2006 (P.06.0018.F), No. 221, *Pas.* 2006, 864, *Arr.Cass.* 2006, 895.
640. Cass. 24 March 1999 (P.98.1479.F), No. 177, *Pas.* 1999, 441, *Arr.Cass.* 1999, 429.

of necessity can also justify behavior that is intended to protect someone else, who is subject to imminent danger.

§4. Others

190. Two other grounds of justification are worth mentioning.

191. First, performing a duty imposed by a rule of law or obeying an order from the government (*fait du prince*) is per definition not wrongful. First, obeying the law is per se reasonable, so it cannot be qualified as negligent. Second, illegal behavior or behavior that violates a specific behavioral rule of law is not wrongful if it was imposed by the government. Therefore, a person executing an order that he is legally required to follow, cannot be held liable for the loss caused by this act.

192. Second, and in practice more importantly, a violation of a behavioral rule of law will not be qualified as wrongful if it is the consequence of an unavoidable and invincible, i.e., an unsurmountable mistake. The error can be about the existence or the specific content of the legal rule that is found to be violated, or about the facts surrounding the case that determine the applicability of the violated rule.

In traffic cases, for instance, a driver who has violated the rule that requires him to give the right of way to another vehicle coming from the right, will not be civilly liable if that other vehicle was driving at such a high speed that the driver reasonably could not expect it to reach the crossing that soon.[641] In such cases, the courts apply the general standard of care, finding the violation of the rule not wrongful if the mistake was not unreasonable, if the defendant's behavior was based on reasonable expectations.[642]

193. In cases involving ignorance of the existence of the violated rule or a mistake about its actual content, the case law uses a higher standard. Mere unawareness of the rule is no excuse. Invoking the principle that one is supposed to know the law, only a so-called unescapable or unsurmountable ignorance of the law—i.e., a mistake that *any* reasonable person would have made—provides an excuse.[643] Mere excusable ignorance—i.e., a mistake *some* reasonable persons would not have made—does not.[644]

In practice, however, one can see that in cases involving government liability, the courts sometimes tend to forgive the executive for having misunderstood the law, when conflicting opinions can be found in case law, which of course shows that the mistake might be excusable because reasonable, but not unsurmountable as in fact surmounted by some courts.[645]

641. Cass. 7 June 2001 (C.99.0308.F), No. 341, *Arr.Cass.* 2001, 1102, *Pas.* 2001, 1064.

642. Cass. 11 December 2015 (C.14.0559.F), No. 742, *Pas.* 2015, 2844, *Arr.Cass.* 2015, 2907.

643. Cass. 2 December 2015 (P.15.0416.F), No. 721, *Pas.* 2015, 2759, *Arr.Cass.* 2015, 2816; Cass. 23 September 2010 (C.09.0220.F), No. 544, *Pas.* 2010, 2367, *Arr.Cass.* 2010, 2275; Cass. 25 October 1999 (S.98.0112.N), No. 559, *Arr.Cass.* 1999, 1327, *Pas.* 1999, 1384.

644. Cass. 20 April 1982, No. 486, *Arr.Cass.* 1981–1982, 1009, *Pas.* 1982, 949.

645. Cass. 8 February 2008 (C.07.0131.F), No. 96, *Pas.* 2008, 382, *Arr.Cass.* 2008, 370.

Chapter 3. Contributory Fault

194. If the harm the victim suffers is not only caused by a fact for which a third party is liable but also the consequence of his own lack of care or reckless behavior, the civil liability of the third party is reduced. This is referred to as "shared liability."[646]

195. Although the damage is often also caused by a fault of the victim consisting in a violation of a behavioral rule imposed by law,[647] which is the case in many traffic accidents, it is also possible that the behavior of the victim which contributed to the occurrence of the harm does not violate such a behavioral rule and is therefore not wrongful in the strict sense. Such behavior cannot really be qualified as negligent, as negligence involves a lack of care for the interests of others. One is not required by law to devote care to one's own interests. While some authors have tried to overcome this dogmatic legal problem by arguing that a victim who behaves carelessly is in fact negligent toward the interests of the liable third party, whose interests are served in avoiding or limiting the damage for which he would be liable, most Belgian courts and authors simply ignore this theoretical issue and qualify the behavior of a victim that did not reasonably cared for its own interests as a "fault."

196. Applying the same principles used when dividing the contribution among two separate third parties that share liability toward a victim,[648] the courts then reduce the third party's liability by subtracting the share the victim would have had to bear in contribution if it were a third party. This results in a division of the burden of the harm between the liable third party and the victim proportionately to the extent to which the fact for which each is liable has contributed to causing the event. Belgian law thus applies a rule of pure comparative negligence.[649] In effect, this means that the fact-finding court decides to what extent the compensation due by the third party is reduced, based on findings of fact in the particular case. This principle is also applied to next of kin claiming compensation for consequential damage suffered by repercussion from the death suffered by the primary victim.[650]

197. Although the gravity of the faults of the victim and the liable third party is not an acceptable criterion to reduce third-party liability, the Court of Cassation has ruled that the liability of a third party that in bad faith intentionally causes harm to a careless victim will not be reduced. The principle of *fraus omnia corrumpit* estops the third party from invoking the rules of comparative negligence, so that he bears full

646. Cass. 9 February 1982, *Arr.Cass.* 1981–1982, 741, No. 346, *Pas.* 1982, 716; Cass. 8 September 1999 (P.99.0472.F), No. 443, *Pas.* 1999, 1096, *Arr.Cass.* 1999, 1056; Cass. 25 January 2002 (C.00.0068.F), No. 54, *Pas.* 2002, 240, *Arr.Cass.* 2002, 253; *see* already Cass. 2 April 1936, *Pas.* 1936, 209.

647. *See supra* Part I, Ch. 1, §3.

648. *See infra* para. 214.

649. Cass. 9 October 2009 (C.07.0080.F), No. 567, *Pas.* 2009, 2195, *Arr.Cass.* 2009, 2266; Cass. 9 September 2015 (P.15.0653.F), No. 497, *Pas.* 2015, 1963, *Arr.Cass.* 2015, 1943.

650. Cass. 19 December 1962, *Pas.* 1963, 491; Cass. 23 January 2012 (C.09.0228.F), No. 62, *Pas.* 2012, 180, *Arr.Cass.* 2012, 202. This was approved by Con.C. No. 111/2014 of 17 July 2014.

liability for the entirety of the harm suffered by the victim, even if its own unintentional fault contributed to the occurrence of the loss.[651]

651. Cass. 6 November 2002 (P.01.1108.F), No. 584, *Pas.* 2002, 2103, *Arr.Cass.* 2002, 2383. On this basis, the master, who is vicariously liable for damage caused by an intentional fault of his servant, cannot invoke the unintentional fault of the victim to claim "shared liability": Cass. 30 September 2015 (P.14.0474.F), No. 568, *Pas.* 2015, 2229, *Arr.Cass.* 2015, 2234.

Chapter 4. Immunity of Employees, Civil Servants and Volunteers

198. Employees enjoy social protection under the Federal Employment Contracts Act of 3 July 1978 (ECA). This Act limits the personal liability of employees to damage caused by his intentional fault,[652] his gross fault or for his customary—i.e., regularly reoccurring—light fault.[653] This immunity applies to extracontractual liability for damage caused to third parties and to contractual liability for harm caused to the employer. Thus, the employer who has compensated the victim[654] cannot have recourse by withholding the same amount on the employee's salary. This also means that a teacher who is an employee can escape his vicarious liability[655] by showing that he did not commit any intentional fault, gross fault or regularly reoccurring light fault.[656] Analogously, an employee will not be liable on the basis of a strict liability when he in the performance of his job is the custodian of a defective object[657] or uses an animal.[658]

199. Originally, no such immunity from civil liability existed for civil servants, who do not have an employment contract and therefore do not enjoy the protection of the ECA. However, the Court of Arbitration (now the Constitutional Court) has ruled that such different treatment of employees and civil servants and such different treatment of victims of harm caused by employees or civil servants violates the constitutional principle of nondiscrimination.[659] To remedy this inequality, substantially similar immunities were inserted in the statutes organizing the status of several types of public servants. In 2003, a federal statute introduced a general immunity regime identical to the one for employees for subordinated members of personnel of public sector entities.[660]

200. Since 2005, a comparable immunity regime exists for volunteers working for certain organizations,[661] with the difference that contrary to the regime for employees

652. An intentional fault requires the person to have wanted to cause harm. *See* Cass. 11 March 2014 (P.12.0946.N), No. 193, *Arr.Cass.* 2014, 723, *Pas.* 2014, 673.
653. Article 18 ECA. This immunity has been judged to be consistent with the constitutional principle of equal treatment: C.Arb. No. 20/99 of 17 February 1999.
654. Often, the employer will as a master be vicariously liable for the damage his employees cause to third parties (*see supra* Part II, Ch. 1, §1), and as a contract party of his customers he will be contractually liable for the harm caused by a bad performance of his contract (*see supra* Part II, Ch. 1, §2).
655. Article 1384, para. 3, CC; *see supra* Part II, Ch. 2, §3.
656. Cass. 25 January 1993, No. 47, *Pas.* 1993, 91, *Arr.Cass.* 1993, 98.
657. Article 1384, para. 1, CC; *see supra* Part III, Ch. 1.
658. Article 1385 CC; *see supra* Part III, Ch. 4.
659. C.Arb. No. 77/96 of 18 December 1996 (a case about the possibility for the employer to recover damages paid to the victim from the member of personnel), and C.Arb. No. 19/2000 of 17 February 1999 (a case about the possibility of the victim to claim damages from the member of personnel).
660. (Federal) Act of 10 February 2003 on the Liability of and for Members of Personnel of Entities in the Public Sector.
661. Article 5 (federal) Act of 3 July 2005 on the Rights of Volunteers.

this immunity is also applicable to volunteers performing leading functions within the organization.[662]

662. Article 3, 1° and 2°, (federal) Act of 3 July 2005 on the Rights of Volunteers.

Chapter 5. Exclusion Clauses

201. Exoneration based on exclusion clauses is an issue that in Belgian literature has mainly been studied in the contractual context. The general rule here is that parties can agree to a limitation or even exclusion of liability subject to three restrictions. First, exclusion or limitation of liability is not possible for losses caused by an intentional breach, fraud or acts in bad faith.[663] However, under Belgian law, a grave wrong is not equivalent to an intentional wrong.[664] In principle, parties can contractually agree to an exclusion or limitation of liability for gross negligence.[665] Second, a clause excluding or limiting liability is not allowed to render the main obligation of the exonerated party nugatory.[666] Third, contractual exoneration is of course not possible for statutorily imposed mandatory liability. Rules of consumer protection, for instance, provide that additional types of exclusion clauses are not valid: in their relation with consumers, suppliers cannot limit or exclude their liability for damage caused by their intentional fault, their gross fault of the gross fault of their servants or representatives,[667] nor can they limit or exclude their liability in the event of the death of a consumer or personal injury to the latter resulting from an act or omission of that seller or supplier.[668]

Given the position of the majority doctrine in Belgium, which considers it to be impossible for parties to a contract to invoke extracontractual liability if the damage is the consequence of behavior or a fact that is an element of the performance of the contract,[669] contractual exclusion clauses in effect can grant total immunity from civil liability for loss caused to a contract party in the performance of the contract.

202. The legal concept of an exclusion clause is often also used to analyze cases in which the victim and the person who he claims compensation from are not bound by a contract, but where the person that is allegedly liable unilaterally declared conditions for entering his premises, using his things, or relying on his statements. A notice warning that no liability will be accepted for any accident at the entrance of a playground or a statement accompanying a rating issued by a credit rating agency are just two examples. In principle, the rules of extracontractual liability are not considered to touch public policy, so private parties can agree to deviations from these rules for their mutual relations.[670] However, the general rule that an exclusion clause cannot include liability for intentionally wrongfully caused harm is also applied in such extracontractual cases.[671] The same can be said of the specific rules of consumer protection, which are applicable even if the consumer has not yet entered into a contract with the supplier.

663. Cass. 28 February 1980, No. 411, *Pas.* 1980, 794, *Arr.Cass.* 1979–1980, 801.
664. Cass. 25 September 1959, *Pas.* 1960, 113, *Arr.Verbr.* 1960, 86.
665. Cass. 5 January 1961, *Pas.* 1961, 483.
666. Cass. 26 March 2004 (C.02.0038.F), No. 170, *Pas.* 2004, 513, *Arr.Cass.* 2004, 537; Cass. 27 September 1990, No. 42, *Pas.* 1991, 82, *Arr.Cass.* 1990–1991, 88.
667. Article VI.83, 13°, CEL.
668. Article VI.83, 25°, CEL.
669. *See supra* General Introduction, §5.
670. Cass. 21 February 1907, *Pas.* 1907, 135.
671. Cass. 3 March 2015 (P.13.1040.N), No. 150, *Arr.Cass.* 2015, 558, *Pas.* 2015, 526; Cass. 29 September 1972, *Arr.Cass.* 1973, 121, *Pas.* 1973, 124; *see* already Cass. 21 February 1907, *Pas.* 1907, 135.

Belgian courts often consider such unilateral declarations to be offers to contract, so that they are only binding if truly accepted by the victim. This allows the courts to be very strict, and most often ignore such notices, justifying this decision by their finding that the fact that the victim could have seen the notice does not imply that he accepted it. Of course, this leads to many factual disputes, resulting in casuistic case law from which no real general rules can be distilled. In the end, it depends on the personal opinion of the judge, who has a large margin to be sympathetic to either party.

203. Unilateral declarations by the allegedly liable party can also be construed as warnings or instructions, which can influence potential liability. In a warning, the potential victim's attention is directed at a specific risk of damage, so that his normally expected behavior will avoid the risk from materializing. An instruction directs or guides the potential victim's behavior in a manner that normally will reduce or avoid the risk from materializing.

Such warnings and instructions can have different legal effects, depending on in which part of the liability analysis they are invoked. First, the warning or instruction can be invoked as an element of the allegedly liable person's behavior constituting the measure of care that in the given circumstances is reasonable, showing that his actions were not negligent, and thereby successfully fending off a claim based on fault liability.[672] However, this does not mean that a person can always avoid liability by warning for the danger he has wrongfully created: in some circumstances, the warning will not be considered sufficiently effective to constitute reasonable behavior, in effect finding the risk creating behavior in itself to be unreasonable and therefore negligent.[673] Second, the warning or instruction can be an element that renders a potentially dangerous product not defective, thus denying a claim based on product liability.[674] The same defense will not be successful in a case based on the general liability of a custodian for damage caused by his defective thing, as the Court of Cassation has ruled that the fact that the victim was warned for the abnormal characteristic[675] or actually had knowledge of the abnormal characteristic of the thing,[676] does not in itself preclude this abnormal characteristic from being a defect. Third, in specific cases such as the liability for harm caused by animals, the Court of Cassation has allowed the lower courts to decide that the damage is not caused by the animal if the victim knowingly and carelessly subjected itself to the risk posed by the normal behavior of the animal.[677] An appropriate warning not to enter the cage of a tiger in a zoo probably will successfully counter a claim for compensation brought by a visitor that was hurt by the tiger after ignoring the warning.[678] Fourth, ignoring a warning or not complying with an instruction

672. *See* e.g. CA Antwerp 17 January 1996, *RW* 1998–1999, 306.

673. *See* e.g. Cass. 7 March 1963, *Pas.* 1963, 744, *RW* 1963–1964, 1115.

674. Article 5, a, PLA, according to which the presentation of the product has to be taken into account when judging whether it provides the safety which a person is entitled to expect.

675. Cass. 17 January 2014 (C.12.0510.F), No. 39, *Pas.* 2014, 143, *Arr.Cass.* 2014, 161; Cass. 21 November 2003 (C.02.0619.F), No. 590, *Pas.* 2003, 1878, *Arr.Cass.* 2003, 2183.

676. Cass. 4 January 2016 (C.15.0191.F), *RGAR* 2016, No. 15,334, *NJW* 2016, 917; Cass. 17 December 2010 (C.10.0193.F), No. 754, *Pas.* 2010, 3275, *Arr.Cass.* 2010, 3060.

677. Cass. 12 October 1984, No. 119, *Arr.Cass.* 1984–1985, 254, *Pas.* 1985, 220; Cass. 6 January 2012 (C.11.0025.F), No. 15, *Pas.* 2012, 49, *Arr.Cass.* 2012, 60.

678. *Cf.* CA Antwerp 11 April 2007, *Revue générale de droit civil belge* 2010, 98.

can be seen as a "fault" of the victim, in effect limiting the third-party liability by applying the principle of comparative negligence.[679] In extreme cases, the courts are willing to completely exclude the third party's liability, and leave the victim that carelessly and thus wrongfully ignored adequate warnings to bear its own loss.[680]

---

679. *See supra* Part IV, Ch. 3.
680. *See* e.g. CA Antwerp 17 January 1996, *RW* 1998–1999, 306, a case involving a pedestrian falling on a street that was under construction, ignoring the clear warning signs.

Part V. Causation

204. Liability only attaches if the fact for which the defendant is responsible is the cause (*cause—oorzaak*) of the damage.[681]

681. Cass. 14 December 2006 (C.04.0582.F), No. 650, *Pas.* 2006, 2667, *Arr.Cass.* 2006, 2605; Cass. 22 April 2004 (C.01.0484.N), *RW* 2004–2005, 827.

Chapter 1. The Traditional Theory

§1. Equivalence of Conditions

205. According to generally accepted theory, Belgian law adheres to the doctrine of equivalence of conditions (*théorie d'équivalence des conditions—equivalentieleer*). Under this theory, the court not only is allowed[682] and required[683] to deny causality if it establishes that the invoked fact was not necessary for the harm to occur, it also is allowed[684] and even required[685] to find causality if it has established the invoked fact to have been necessary (*conditio sine qua non*) in the given circumstances for the damage to occur.

206. Causation (*relation causale—oorzakelijk* or *causaal verband*) cannot be denied just because the harm could also have occurred without the invoked fact but in circumstances not present in this particular case.[686] A fact that *in concreto* was necessary for the harm to occur, is a cause even if a later intervening fact was also necessary.[687] Also, a fact that was a necessary condition for the damage to occur the way it did is a cause even if this damage was not a necessary consequence,[688] this harm is not the normal consequence,[689] or this harm was not a foreseeable consequence of this fact.[690]

207. To apply this doctrine, the court has to verify whether the occurrence of the harm can be explained by applying the generally known patterns of events to all the other circumstances in the case apart from the invoked fact. If so, those other circumstances apparently are a sufficient condition for the damage and thus its cause, allowing the court to exclude the element left out in the thought experiment as a cause. Whether the other circumstances of the case are sufficient to explain the occurrence

682. Cass. 7 March 2013 (C.10.0741.F), No. 153, *Pas.* 2013, 565, *Arr.Cass.* 2013, 598; Cass. 11 May 1956, *Arr.Verbr.* 1956, 757, *Pas.* 1956, 962.
683. Cass. 5 June 2008 (C.07.0199.N), No. 350, *Arr.Cass.* 2008, 1462, *Pas.* 2008, 1425; Cass. 28 May 1951, *Pas.* 1951, 645, *Arr.Verbr.* 1951, 554.
684. Cass. 17 December 2009 (C.08.0145.N), No. 757, *Arr.Cass.* 2009, 3056, *Pas.* 2009, 3045; Cass. 4 December 1950, *Pas.* 1951, 201, *Arr.Verbr.* 1951, 158.
685. Cass. 6 June 2011 (C.10.0095.F), No. 377, *Pas.* 2011, 1599, *Arr.Cass.* 2011, 1478; Cass. 11 June 1956, *Pas.* 1956, 1096.
686. Cass. 24 March 2005 (C.04.0016.F), No. 185, *Pas.* 2005, 703, *Arr.Cass.* 2005, 703; Cass. 11 June 1956, *Pas.* 1956, 1094.
687. Cass. 5 March 1953, *Arr.Verbr.* 1953, 457, *Pas.* 1953, 516; Cass. 28 May 1991, No. 497, *Arr. Cass.* 1990–1991, 959, *Pas.* 1991, 843.
688. *See* e.g. Cass. 19 December 1979, *Pas.* 1980, No. 252, 487, *Arr.Cass.* 1979–1980, 488; *see* already Cass. 22 December 1947, *Pas.* 1947, 555, *Arr.Verbr.* 1947, 425.
689. *See* e.g. Cass. 23 September 2011 (C.10.0744.F), No. 496, *Pas.* 2011, 2034, *Arr.Cass.* 2011, 1909.
690. *See* e.g. Cass. 15 November 2006 (P.06.0308.F), No. 561, *Pas.* 2006, 2336, *Arr.Cass.* 2006, 2302.

of the loss, allowing the conclusion that the invoked fact was not necessary for the loss to occur, is a question of fact, to be judged by the fact-finding court.[691]

§2. Causal Uncertainty

208. Sometimes, applying the generally known patterns to the other facts of the case leaves several outcomes possible, some involving the occurrence of the harm while others not. In that case, the court cannot award full compensation for the ultimate disadvantage the victim claims to suffer. While in some cases, the courts will then decide that there is insufficient certainty to establish causality and therefore refuse to impose any liability,[692] in others they find a way around this problem by considering the chance the victim had to avoid the harm as an interest that was lost because of the invoked fact.

209. The Court of Cassation does allow courts to award compensation for the value of the lost chance the victim had of not suffering the disadvantage.[693] The value of this lost chance will be estimated as a fraction—i.e., an expression of the chance the victim had—of the value of the disadvantage the victim ultimately has suffered.[694] Thus, an underlying causal uncertainty is conceptually reframed as an issue relating to the requirement of damage, to allow the courts to in effect apply proportional liability in certain cases of causal uncertainty.

---

691. Cass. 20 June 1961, *Pas.* 1961, 1148.
692. *See* e.g. Cass. 23 September 1974, *Arr.Cass.* 1975, 97, *Pas.* 1975, 87; recent: Cass. 29 October 2014 (P.14.0820.F), No. 644, *Pas.* 2014, 2364, *Arr.Cass.* 2014, 2374.
693. *See* e.g. Cass. 15 March 2010 (C.09.0433.N), No. 182, *Arr.Cass.* 2010, 767, *Pas.* 2010, 839; Cass. 5 June 2008 (C.07.0199.N), No. 350, *Arr.Cass.* 2008, 1462, *Pas.* 2008, 1425; Cass. 19 January 1984, No. 266, *Pas.* 1984, 548, *Arr.Cass.* 1983–1984, 585.
694. Cass. 21 October 2013 (C.13.0124.N), No. 537, *Arr.Cass.* 2013, 2159, *Pas.* 2013, 1999; Cass. 17 December 2009 (C.08.0145.N), No. 757, *Arr.Cass.* 2009, 3056, *Pas.* 2009, 3045.

Chapter 2. Legal Reality: Not Equivalence of Conditions?

210. The doctrine of equivalence of conditions necessarily leads to inacceptable decisions. In theory, it allows any fact that occurred a very long time before the actual loss occurrence to remain a cause of the loss, as long as history would have taken another turn if it would not have happened. Jokingly, one often says that this theory allows a court to find Eve to be liable for all harm suffered by humanity… This objection against the theory, however, is not a criticism on Belgian law, as Belgian courts in reality do not apply the theory rigorously in cases of remote facts.

211. For instance, a passenger who knowingly takes a ride with an intoxicated driver or a person that is not allowed to drive or not to transport a passenger and who subsequently is hurt in an accident, will still be able to recover full compensation from the third party liable for that accident if it was not caused by the state of intoxication of the driver or the reason why he was not allowed to drive or move a passenger.[695] In another category of cases, the harm results from a wrongful failure by a person to avoid a visible irregular circumstance caused by a previous accident or fact.[696] Thus, a careless driver who hits the back of a cue that was caused by an earlier accident will not be allowed to recover from the person liable for the initial accident that resulted in the traffic jam.[697] Also, if a necessary condition is too remote, the courts tend to neglect it.[698] A typical example is the court finding that a car driving too fast was not a cause of the accident when the accident according to the court would also have happened if that car had been driving slower,[699] ignoring the fact that this car of course would not have reached that position if it had been driving slower.

212. A large category of cases where the courts systematically take decisions that do not conform to the doctrine of equivalence of conditions, involve wrongful behavior of the victim that did not cause the accident that resulted in the harm[700] but that did cause this damage after it first occurred to increase. The typical example is the passenger not wearing a seat belt or the motorcycle rider not wearing a helmet. A similar set of cases relate to a victim not making reasonable efforts to reduce or limit the damage caused by an event for which a third party is liable.[701] Courts decide in

---

695. Cass. 10 June 2003 (P.02.1358.N), No. 341, *Arr.Cass.* 2003, 1355, *Pas.* 2003, 1143; Cass. 16 September 1986, No. 24, *Arr.Cass.* 1986–1987, 56, *Pas.* 1987, 53.
696. Cass. 12 October 2001 (C.00.9487.N), *Droit de la circulation* 2002, 414; Cass. 5 November 1996 (P.95.0122.N), No. 413, *Arr.Cass.* 1996, 993, *Pas.* 1996, 1066; Cass. 5 November 1996 (P.95.1329.N), No. 414, *Arr.Cass.* 1996, 997, *Pas.* 1996, 1070.
697. Cass. 17 June 2003 (P.03.0188.N), not published.
698. *See* e.g. Cass. 23 January 2013 (P.12.0089.F), No. 50, *Pas.* 2013, 164, *Arr.Cass.* 2013, 188, a case involving a driver who had committed a hit-and-run after a first accident and was then involved in a second accident.
699. Cass. 23 February 2000 (P.99.1574.F), No. 140, *Pas.* 2000, 469, *Arr.Cass.* 2000, 474; Cass. 3 October 1984, No. 87, *Arr.Cass.* 1984–1985, 194, *Pas.* 1985, 167.
700. For such cases, *see infra* para. 215.
701. A victim does not have to reduce or limit the damage to the extent possible, but if the damage is or remains larger because of his unreasonable behavior, there is “shared liability,” which means the liability of the third party is reduced. Cass. 14 May 1992, No. 478, *Arr.Cass.* 1991–1992, 855, *Pas.* 1992, 798.

such cases that the victim cannot recover any of this extra harm (pure contributory negligence), even though the equivalence theory would require this extra harm to be partially compensated by the third party liable for the original harm to occur (pure comparative negligence).

213. One could therefore conclude that, even though the quasi-unanimous Belgian scholarly community keeps repeating the theory that causality is governed by the equivalence of conditions, this might be more a myth than a reality, and that Belgian positive law is not well described by the simple rule of the *conditio sine qua non.*

Chapter 3. Plurality of Liable Parties

214. If the harm can be divided into separate injuries caused by different persons, each of them is liable for the specific injury he has caused. The causality requirement applied in Belgian law, however, also allows for several facts attributable to different persons to be the cause of a single indivisible loss. In that case, the victim is entitled to sue any or all of them for the full amount of his damage, and each is said to be *in solidum* liable for the whole damage.[702]

If one of the liable parties compensated the victim, he can seek "contribution" from the others.[703] The fraction of the damage each liable party has to bear is measured based on the relative role the fact for which it is liable played in causing the harm, which is called its "causal contribution."[704]

215. If the victim is also responsible for the harm-causing event, "shared liability" applies,[705] reducing the liability of third parties to the extent the victim has contributed to causing the event (pure comparative negligence).[706] This principle is also applied to next of kin claiming compensation for damage suffered by repercussion.[707]

216. If a person intentionally inflicts harm to the victim—for instance to obtain an advantage by illegally taking something from the victim—in circumstances in which this could only succeed because of the unintentional fault of the victim, applying the principle *fraus omnia corrumpit* results in the bad faith wrongdoer not being allowed to invoke comparative negligence and hence having to fully compensate the good faith victim that has been taken advantage of.[708] However, if the harm is caused by a combination of intentional and unintentional faults of third parties, they are both *in solidum* liable toward the victim for the entire loss and in dividing the contribution

702. Cass. 13 February 1970, *Arr.Cass.* 1970, 545, *Pas.* 1970, 511; recent: Cass. 16 February 2011 (P.10.1232.F), No. 137, *Pas.* 2011, 529, *Arr.Cass.* 2011, 524.
703. Cass. 19 February 1999 (C.94.0246.N), No. 97, *Arr.Cass.* 1999, 225, *Pas.* 1999, 232; Cass. 18 January 2007 (C.05.0529.F), No. 27, *Pas.* 2007, 93, *Arr.Cass.* 2007, 97.
704. Cass. 4 February 2008 (C.06.0236.F), No. 81, *Pas.* 2008, 329, *Arr.Cass.* 2008, 315; Cass. 21 October 2008 (P.08.0561.N), No. 567, *Arr.Cass.* 2008, 2322, *Pas.* 2008, 2319; Cass. 2 October 2009 (C.08.0168.F), No. 548, *Pas.* 2009, 2110, *Arr.Cass.* 2009, 2190; Cass. 3 May 2013 (C.12.0378.N), No. 278, *Arr.Cass.* 2013, 1099, *Pas.* 2013, 1053.
705. Cass. 9 February 1982, *Arr.Cass.* 1981–1982, 741, No. 346, *Pas.* 1982, 716; Cass. 8 September 1999 (P.99.0472.F), No. 443, *Pas.* 1999, 1096, *Arr.Cass.* 1999, 1056.
706. Cass. 9 October 2009 (C.07.0080.F), No. 567, *Pas.* 2009, 2195, *Arr.Cass.* 2009, 2266; Cass. 9 September 2015 (P.15.0653.F), No. 497, *Pas.* 2015, 1963, *Arr.Cass.* 2015, 1943.
707. Cass. 19 December 1962, *Pas.* 1963, 491; Cass. 23 January 2012 (C.09.0228.F), No. 62, *Pas.* 2012, 180, *Arr.Cass.* 2012, 202. This was approved by Con.C. No. 111/2014 of 17 July 2014.
708. Cass. 6 November 2002 (P.01.1108.F), No. 584, *Pas.* 2002, 2103, *Arr.Cass.* 2002, 2383. On this basis, the master, who is vicariously liable for damage caused by an intentional fault of his servant, cannot invoke the unintentional fault of the victim to claim "shared liability": Cass. 30 September 2015 (P.14.0474.F), No. 568, *Pas.* 2015, 2229, *Arr.Cass.* 2015, 2234.

among these third parties, the court can only take the relative causal contribution into account, not the intentional character of one of the faults.[709]

---

709. Cass. 2 October 2009 (C.08.0168.F), No. 548, *Pas.* 2009, 2110, *Arr.Cass.* 2009, 2190. The same rule is applied when one of the liable parties is held on the basis of vicarious liability for a person that has committed the *fraus*: Cass. 16 May 2011 (C.10.0214.N), No. 319, *Arr.Cass.* 2011, 1227, *Pas.* 2011, 1337.

Part VI. Remedies

Chapter 1. General Principles

217. Civil liability is a source of a legal obligation, constituting for the victim a right to "reparation" and for the person that is liable a corresponding duty to "undo" the loss (*réparation du dommage—schadeloosstelling*). The injured party is to be restored into the situation it would have been in if the event would not have occurred.[710]

218. In principle, the harmed party has the right to demand specific restoration.[711] However, this also means that the victim will have to accept restoration in kind if offered.[712] In case of reputational harm, for instance, the imposed remedy often takes the form of public apologies or a retraction of the wrongful insult or the unwarranted accusation, or the publication of the court's decision.

219. If actual restoration is not possible, the victim still has a right to restoration, which then takes the form of compensation by damages.[713] In practice, civil liability almost always results in the court awarding the victim damages (*dommages-intérêts—schadevergoeding*). Only rarely can a case imposing restoration in kind be found. Still, the Belgian standard theory of liability considers damages to be a subsidiary remedy, only available: (1) if specific restoration is conceptually impossible, such as for harm already suffered and for moral damage; (2) if restoration in kind is in the particular circumstances of the case physically impossible, as in the case of constructive total loss (*perte totale constructive*); or (3) if invoking the right to specific restoration would place an extremely unreasonable burden on the person held liable to that it by claiming this remedy, the victim would abuse its right to restoration,[714] as in case of economic total loss (*perte totale économique*), i.e., when the cost of physical reparation is higher than the value of the repaired object.[715] In this view, damages are functionally a substitute for specific restoration and thus must be "equivalent" to restoration, usually referred

710. Cass. 9 April 2003 (P.03.0049.F), No. 235, *Pas.* 2003, 765, *Arr.Cass.* 2003, 919; Cass. 2 May 1974, *Pas.* 1974, I, 906, *Arr.Cass.* 1974, 633.
711. Cass. 21 April 1994 (C.93.0225.F), No. 189, *Pas.* 1994, I, 388, *Arr.Cass.* 1994, 392; Cass. 26 June 1980, No. 686, *Pas.* 1980, I, 1341, *Arr.Cass.* 1979–1980, 1365 ; Cass. 5 May 2011 (C.10.0496.F), No. 299, *Arr.Cass.* 2011, 1157, *Pas.* 2011, 1272.
712. *See* e.g. Comm. Antwerp 22 April 1993, *Rechtspraak van de Haven van Antwerpen* 1994, 176.
713. Cass. 17 December 2012 (S.11.0099.F), No. 695, *Pas.* 2012, 2532, *Arr.Cass.* 2012, 2873, ruling that a court cannot refuse the victim compensation on the basis of the fact that the loss in the past in fact cannot be undone anymore.
714. On abuse of right, *see supra* Part I, Ch. 2, §2.
715. Cass. 23 October 1986, No. 118, *Pas.* 1987, 249, *Arr.Cass.* 1986–1987, 266; Cass. 5 May 2011 (C.10.0496.F), No. 299, *Arr.Cass.* 2011, 1157, *Pas.* 2011, 1272.

to as "integral compensation" (*restitutio in integrum*). The standard expression is that damages compensate the loss and nothing but the loss.[716] This also means that any advantage the victim might have obtained because of the incident, or costs that the victim can save because of the incident, has to be deducted from the amount that can be awarded.[717]

220. For some specific liabilities, statutory provisions deviate from this general principle of full compensation. For some, the amount of damages that can be awarded is limited. As will be discussed further, the liability of mentally ill can be limited based on equitable grounds.[718] Another example is the strict liability for fires or explosions in public establishments, which is limited to amounts that at present equal approximately EUR 24 million for bodily harm and EUR 1.2 million for property damage.[719] For other liabilities, the obligation to compensate the victim is restricted to specific types of damage. A good example is product liability, which is limited to personal injuries and damage to property that is intended for private use or consumption and that was used by the injured person mainly for his own private use or consumption, thus excluding damage to professionally used property.[720]

221. The victim is free to use the damages he receives as he pleases. There is no obligation to use this sum to pay for actual reparation of the loss. How the victim uses the awarded sum in no way influences the amount the court can award.[721]

716. Cass. 17 January 1929, *Pas.* 1929, 63; Cass. 15 May 1941, *Pas.* 1941, 195; Cass. 26 October 2005 (P.04.1258.F), No. 542, *Pas.* 2005, 2044, *Arr.Cass.* 2005, 2045.
717. *See* e.g. Cass. 5 March 2015 (C.14.0017.F), No. 162, *Pas.* 2015, 578, *Arr.Cass.* 2015, 595, ruling that household expenses saved because the spouse of the claimant has died have to be deducted from the amount of household damage the claimant can obtain because of the loss of the household efforts from the spouse; Cass. 1 February 2013 (C.12.0205.N), No. 78, *Arr.Cass.* 2013, 317, *Pas.* 2013, 300, allowing the lower court to substract the saved salary of the incapacitated company director from the damages awarded to the company for the salary it had to pay to a temporary substitute director taking his place.
718. *See infra* paras. 255–256.
719. *See supra* Part III, Ch. 7.
720. Article 11 PLA.
721. Cass. 13 April 1988, No. 489, *Pas.* 1988, 936, *Arr.Cass.* 1987–1988, 1016; Cass. 15 February 2010 (C.09.0028.N), No. 101, *Arr.Cass.* 2010, 431, *Pas.* 2010, 455.

Chapter 2. Types of Losses

222. The concept of damage, as it is used in Belgian civil liability law, has been discussed earlier.[722] As was mentioned there, damage consists of a sufficiently certain injury to a legitimate personal interest.

§1. Individual and Collective Losses

223. Harm is thus only considered damage recoverable based on liability if the injured interest is personal to the claimant.[723] Several persons suffering losses caused by the same event each suffer separate damage, consisting of the injury to their personal interest. They cannot, for purposes of civil liability, be considered as claimants exercising one claim against the wrongdoer, the proceeds of which would then later have to be divided among them. They each have to exercise their individual claim, and the court has to rule on each individual claim.[724]

224. Legal entities are recognized as persons that have personal interests.[725] A legal entity, therefore, can suffer damage and can claim compensation based on civil liability. However, the interests of the legal entity are distinguished from the interests of the members, the partners, the associates or the shareholders of the entity. As a result, shareholders of a corporation cannot claim compensation for the loss in value of their shares as a result of harm suffered by the corporation, for which only the corporation can claim compensation.[726] For the same reason, the legal entity cannot claim compensation for the losses suffered by its members. However, this principle does not preclude a victim's right to compensation for an injury to its personal interest, which is based on civil liability, to be transferred to another person, either by succession, subrogation[727] or contract.[728] This makes it possible for multiple victims of damage caused by the same event to pool their claims for compensation by transferring them to an interest group with legal personality, which as the new holder of their right to compensation can claim from the person that is liable for the damage.

225. Recently, a procedure for mass claims has been created for collective damage.[729] Collective damage is the total of all individual damage suffered by members

722. *See supra* General Introduction, §6.

723. *See* e.g. Cass. 6 January 2010 (P.09.1152.F), No. 5, *Pas.* 2010, 20, *Arr.Cass.* 2010, 19, ruling that the victim who is in hospital cannot claim damages for the loss of his household work, as this loss is suffered by his family members, not by himself.

724. Cass. 10 December 2008 (P.08.1201.F), No. 716, *Pas.* 2008, 2915, *Arr.Cass.* 2008, 2994.

725. Cass. 19 September 1996 (C.95.0386.F), No. 319, *Pas.* 1996, 830, *Arr.Cass.* 1996, 775.

726. Cass. 23 February 2012 (C.11.0459.N), No. 131, *Arr.Cass.* 2012, 459, *Pas.* 2012, 431.

727. In practice, much damage is first compensated by a first-party insurer of the victim, who by statute is subrogated in the claims this victim had against the persons liable for the damage (Article 95 Federal Insurance Act of 4 April 2014).

728. Cass. 30 June 1930, *Pas.* 1930, 281; Cass. 26 September 1955, *Pas.* 1956, 38, *Arr. Verbr.* 1956, 28.

729. Book XVII, Title 2, CEL (Articles XVII.35–69).

of a group that has a common cause.[730] Such proceedings, however, are limited to harm suffered by consumers[731] as a result of a fault committed by an undertaking.[732] Also, the mass claim is only available for damage caused by either a breach of contract or by the violation of a specifically listed statute.[733] Thus, no collective claim is possible in case of extracontractual liability based on negligence.

§2. Direct and Indirect Losses

226. Damage, consisting of an injury to a personal legitimate interest, can be directly caused by a fact, consisting of a fault or another person or of an act or thing happening for which a rule of law holds another person strict liable. However, a person's interest can also be injured as a result of a fact which itself is also considered damage. Thus, the physical injury of a person as a result of a fault of someone else, of an act of an animal used by someone else, or of an accident caused by a defect in a thing under the custody of someone else, constitutes damage as a direct loss suffered by this primary victim. The loss of income this person may suffer because of this physical injury is a loss that indirectly follows from that fault, that act or that defect, as it is the direct consequence of the primary direct loss, the physical injury. If the primary victim suffering the physical injury dies, the loss of income or support for his or her family members or the emotional distress they may suffer is again an indirect loss, as it is a direct consequence of the death and not of the fault, the act or the defect. Such indirect loss suffered by another person than the primary victim is called damage by repercussion.

227. Belgian tort law does not restrict the concept of damage to direct losses. Any injury to a legitimate personal interest is damage. Whether or not there is an injury, is decided based on a comparison of the victim's *actual* interest position after the fact with the *hypothetical* position this victim would have enjoyed if the fact had not happened.[734] As a result, the indirect losses—which just as well would not have occurred but for the fault, the act or the defect causing the direct losses—are considered damage. Because of the very broad concept of causality used in Belgian tort law, the requirement of a causal link between the fact on which liability is based and the damage can also not systematically limit or exclude the liability for indirect losses.

§3. Pecuniary and Nonpecuniary Losses

228. The Civil Code does not contain any specific rules relating to different kinds of losses in relation to extracontractual liability. Traditionally, however, a distinction is made between material damage and moral damage. Both types of damage

730. Article I.21, 1°, CEL.
731. A consumer is defined as any natural person who is acting for purposes which are outside his trade, business, craft or profession (Article I.1, 2°, CEL).
732. An undertaking is defined as any natural or legal person who is pursuing an economic goal (Article I.1, 1°, CEL).
733. Article XVII.36, 1°, CEL. The list of statutes can be found in Article XVII.37 CEL.
734. *See supra* para. 56.

are subject to the principle of integral compensation, but the manner of measuring their extent and establishing their value is different.

229. Material damage consists of the injury to the pecuniary interests of the victim, usually referred to as "patrimonial." The patrimony of a person is the aggregate totality of its rights and duties that are transferrable. Items in a person's patrimony are in principle subject to potential seizure by his creditors, who have a statutory implicit lien on these items.[735]

Such harm can occur when property is damaged or destroyed, in which case both the reduction in value of the object or the cost of repair are considered to be damage, as well as the fact that the object has to be missed for a time period, which can entail loss of income or loss of enjoyment, or has to be replaced, which can entail extra costs. Material damage can also occur in cases of personal injury. Loss of income or additional (medical) costs are examples. Both *damnum emergens* and *lucrum cessans* are recoverable under civil liability.

As such material interests are transferrable, they can be traded on a market and usually have a price that can be used as a proxy for the value of the damage.[736]

230. Moral damage consists of the injury to a nonpecuniary interest of the victim. According to the Court of Cassation, moral damage consists of physical pain, sadness or any other type of moral, emotional or psychological discomfort, distress or suffering, and such harm is in principle also subject to integral compensation.[737]

Cases of personal injury very often contain claims for compensation of moral damage, such as physical pain, loss of pleasure, loss of self-esteem, esthetical damage, loss of sexual pleasure, infertility, and loss of chances to start a relationship or get married. Such moral loss can be suffered by the person that is physically injured, but also by other persons surrounding him or her that have an emotional or other relationship with him or her. Although legal entities cannot suffer physical injury, pain or emotional distress, they can suffer moral damage constituting of an injury to an immaterial interest, such as their honor or good name.[738] Less often but sometimes, moral damages are recognized in cases involving nonpersonal injuries, such as in case of emotional distress because of the death of or injury to a pet or horse.

As these nonpecuniary interests cannot be transferred from one person to another, they are not traded on a market and they do not have a "price," which can serve as the basis for establishing their value.[739]

---

735. Articles 7 and 8 of the (federal) Mortgage Act of 16 December 1851, which is codified as Book III, Title XVIII of the Civil Code.

736. *See infra* para. 251.

737. Cass. 10 October 1972, *Arr.Cass.* 1973, 146, *Pas.* 1973, 147; Cass. 3 February 1987, No. 322, *Arr.Cass.* 1986–1987, 724, *Pas.* 1987, 644; Cass. 13 October 1999 (P.99.0861.F), No. 528, *Pas.* 1999, 1308, *Arr.Cass.* 1999, 1255; Cass. 20 February 2006 (C.04.0366.N), No. 100, *Arr.Cass.* 2006, 414, *Pas.* 2006, 413.

738. *See* e.g. CA Antwerp 4 February 1992, *RW* 1992–1993, 258.

739. *See infra* para. 252.

§4. Pure Economic Loss

231. As was mentioned earlier, Belgian civil liability uses a very broad concept of damage, resulting in the absence of any *a priori* exclusion of claims for economic losses.[740] Of course consequential economic loss—i.e., a financial loss, consisting in extra out of pocket expenses or a reduction of income, which is the consequence of a personal injury or property damage—can be recovered. Different than in many other legal systems, however, Belgian tort law contains no *a priori* exclusion of pure economic loss—i.e., lost income or increased costs that are not the repercussion or consequence of a personal injury or property damage. Injury to a personal legitimate interest is damage, even if this interest is nothing more than the interest in avoiding the cost or obtaining the gain.

232. The broad concept of damage causes difficulties in Belgian tort theory when justifications have to be given for limiting the recoverability of the cost of complying with a preexisting legal or contractual obligation triggered as a consequence of the incident. Typical examples are the loss suffered by an insured party because of the contractual obligation to pay a higher premium as a result of the loss of a no-claims discount, the contractual obligation of an insurance company to pay out a life insurance, the statutory obligation of the government to intervene to keep the roads or waterways open to traffic, or the statutory obligation of a (public) employer to continue to pay the salary of a member of personnel that is temporarily unable to work or to pay benefits to a disabled member of staff.

Although it has used different types of reasoning to solve the question, the Court of Cassation now rules that expenses that according to the meaning of the contract, regulation or statute are not supposed to remain for the charge of the person who is legally required to make them, constitute recoverable damage.[741] However, careful analysis of the facts reveals that this given rationale is not capable of explaining the actual decisions in all cases, showing that the Court in fact only has allowed the public sector employer to recover the gross salary cost—including social security contributions and paid medical costs—of a civil servant who is disabled because of an accident for which a third party is liable. In all other factual settings, the Court ends up ruling that the performance of a legal duty *in itself* is not recoverable damage.[742] If, however, a person had the legal obligation to restore a loss suffered by himself or to restore or compensate a loss suffered by a victim for which someone else is liable, the Court allows this person to recover the cost of this restoration from the person held liable

740. *See supra* para. 58.
741. Cass. 19 February 2001 (C.98.0119.N), No. 96, *Arr.Cass.* 2001, 318, *Pas.* 2001, 316; recent: Cass. 4 February 2014 (P.13.0992.N), No. 92, *Arr.Cass.* 2014, 352, *Pas.* 2014, 365; Cass. 8 February 2016 (C.15.0170.N).
742. For the obligation of insurance companies, *see* Cass. 1 April 2015 (P.13.2051.F), No. 234, *Pas.* 2015, 891, *Arr.Cass.* 2015, 921; Cass. 26 March 2003 (P.02.1609.F), No. 204, *Pas.* 2003, 638, *Arr.Cass.* 2003, 764. For the obligation to pay benefits by mutual health insurers, *see* Cass. 3 September 2003 (P.03.0256.F), No. 410, *Pas.* 2003, 1346, *Arr.Cass.* 2003, 1583. For the obligation of the insurer or the government to pay benefits in case of incapacity to work of members of personnel, *see* Cass. 9 January 2006 (C.05.0007.N), No. 22, *Arr.Cass.* 2006, 96, *Pas.* 2006, 95; Cass. 24 April 2002 (P.01.1623.F), No. 248, *Pas.* 2002, 991, *Arr.Cass.* 2002, 1104.

for the original loss. The Court even allows such recovery if there was no legal obligation to help the victim in this way, but the voluntary intervention was reasonable.[743] This also means that a victim whose harm has been restored by a third party free of charge, cannot claim compensation anymore, as its harm has been undone and the remaining damage, i.e., the cost of the restoration, are not an injury to the victim's interest but to the interests of this third party.[744]

§5. Actual and Future Losses

233. Under Belgian tort law, the distinction between actual losses or losses already suffered (*damnum emergens*) and future losses (*lucrum cessans*), is less relevant than in some other legal systems. In principle, both types of loss are recognized as damage and are fully recoverable in tort.

However, for a loss to be recognized as damage it has to be sufficiently certain.[745] Of course, losses already suffered are in practice much more easily proved than future losses, for which there always remains some doubt about what is to happen in the future as well as what would have happened in the future but for the fact serving as a basis for the liability. Also, actual losses may be easier to measure and can thus more easily be exactly valued, while future losses in practice very often can only be estimated.[746]

234. When future losses are compensated by a lump sum payment, the fact that this early payment gives the victim an advantage has to be taken into account when setting the amount of damages. A court cannot award damages equal to the full amount of the victims (lost) future salary to be paid in advance, but has to discount this amount and award only its present day value.[747]

§6. Other Costs

235. The costs the victim has to make to successfully claim compensation were traditionally not considered damage caused by the fact that serves as a basis for the liability. They were seen as costs that were caused by the dispute, i.e., by the fact that the opposing party exercises his right to dispute his liability. As it is a fundamental right of each person to choose a legal position and defend it in court, those costs were not considered to be caused wrongfully, and therefore could not be recovered based on liability.

743. Cass. 6 November 2001 (P.99.1703.N), No. 600, *Arr.Cass.* 2001, 1856, *Pas.* 2001, 1790; Cass. 4 March 2002 (C.01.0284.N), No. 154, *Arr.Cass.* 2002, 678, *Pas.* 2002, 632.
744. Cass. 25 May 2012 (C11.0494.F), No. 340, *Pas.* 2012, 1201, *Arr.Cass.* 2012, 1432.
745. *See supra* Part V, Ch. 1, §2.
746. *See infra* para. 251.
747. Cass. 24 September 2010 (C.09.0517.N), not published but discussed in G. Jocqué, "Actualia schade en schadeloosstelling", *CRA* 2014/3, 3-18, para. 35, pp. 9–10, a review written by one of the justices of the Court.

This view changed after the Court of Cassation in 2001 ruled that the cost of performing a statutory, regulatory or contractual obligation are caused by the fact because of which they had to be performed.[748] Such costs can be recovered in liability, according to the Court, if the statute, regulation or contract does not require this burden to remain for the charge of the person who is legally required to perform the obligation.[749]

236. Based on this reasoning, parties in disputes started to claim compensation for the fees they needed to pay to experts to establish the existence of their loss and the cause of such loss in a dispute with the allegedly liable person. These expert fees where the cost of performing their obligation from their contract with the expert, but as this contract does not require or even intend these costs to remain with the client, these fees qualify as recoverable damage under the new interpretation. As a result, the Court of Cassation recognized that expert fees can be recovered as damage caused by the fact that has caused the loss the expert was examining.[750]

Soon thereafter, the Court of Cassation also decided that attorney fees paid by the victim in the dispute with the defended who is found to be liable by the court, qualified as recoverable damage caused by the fact that has caused the loss for which the victim claimed compensation from the defendant.[751]

237. This new line of case law was, however, ruled to be based on an unconstitutional interpretation of the law. The line chosen by the Court of Cassation allows the claimant of a dispute—who is the victim of a primary loss claiming compensation based on civil liability—to recover his attorney fees if he wins the case, as this win implies the court finding the defendant liable for the primary loss and hence also for the loss consisting of the costs required to obtain compensation for that primary loss. However, the defendant in that same dispute would not be able to recover his attorney fees if he wins the case, as the court's decision that he is not liable does not imply that the claimant who unsuccessfully brought the case committed a fault. This inability of the defendant to recover the fees was found to be in violation of the constitutional principle of equal treatment and Article 6, paragraph 1, of the ECHR (principle of equality of arms).[752]

In reaction to this decision of the Court of Arbitration (now the Constitutional Court), the legislature intervened and created specific statutory rules for attorney fees. First, the recovery of such fees on the basis of civil liability is now statutorily excluded. Instead, a system of compensation is included in the procedural rules, allowing the winning party, irrespective of whether this was the claimant or the defendant, to recover a reduced amount, set by royal decree.[753]

748. *See* Cass. 19 February 2001 (C.98.0119.N), No. 96, *Arr.Cass.* 2001, 318, *Pas.* 2001, 316.

749. *See supra* para. 232.

750. Cass. 28 February 2002 (C.99.0193.N), No. 147, *Arr.Cass.* 2002, 642, *Pas.* 2002, 609.

751. *See* for contractual liability Cass. 2 September 2004 (C.01.0186.F), No. 375, *Pas.* 2004, 1217, *Arr.Cass.* 2004, 1271, and for extracontractual liability Cass. 16 November 2006 (C.05.0124.F), No. 568, *Pas.* 2004, 2372, *Arr.Cass.* 2004, 2325.

752. C.Arb. No. 57/2006 of 19 April 2006.

753. Articles 1017–1024 JC, as revised by the (federal) Act of 21 April 2007 on the Recovery of Attorney Fees and Costs; Art. 30/1 of the (federal) Coordinated Act of 12 January 1973 on the Council of State, as inserted by the (federal) Act of 20 January 2014 Reforming the Jurisdiction, Procedure and Organisation of the Council of State.

238. These new statutory rules, however, create a new unequal treatment. Now the recovery of attorney fees is capped but granted to both the victim in a suit that ends in the court finding the defendant liable and the defendant in a suit that ends in the court finding the defendant not to be liable. The recovery of expert fees and other costs in disputes relating to civil liability, however, are not specifically regulated by statute, so the general rules, as interpreted by the Court of Cassation in its decision of 2002,[754] remain applicable, allowing the victim to recover such costs if the defendant is found liable,[755] but not allowing a defendant that the court finds not to be liable to reclaim the same costs from the claimant. The Constitutional Court has ruled that this unequal treatment does not violate the constitution, as Article 6 of the ECHR is not applicable to such fees and the services of an attorney and an expert as essentially different.[756]

239. These Belgian rules were challenged in front of the ECJ for disputes relating to infringements of intellectual property rights. For such infringements, an EU directive requires national law to ensure that reasonable and proportionate legal costs and other expenses incurred by the successful party shall, as a rule, be borne by the unsuccessful party, unless equity does not allow this.[757] The ECJ found that EU law precludes national legislation providing flat-rates which, owing to the low maximum amounts it contains do not ensure that, at the very least, a significant and appropriate part of the reasonable costs incurred by the successful party are borne by the unsuccessful party. It also decided that EU law precludes national rules restricting the reimbursement of the costs of a technical adviser to instances where the unsuccessful party was at fault.[758] As such, this means that the Belgian statutory and regulatory rules will not be applied to disputes relating to intellectual property rights. However, at the time of writing this report, it remains to be seen whether this means that under the Belgian equal treatment principle the EU rule applicable to liability suits in cases of infringements of intellectual property rights will also have to be applied in other civil liability disputes. According to the general principle followed by the Constitutional Court, a different treatment of comparable cases is allowed if this difference results from certain cases being ruled by EU law and others not, but such difference should not be too large.[759]

§7. Mitigation of Damages

240. In principle, a victim has a right to full integral compensation of the loss it has suffered.[760] Belgian law does not impose a real duty on the victim to minimize

754. *See supra* footnote 750.
755. *See* e.g. Cass. 1 March 2012 (C.10.0425.N), No. 142, *Arr.Cass.* 2012, 489, *Pas.* 2012, 463.
756. Con.C. No. 15/2009 of 5 February 2009.
757. Article 14 of Directive 2004/48/EC of the European Parliament and of the Council of 29 April 2004 on the enforcement of intellectual property rights, *Official Journal* L157/45 of 30 April 2004.
758. ECJ, *United Video Properties Inc. v. Telenet NV*, Case No. C-57/15, ECLI:EU:C:2016:611, decision of 28 July 2016.
759. Con.C. No. 182/2008 of 18 December 2008.
760. *See supra* para. 219.

or reduce harm it suffers. Nor does a victim lose its right to full compensation because it had the *possibility* to limit or reduce the harm it suffered and did not do it. However, a victim that does not *reasonably* take the measures to limit its damage is considered to behave negligently.[761] In that case, the liability of the third party that is liable for the occurrence of the loss will be reduced to the extent the damage would have been reduced or restricted if the victim had behaved reasonably.[762]

241. Although this is explained in the literature as if it were a mere application of the general principle applicable when the harm is also caused by a fault of the victim,[763] one can notice a difference. In these cases, the courts tend to leave the burden of the harm that could have been avoided completely for the victim, allowing it to recover only that part of the damage that it also would have suffered if it would have behaved reasonably.[764] This in effect amounts to applying a principle of pure contributory negligence instead of the general system of comparative negligence, even though most authors do not explicitly recognize it as such.

242. This principle is also applied in cases where the victim refuses to undergo medical treatment that would normally reduce its physical injury,[765] even though the victim as a patient in principle has the right to refuse any treatment.[766] Sometimes the court explicitly states that in that case, the damage is the consequence of the choice of the victim, and for that reason, no compensation can be claimed.[767] The Court of Cassation, however, continues to stress that the victim can only be denied damages if its choice can be found to be differing from the choice a normally reasonable person would have made in the circumstances.[768]

761. Cass. 14 May 1992, No. 478, *Pas.* 1992, 798, *Arr.Cass.* 1991–1992, 855.
762. Cass. 25 October 1991, No. 113, *Arr.Cass.* 1991–1992, 192, *Pas.* 1992, 158, a case where the victim received no compensation at all because the damage subsisted because of the refusal of the victim to do what would have allowed the damage to be restored.
763. *See supra* para. 212.
764. Clear examples are the cases where interests are refused because the court finds the victim to have waited too long to bring its claim. *See* Cass. 18 September 1996 (P.96.0127.F), No. 316, *Pas.* 1997, 824, *Arr.Cass.* 1996, 769; Corr. Dinant 7 June 2006, *Droit de la circulation* 2006, 727; Pol. Ghent 7 March 2005, *Bull.Ass.* 2005, 783; Pol. Mechelen 3 June 2002, *Bull.Ass.* 2002, 969; CA Brussels 7 February 2001, *Journal des juges de paix* 2001, 381; Pol. Bruges 16 September 2004, *Tijdschrift voor Gentse rechtspraak* 2004, 306.
765. *See* e.g. Cass. 17 September 1964, *Pas.* 1965, 60; LC Ghent 1 March 2010, *Bull.Ass.* 2010, 290; Pol. Bruges 18 October 2004, *Bull.Ass.* 2005, 384; CA Brussels 21 December 1988, *RGAR* 1990, No. 11,609; CFI Liège 26 June 1990, *Bull.Ass.* 1990, 830.
766. Article 8 (federal) Act of 22 August 2002 on the Rights of Patients.
767. *See* e.g. CFI Dendermonde 7 March 2002, *Revue de droit de la santé* 2004–2005, 238; Pol. Huy 6 February 2012, *Evaluation du préjudice corporel: commentaire au regard de la jurisprudence* 2013, III.3. Huy., 113.
768. Cass. 13 June 2016 (C.15.0305.N), *RDC* 2017, 407, *RGAR* 2017, No. 15,359, a case where the victim continued to visit the same physician to treat its injuries caused by an accident after having moved away more than 100 km, and subsequently claimed the cost of transport to and from the medical cabinet of this physician as damage caused by the accident.

Chapter 3. Compensation and Assessment of Damages

§1. Concrete Versus Abstract

243. The basic general rule of Belgian tort law is that the victim has a right to actual reparation, i.e., restoration of the situation it would have been in but for the event that triggered liability (reparation in kind).[769] Only if this is practically impossible or would be manifestly unreasonable to demand (abuse of right), the victim's right is reduced to a claim for damages (reparation by equivalent). This compensation, however, has to place the victim in a situation that is in value equivalent to having the harm itself be undone. This means that the awarded damages have to provide "integral compensation" for the loss suffered. Integral compensation requires damages to be assessed *in concreto*. All specific circumstances of the case or the victim's situation have to be taken into account to value his injured interest or to determine which specific measures (at what cost) would be required to undo the damage.

244. In case of harm consisting in a future loss of income, for instance, the damages have to be equivalent to what this particular victim would earn, and cannot be based on what a person of the age and qualification of the victim in general or on average earns or on what income would be required to be able to lead a normal life.[770] It also means that the wrongdoer must take the victim as he finds him: if the victim has particular needs that result in a higher value of a certain interest, then injuring this interest will result in higher damages to compensate for this particular loss. The schoolbook example is the person with only one eye losing this eye suffering more recoverable damage than a person with two functioning eyes who loses one eye.[771] If a particular victim because of impaired mental capacities does not realize his loss, the amount of damages awarded to compensate for moral loss will be lower than it would be in standard cases.[772] The victim is thus to be compensated for its actual specific loss, not for the loss a standard person would have suffered in this kind of situation.

245. More and more, however, courts are in fact assessing damages in an abstract way, taking as a starting point for valuation the normal value of an interest. This, of course, has obvious procedural economic advantages. It also has the advantage that equal protection by the different courts, whose valuation of interests *in concreto* might vary widely, can be better observed.

When in a reform of civil procedure all civil liability cases relating to traffic accidents were reappointed to the police courts, which have jurisdiction over the criminal liability that almost always is involved in such cases, the fear was that this would result in insufficient unification in the courts' decisions. Before the reform,

---

769. *See supra* paras. 217–218.

770. Cass. 13 April 1995 (C.94.0126.F), No. 201, *Pas.* 1995, 423, *Arr.Cass.* 1995, 409.

771. *Cf.* Cass. 6 January 1993, No. 7, *Pas.* 1993, 11, *Arr.Cass.* 1993, 11; Cass. 25 May 1977, *Pas.* 1977, 978, *Arr.Cass.* 1977, 981; Cass. 1 April 1985, No. 464, *Arr.Cass.* 1984–1985, 1051, *Pas.* 1985, 963.

772. Cass. 13 October 1999 (P.99.0861.F), No. 528, *Pas.* 1999, 1308, *Arr.Cass.* 1999, 1255.

these cases were heard on appeal by the courts of appeal, of which there are only five in the country, but now the appellate decisions would be spread over twenty seven courts (at the time). At the initiative of police court judges, working together with other stakeholders in civil liability litigation, a nonbinding so-called Indicative Table was agreed, setting standard amounts for particular types of damage. The first such table was published in 1995, and in 2016, the seventh edition was published. Over the years, the content of the table has been widened, nowadays not only covering damage occurring in traffic accidents but more generally treating most kinds of damage which can occur.

These tables are not binding; they are not law. A court, therefore, cannot dismiss a claim for damages merely because the type of loss claimed is not mentioned in these tables or the tables mention conditions not fulfilled in the case.[773] However, as the burden of proof rests on the claimant, courts can apply these guidelines if the victim has not provided evidence that its particular harm differs from the injury normally occurring in similar cases.[774]

§2. Objective Versus Subjective

246. Belgian courts and authors do not pay attention to the distinction between objective and subjective valuation of damage. Of course, the value of the damage in extracontractual liability is set by the court, and not unilaterally decided by the victim. Therefore, civil liability corresponds to what Calabresi and Melamed called "liability rules," as opposed to property rules, which give the holder of an entitlement the right to unilaterally decide on the value of the interest himself.[775] In that sense, Belgian tort law uses an objective valuation of the concrete loss. The extent of the damage is determined by the specific concrete interests of the victim,[776] but the value attached to this specific injury is determined by the court based on a general view on such values.[777]

247. A hypothetical example can make this clear. If a dog and a cat are wrongfully killed, the owner has a right to full compensation. Concrete assessment of damages means that the value of the animals for the victim will depend on his particular situation. If this person is blind and the dog guides him, the damages awarded will be higher for the loss of the dog than for the loss of the cat. However, the victim cannot claim millions of euros in damages for the loss of the cat based on the argument that he would maybe have been prepared to let his dog go but would never have been willing to sell the cat, not for any price. This shows that damages are assessed on an objective basis, not subjective.

773. Cass. 6 March 2013 (P.12.1596.F), No. 146, *Pas.* 2013, 534, *Arr.Cass.* 2013, 575.

774. Cass. 11 September 2009 (C.08.0031.F), No. 490, *Pas.* 2009, 1847, *Arr.Cass.* 2009, 1995.

775. *See* G. Calabresi & A.D. Melamed, "Property Rules, Liability Rules, and Inalienability: One View of the Cathedral", *Harvard Law Review* 1972, vol. 85, 1089–1128.

776. *See supra* footnote 772.

777. *Cf.* Cass. 4 April 1990, No. 468, *Pas.* 1990, 913, *Arr.Cass.* 1989–1990, 1025, where the Court ruled that damages cannot be set at a lower amount just because the victim suffering a loss does not fully realize that this money serves to compensate for its emotional distress.

248. The amount of damages due is based on the actual concrete loss, as it is objectively valued. The type of fact that caused the loss and that serves as a basis for liability has no influence on the extent of damages due. Under Belgian law, a victim that suffers a loss caused by an intentional wrong or a very grave fault has no different right to compensation than a victim suffering the same loss caused by an unintentional wrong, a very light fault, or a fact which is not wrongful but for which the defendant bears a strict liability. However, it is possible that the emotional distress a victim suffers from an event is more severe because of the heinous character of the fault. In that case, higher moral damages are not revealing a valuation of the damages based on the graveness of the fault, but a consequence of the harm resulting from such fault being greater.

§3. Methods of Assessing Damages

249. As the general rule requires integral compensation, the court in principle has to establish the exact extent of the losses in the particular case. This requires the consideration of all relevant circumstances of the instance—i.e., *in concreto* and not *in abstracto*—on an objective basis.[778] In principle, the fact-finding court has the full competence to establish what losses are present, and what their value is.[779]

250. The amount of the damages awarded is set case by case by the fact-finding court, based on the evidence presented by the parties.[780] The burden of proof rests on the claimant:[781] he who claims an amount of compensation has to show that the damage he has suffered can be valued at this amount. As the defendant has to receive the opportunity to dispute the facts introduced by the claimant, the victim of a loss has to make sure that the loss is established in a manner respecting the procedural rights of the defendant. Thus, a victim cannot unilaterally decide to have the damage repaired and provide the invoice as the only evidence of the extent of the damage. For damage caused by traffic accidents, the insurance companies active on the Belgian market have concluded an agreement containing mutual recognition of expert witnesses, allowing for a fast and direct settlement of such cases.[782]

Because the court in a civil procedure cannot decide *ultra petita*, the damages awarded cannot be higher than the amount claimed by the victim, even if the court comes to the conclusion that the actual loss has a higher value.

251. Losses already suffered can usually be exactly valued on the basis of market prices for goods and services needed for the repair or replacement of the loss. This is

778. Cass. 8 January 2016 (C.15.0271.F), *RGAR* 2016, No. 15,291; *Bull.Ass.* 2016, 486; Cass. 16 April 2015 (C.13.0305.F), No. 254, *Pas.* 2015, 961, *Arr.Cass.* 2015, 999.

779. Cass. 18 September 2013 (P.13.0732.F), *JT* 2013, 629, *RGAR* 2014, No. 15,089.

780. Cass. 3 February 1987, No. 322, *Arr.Cass.* 1986–1987, 724, *Pas.* 1987, 644.

781. Article 870 JC states that any party relying on a fact has to prove the existence of this fact if it is disputed. Article 1315 CC requires the person demanding the performance of an obligation—*in casu* the obligation to pay damages—to prove the existence of this obligation, which in case of an obligation based on civil liability requires the establishment of a loss.

782. *See Convention d'expertise et RDR—Expertise en RDR-overeenkomst*, available at http://assuralia.be.

not the case for future losses: the necessary element of uncertainty involved in those kind of losses force the court to always use an estimate of the value of the loss, even though it can be based on objective elements such as current market values.

252. When the court has acknowledged that a loss has occurred but it is not possible for the court to calculate the value of the damage on the basis of objective elements, the court will not be allowed to deny the claimant any compensation, as this would per se not constitute integral compensation.[783] In such a case, the court is therefore obliged to set damages on the basis of equity and conscience, awarding a more symbolic amount that serves to recognize the existence of the loss without having the pretention to undo it, usually referred to as setting the damages *ex aequo et bono.*

This is the only option for injuries to interests for which no market values exists, such as for moral damage[784] and for personal injuries as such, i.e., not for the economic consequences of such injuries.[785] However, this is also the case for other types of losses if the claimant does not offer sufficient evidence showing the value of the harm.[786] When one of the parties proposed a method for an objective calculation of the loss, the court cannot award a lump sum equitable amount without first establishing by a reasoned decision that the proposed valuation is not suitable.[787]

As mentioned previously, courts often rely on the periodically published indicative tables,[788] which contain standard amounts for different types of loss categories that cannot be exactly valued on the basis of objective elements such as market prices.

253. Future losses can be compensated in different ways: by a series of periodic payments compensating the future losses as they will occur, by an immediate lump sum payment of an amount equal to the present day value of the future stream of losses, and by a lump sum payment of an amount set as an estimate of the total value of the loss *ex aequo et bono*. In principle, the fact-finding court can choose among those three possibilities, based on which of these methods results in the most accurate integral compensation of the loss in the light of the evidence presented. These methods will be discussed in more detail further on.[789]

§4. Equitable Limitation of Damages

254. Belgian law does not contain a general rule allowing the court to limit damages based on equitable grounds. The only measure of the damages awarded is the objective extent of the harm or the loss. The seriousness or gravity of the fault is

783. Cass. 15 January 2008 (P.07.1247.N), No. 27, *Arr.Cass.* 2008, 119, *Pas.* 2008, 117; Cass. 9 October 2009 (C.07.0545.F), No. 568, *Pas.* 2009, 2204, *Arr.Cass.* 2009, 2276.
784. *See supra* para. 230.
785. *See infra* para. 270.
786. Cass. 2 March 2016 (P.15.0929.F), *RGAR* 2016, No. 15,336, *JT* 2017, 400; Cass. 9 October 2009 (C.07.0545.F), No. 568, *Pas.* 2009, 2204, *Arr.Cass.* 2009, 2276; Cass. 3 March 2008 (C.07.0090.F), No. 149, *Pas.* 2008, 597, *Arr.Cass.* 2008, 623.
787. *See* e.g. Cass. 15 January 2014 (P.13.1110.F), No. 31, *Pas.* 2014, 126, *Arr.Cass.* 2014, 128; Cass. 20 November 2012 (P.12.0499.N), No. 624, *Arr.Cass.* 2012, 2602, *Pas.* 2012, 2268; Cass. 4 October 2010 (C.09.0475.N), No. 572, *Arr.Cass.* 2010, 2387, *Pas.* 2010, 2472.
788. *See supra* para. 245.
789. *See infra* Part VI, Ch. 3, §5.

in principle not relevant. Thus, a very minor or light fault may result in enormous damages if it caused a very big loss, and, vice versa, a very grave fault may result in minute damages, if the loss caused happened to be very small. The disproportion between the gravity of the fault and the burden of the remedy is not an element to be taken into account when setting damages.

255. There is, however, one notable exception to this general rule. Article 1386*bis* of the Civil Code, which makes it possible to hold a person with a mental condition impairing his judgment or limiting his control over his actions civilly liable for the loss he wrongfully causes.[790] Article 1386*bis* of the Civil Code allows the court to leave the burden of the harm completely on the shoulders of the victim or to partially or completely shift it to the wrongdoing mentally ill person based on an equitable judgment, taking into account the (financial) situation of both parties. Although this has been criticized by scholars, the Court of Cassation has ruled that when the mentally ill person has civil liability insurance, this insurer will be held to full compensation of the harm that was wrongfully caused, as the insurer—as opposed to the insured mentally ill person—cannot invoke the ground for limiting this liability.[791]

256. This provision was inserted in the Civil Code in the thirties of the previous century, when the legislature also created the possibility to intern persons that have committed a criminal offense but that cannot be punished for it because of their insanity defense. As these persons might still pose a danger for society, the alternative measure of involuntary commitment was introduced.[792] Article 1386*bis* Civil Code was intended to cover the civil liability in these cases, and is thus only applicable to persons suffering from a mental disorder. Of course, one can wonder whether from a civil law perspective, there are appropriate reasons to limit the remedy of equitable relief of a victim of damage which was wrongfully caused to cases where the person who caused the loss suffers from a mental condition, and not also apply the same remedy in cases where this person has lost control over his actions because of a physical condition.[793] Even more, one can question the constitutionality of this difference in treatment of the victims of a loss depending on the cause of the lack of culpability of the person that wrongfully caused it. Why should the same principle not apply in cases where the person that wrongfully caused the loss is not liable because he is not old enough to have the capacity to be culpable,[794] or where that person committed the wrong because of a ground of exclusion of liability that renders the person not guilty of his wrongful act?[795] So far, however, the Constitutional Court has not yet ruled on the question.

790. *See supra* para. 79.

791. Cass. 22 September 2000 (C.98.0090.N), No. 489, *Arr.Cass.* 2000, 1420, *Pas.* 2000, 1390.

792. Originally organized by the Act of 9 April 1930 on the Protection of Society against Abnormal People, Recurrent Criminals and Sexual Offenders, nowadays organized under the Act of 5 May 2014 on Involuntary Commitment.

793. Cass. 20 June 1979, *Arr.Cass.* 1978–1979, 1258, *Pas.* 1979, 1217, vacating a judgment that had applied Art. 1386*bis* CC in a case where the loss was caused by a person while suffering from a heart attack; *see also* Cass. 24 April 1980, No. 542, *Pas.* 1980, 1055, *Arr.Cass.* 1979–1980, 1065, vacating a judgment that had applied Art. 1386*bis* CC in a case where the loss was caused by a person while suffering diminished consciousness caused by a vascular problem.

794. *See supra* para. 78.

795. *See supra* Part IV, Ch. 2, §2–4.

§5. Methods of Payment

I. Lump Sum

257. The standard method of payment of damages is the payment of one global sum representing the total value of the loss. In simple cases of property damage, patrimonial damage consisting of costs already incurred, and nonpecuniary losses already suffered, this is the only method available.

258. In cases involving future losses, damages in the form of a lump sum are also possible. To estimate the amount to be awarded, the court will calculate the cumulative present value of the stream of periodic future losses in a process called "capitalization." The sum awarded should allow the victim to periodically withdraw an amount equal to the loss he suffers in a specific period of time for as long as he was expected to suffer the damage at the time of the decision. Capitalization places the market risk of the future value of the awarded sum with the victim. The amount awarded has to take the advantage of the earlier payment into account, as the victim can invest the received moneys and thus earn capital income, which also serves to compensate his future losses.[796] In practice, courts use tables to calculate the amount to be awarded.[797]

This method of payment is most often used for the compensation of future losses caused by permanent personal injury, such as lost income and anatomic reduction or diminished functionality. Since 2010, the Court of Cassation has allowed this method also to be used for moral damages, which are then calculated as the present capital value of a stream of sums compensating for the moral damages to be suffered in the future.[798] However, the fact-finding court can refuse such capitalization if it motivates its decision on the facts of the case, for instance if there are serious indications that the mental suffering will most likely diminish over time.[799] Only future losses can be included in this capitalization.[800] Income or opportunities already lost at the time of the court's decision cannot be included in the calculation, and have to be compensated by separately calculated damages, which can be set on a concrete basis.[801]

When used, the possible early death of the victim, which in effect reduces the loss he has actually suffered, will not reduce the compensation due on the basis of liability. In the same way, a potential survival of his normal life expectancy may result

796. Cass. 24 June 2003 (P.03.0232.), No. 375, *Arr.Cass.* 2003, 1488, *Pas.* 2003, 1263; Cass. 14 January 1998 (P.97.1060.F), No. 25, *Pas.* 1998, 76, *Arr.Cass.* 1998, 69; Cass. 22 January 1968, *Arr.Cass.* 1968, 694, *Pas.* 1968, 648; *see also supra* footnote 747.

797. *See* e.g. www.tafelsschryvers.be.

798. Cass. 15 September 2010 (P.10.0476.F), No. 522, *Pas.* 2010, 2270, *Arr.Cass.* 2010, 2193; *see also* e.g. Cass. 4 October 2010 (C.09.0475.N), No. 572, *Arr.Cass.* 2010, 2387, *Pas.* 2010, 2472; Cass. 17 February 2012 (C.11.0451.F), No. 120, *Pas.* 2012, 374, *Arr.Cass.* 2012, 409; Cass. 19 November 2014 (P.14.1121.F), No. 707, *Pas.* 2014, 2580, *Arr.Cass.* 2014, 2645.

799. Cass. 7 May 2014 (P.13.0638.F), *JLMB* 2015, 598, *Bull.Ass.* 2014, 436; Cass. 24 September 2014 (P.14.0608.F), *JLMB* 2014, 1800.

800. Cass. 23 October 2009 (C.07.0638.F), No. 616, *Pas.* 2009, 2423, *Arr.Cass.* 2009, 2481.

801. Cass. 25 March 2003 (P.02.0417.N), No. 196, *Arr.Cass.* 2003, 746, *Pas.* 2003, 615; Cass. 21 September 2005 (P.05.0452.F), No. 447, *Pas.* 2005, 1686, *Arr.Cass.* 2005, 1685; Cass. 22 November 2005 (P.05.0963.N), No. 616, *Arr.Cass.* 2005, 2322, *Pas.* 2005, 2321.

in the awarded sum not to fully compensate the losses actually suffered. In a way, the use of normal life expectancy in the calculation of the amount due means that abstract damages are awarded instead of the normally required concrete damages. However, the life expectancy tables used in the capitalization method make a distinction between men and women, thus rendering this calculation method more concrete than using the method of compensation by a fixed amount set per "point" of disability,[802] which does not distinguish different categories of people that have a varying life expectancy.

II. Annuities

259. Permanent loss of income can also be compensated by awarding annuities. During the expected period of suffering the loss, the victim will receive a periodical payment of an amount that at the time of the court's judgment was estimated to be equal to his damage. The rent can consist of monthly payments or of yearly sums. Such a rent will be indexed, to make sure future fluctuation of the value of money will not inflate or deflate the real value of the compensation the victim receives.

260. When this method is used, the possible early death of the victim will stop the payments while the possible late death of the victim who survives his normal life expectancy will oblige the liable party to continue to pay. Thus, this method is considered to result in a more correct or more integral compensation of the loss actually suffered. This method also protects the victim against spending the awarded damages too early and against the market risk, resulting in potential financial problems in the future. Notwithstanding these advantages, courts tend to use this method less and less, not at the least because insurance companies, who in reality pay the bulk of damages awarded, strongly prefer and insist on a fast and complete final resolution of their cases, so that they do not have to carry the financial burden of continuously administering all accident cases for long periods of time.

III. Others

261. In case of permanent economic disability, Belgian courts also apply a method of payment of a fixed sum per "point," i.e., per percentage point of disability on the official scale used in matters of social security.[803] In practice, this method is mostly used to compensate for mixed pecuniary and moral losses. The indicative tables[804] mention amounts per point that decrease with the age of the victim. This method is only used in cases of smaller percentages of disability, mostly below 15%. When using this method, no distinction has to be made between income already lost and future losses: it is considered an estimated compensation for the totality of the

802. *See infra* Part VI, Ch. 3, §5, III.
803. The Official Belgian Scale determining Invalidities (*Barème Officiel Belge des Invalidités* (*BOBI*)—*Officiële Belgische Schaal ter bepaling van de graad van Invaliditeit* (*OBSI*)).
804. *See supra* para. 245.

loss.[805] For more serious cases, the capitalization method is preferred, awarding a lump sum based on a calculation of the present value of a stream of future missed income.

805. Cass. 17 March 1999 (P.98.0510.F), No. 159, *Pas.* 1999, 400, *Arr.Cass.* 1999, 389.

Chapter 4. Personal Injury and Death

262. Personal injury consists in loss of physical or psychological integrity, resulting in bodily or mental harm. Primarily, it consists in an invalidity or personal disability. This is a medical concept, indicating the anatomic or functional reduction itself. This disability can be temporarily or permanently, partially or completely. Most often, the level of disability is established by a medical expert on the basis of an official scale used in matters of social security.[806] The injury can cause a reduction in the victim's ability to engage in lucrative activities, but this economic disability is not necessarily equal to the invalidity.[807]

263. Personal harm can also cause losses for other persons than the direct victim of the injury. Belgian law does not contain any *a priori* restrictions for harm suffered by repercussion. Therefore, personal injury in many cases also leads to claims for compensation by other secondary victims. These secondary victims can also suffer pecuniary ("patrimonial") and/or nonpecuniary ("extra-patrimonial") damage.

264. Death is not considered recoverable harm for the person that has died. Of course, a person may have suffered loss because of personal injury prior to dying, which would constitute recoverable damage. If the victim subsequently dies, the right to compensation for this harm will be inherited, so his heirs can claim these damages. The mere fact of dying, however, is not considered to constitute damage for the deceased, so just the fact that someone has died does not create a claim for compensation for his heirs. However, as there is no principled restriction on who can suffer recoverable losses by repercussion, heir or other next of kin can claim damages for the harm they suffer as a consequence of the death.

§1. Pecuniary Losses

265. Personal injury very often leads to medical costs and other expenses of care. Such losses are fully recoverable. In Belgium, many of these costs are in fact borne by mutual insurance that is part of the social security system. The insurer that has had to bear such costs, however, is subrogated in the rights of the insured and thus will be able to recover the loss from the person that is liable for the event causing the personal injury.[808] Private insurers, covering extra medical costs that are not part of the standard coverage of the social health insurance scheme, also benefit from statutory subrogation.[809] If the house or the car of the victim have to be adapted to allow him to use it with his invalidity, the cost of this adaptation is recognized as damage that has to be compensated by the person that is liable for the accident that caused the injury.

266. Personal injury can also cause disability to work (economic disability) and hence loss of potential income. This is fully recoverable under Belgian tort law. Loss

806. *See supra* footnote 803.
807. Cass. 11 January 1983, No. 276, *Arr.Cass.* 1982–1983, 633, *Pas.* 1983, 556.
808. *See infra* para. 280.
809. *See infra* para. 277.

of income earning capacity is recoverable damage even if the victim was unemployed at the time of the accident: it is sufficient that he had the capacity to earn and that his capacity is diminished.[810] A distinction is made between temporary and permanent economic disability. For permanent economic disability, the courts use the three mentioned methods of estimation, i.e., by awarding a capitalized sum, covering all future loss of income, by awarding a rent that is indexed, or by awarding an amount per point of invalidity. Temporary disability to work results in loss that in principle can be estimated and valued much easier *in concreto*. The victim in theory has a right to damages equal to the difference between the salary he actually earns while disabled and the salary he would have earned if the accident had not happened. However, some courts have awarded damages equal to a fraction of the victim's income calculated using his percentage of invalidity set by a medical expert. As such, damages do not necessarily equal the actual loss, these decisions are considered to violate the fundamental principle of integral compensation. When social security benefits are substituted for the lost income, the insurer will be statutorily subrogated, allowing him to claim damages from the liable party based on the right to compensation of the primary victim.

267. The victim of personal injury can also be incapable of working in the household. This work can be valued at market prices, and is as such a pecuniary loss that is recoverable.[811] Temporary disability can also mean that the victim can continue his normal work or other activities but only thanks to the application of extra efforts. The cost of these efforts is in principle recoverable damage.[812] Help to the victim to overcome problems caused by the disability provided by third parties is also accepted as recoverable damage.[813] If the victim is incapable of doing some of the household work and receives help from a third person, the court will have to establish to what extent this outside help, the cost of which is recoverable damage, in fact relieves the victim of the household work, so that the incapacity to do this household work cannot be compensated twice.[814]

268. As was already mentioned, death itself does not constitute a pecuniary loss for the deceased. It can, of course, cause pecuniary losses for others. The partner, children and other dependents[815] of the deceased may lose the benefit of enjoying the support of the deceased. This can be a loss of income[816] and/or a loss of other types

810. Cass. 21 November 1994 (C.94.0073.N), No. 502, *Arr.Cass.* 1994, 996, *Pas.* 1994, 990.

811. Cass. 15 June 1959, *Arr. Verbr.* 1959, 845, *Pas.* 1959, 1050.

812. Cass. 30 November 1970, *Arr.Cass.* 1971, 307, *Pas.* 1971, 289; Cass. 7 January 1999 (C.97.0425.F), No. 7, *Pas.* 1999, 7, *Arr.Cass.* 1999, 7.

813. Cass. 30 November 1977, *Pas.* 1978, 351, *Arr.Cass.* 1978, 368.

814. Cass. 11 March 1999 (C.98.0145.F), No. 147, *Pas.* 1999, 367, *Arr.Cass.* 1999, 358.

815. In Cass. 16 January 1939, *Pas.* 1939, 15, the Court ruled that a sibling that in fact shared living arrangements with the deceased brother or sister can recover damages for the loss of support.

816. Cass. 15 February 2011 (P.10.1244.N), No. 133, *Arr.Cass.* 2011, 506, *Pas.* 2011, 517; Cass. 16 March 2006 (C.05.0299.N), No. 156, *Arr.Cass.* 2006, 635, *Pas.* 2006, 620. The fact that the children still continue to have a right to financial support by the surviving parent does not exclude that they suffer pecuniary loss because of the death of their parent. Cass. 26 January 1973, *Arr.Cass.* 1973, 539, *Pas.* 1973, 515; Cass. 7 November 1978, *Arr.Cass.* 1978–1979, 275, *Pas.* 1979, 288.

of support, such as help in the household.[817] Their damage will not be equal to the total income of the deceased, but only that part of this income that they would have enjoyed.[818] Others who had economic relations with the deceased may suffer harm because they lose the enjoyment of his work or efforts. Employers, for instance, can be confronted with pecuniary losses when an employee dies. As such, these losses by repercussion are fully recoverable under Belgian tort law.[819]

269. Funeral and ceremonial expenses are in principle damage.[820] However, they will not always be recoverable in full. If the person who has paid for the service under normal circumstances would not have had to bear these costs, these expenses meet the criteria to be damage in civil liability. This will for instance be the case if a young person dies and his parents or spouse have to organize the service.[821] This is different, however, if the deceased would under normal circumstances also have had to receive a funeral funded by the person that has paid the costs but at a later point in time, such as is the case when a parent dies and is buried by his children. In that case, the damage the children suffer from paying for the funeral is not equal to the expenses actually paid, but is limited to the fact that they had to make these expenses earlier, now instead of much later. The recoverable loss will in that case be restricted to the time value of the money spent earlier than normally expected.

§2. NONPECUNIARY LOSSES

270. As was mentioned, personal injury can entail a loss of functionality. This loss, quite separately from the potential economic consequences, is also recognized as recoverable damage. Anatomic reduction or diminished functionality can also lead to other losses which do not have a market price, but which are recognized as injuries to legitimate personal interests and for which damages can be obtained. Examples are pain and suffering, loss of self-esteem, loss of pleasure, esthetical loss, sexual loss, and infertility. Such losses are in principle fully recoverable.[822]

---

817. *See* e.g. Cass. 5 March 2015 (C.14.0017.F), No. 162, *Pas.* 2015, 578, *Arr.Cass.* 2015, 595, in which case the Court ruled that the household work that is saved because of the death of a family member will have to be subtracted from the loss of the contribution because of the death of this member.

818. Cass. 22 October 1974, *Arr.Cass.* 1975, 248, *Pas.* 1975, 227; Cass. 4 March 1980, No. 418, *Arr.Cass.* 1979–1980, 826, *Pas.* 1980, 816.

819. *See* e.g. Cass. 10 December 1996, *Le droit des affaires (Revue internationale du droit des affaires)* 1997, 83, allowing a corporation to recover damages for the loss of the work performed by the managing director of the company; Cass. 24 March 1969, *Arr.Cass.* 1969, 690, *Pas.* 1969, 655, allowing a religious community to recover damages for having lost the part of the income that a deceased member voluntarily contributed to the community.

820. Cass. 7 May 2002 (P.01.0272.N), No. 276, *Arr.Cass.* 2002, 1233, *Pas.* 2002, 1106.

821. *See* e.g. Cass. 16 December 2004 (C.02.0212.N – C.02.0251.N), No. 614, *Arr.Cass.* 2004, 2054, *Pas.* 2004, 2014.

822. Cass. 10 October 1972, *Arr.Cass.* 1973, 146, *Pas.* 1973, 147; Cass. 3 February 1987, No. 322, *Arr.Cass.* 1986–1987, 724, *Pas.* 1987, 644; Cass. 13 October 1999 (P.99.0861.F), No. 528, *Pas.* 1999, 1308, *Arr.Cass.* 1999, 1255; Cass. 20 February 2006 (C.04.0366.N), No. 100, *Arr.Cass.* 2006, 414, *Pas.* 2006, 413.

271. Belgian courts also recognize that others than the victim of the personal injury, such as relatives or friends, can suffer moral losses by repercussion. Psychological grief and suffering from seeing a relative or close friend suffering is recognized as affectionate damage.[823] Parents of a seriously injured child will suffer moral loss by being confronted with the condition of the child but also by feelings of uncertainty over its future prospects.[824] Also, a spouse can claim compensation for his or her own moral loss that is caused by the primary victim's injuries, such as sexual loss because of the loss of ability or appetite of his or her partner or for damage caused by the infertility of his or her partner. The existence of a legal obligation of spouses to support each other does not stand in the way of recognizing their moral damage from witnessing their partner suffer.[825]

272. Death in itself does not constitute a moral loss for the deceased. However, emotional distress from realizing one is about to die, is damage. Thus, the courts tend to award moral damages to the estate if the deceased during the period of time between the accident and his death was aware of his fate.

In many cases, the surviving family members will suffer emotional distress, and this moral damage by repercussion is fully recoverable under Belgian law. However, courts struggle with the valuation of this moral damage, recognizing that this suffering cannot be measured nor undone by financial means. In general, Belgian courts are liberal in recognizing emotional suffering by others because of a death as damage, but in general award only relatively moderate amounts of damages.

823. Cass. 4 December 1967, *Arr.Cass.* 1968, 480, *Pas.* 1968, 448.
824. Cass. 3 February 1987, No. 322, *Arr.Cass.* 1986–1987, 724, *Pas.* 1987, 644.
825. Cass. 20 February 2006 (C.04.0366.N), No. 100, *Arr.Cass.* 2006, 414, *Pas.* 2006, 413.

Chapter 5. Various Damages (Property)

273. Property damage consists of the damage to a movable or immovable good or the destruction of such an object. The principle of integral compensation applies, and the Court of Cassation insists that the victim has to be placed back in the circumstances that he would have been in but for the accident.[826] Most often, property damage is patrimonial or pecuniary.

274. In case of destruction of a good, the awarded damages will equal the value of this good, estimated at the normal market price for its replacement by an object of the same type in the same state. In principle, this means that damages will be lower than the market price of a new object, as the actual loss was lower because the lost object was not new and had a value that had already diminished because of its age or wear and tear. In case of a divergence between the purchase price of a replacement of the lost object and the sale price for which the object could have been sold at the time it was damaged, the basic principle that the loss that has to be undone consists in the lost object itself and not in the loss of its price, requires the damages to be equal to the replacement value of the object and not to its sale value.[827] However, when the lost object was to be sold by the victim, which sale could not go through because of its destruction, his damage will be recognized to be equal to the lost sale price of the object.[828]

The valuation of damage to an object is set using the normal market cost of repair. If this cost is higher than the resulting value of the repaired good, insisting on reparation in kind is considered to constitute an abuse of right,[829] and therefore the awarded damages are reduced to the value of the lost good.[830] The lost use of the good during the time period needed for its repair or replacement is also recognized as damage, and so is the cost of temporary replacement during that period. If the damaged property has to be stored, the cost for this storage is also recoverable.

275. The victim of a damaged thing is free to use the awarded damages for actually having the object repaired or replaced or for other uses.[831] The amount awarded does not differ according to what the victim intends to do with it or has done.[832] This means, for instance, that damages for the total loss of an object have to equal the purchase price of a replacement object with the same characteristics, including the tax

826. Cass. 13 April 1988, No. 489, *Pas.* 1988, 936, *Arr.Cass.* 1987–1988, 1016; Cass. 5 May 1992, No. 461, *Arr.Cass.* 1991–1992, 834, *Pas.* 1992, 653; Cass. 20 February 2009 (C.07.0305.N), No. 146, *Arr.Cass.* 2009, 606, *Pas.* 2009, 553; Cass. 18 November 2011 (C.09.0521.F), No. 625, *Pas.* 2011, 2539, *Arr.Cass.* 2011, 2340.

827. Cass. 8 May 1952, *Arr. Verbr.* 1952, 499, *Pas.* 1952, 570; Cass. 13 January 1983, No. 283, *Pas.* 1983, 573, *Arr.Cass.* 1982–1983, 651; Cass. 28 September 1994 (P.94.611.F), No. 404, *Pas.* 1994, 774, *Arr.Cass.* 1994, 791.

828. Cass. 25 September 1979, No. 56, *Arr.Cass.* 1979–1980, 103, *Pas.* 1980, 117.

829. *See supra* Part I, Ch. 2, §2 and para. 219.

830. Cass. 23 October 1986, No. 118, *Pas.* 1987, 249, *Arr.Cass.* 1986–1987, 266.

831. This principle is statutorily only expressed for insurance payments received for losses suffered (Art. 147 of the (federal) Insurance Act of 4 April 2014), but is generally recognized also for damages in contractual or extracontractual liability.

832. Cass. 23 December 1992, No. 812, *Pas.* 1992, 1406, *Arr.Cass.* 1992, 1466.

that would be due on such a purchase, even though the victim is not required to use the damages to finance such purchase and is perfectly free to choose not to replace the destructed object and to use the amount awarded for another purpose.

276. Nonpecuniary losses are less likely in cases of property damage. However, there is no principled objection to such losses being recoverable in liability if they in fact can be shown to exist. In cases of hurt or killed pets, for instance, courts are not unwilling to recognize moral suffering of their owner. Through the acceptance of the existence of moral damages in case of property damage, the courts in effect can to some extent allow for a subjective valuation of the damage, recognizing the extra loss the victim suffers because he attaches a higher value to the lost object than society in general does as a separate item of damage, which can be valued on an objective basis.

Chapter 6. Interference with Collateral Benefits

§1. Insurance

277. Commercial first-party insurance is very widespread in Belgium. It allows victims of many types of harm to shift the burden of their loss to their insurer. The Court of Cassation has systematically ruled that an insurer that performs his contractual obligation by paying benefits to the insured, as such does not suffer damage that can be recovered on the basis of civil liability.[833] However, insurance legislation contains a provision that transfers the right to compensation the insured had on the basis of civil liability to the insurer to the extent it has compensated its loss (subrogation).[834]

278. Also third-party insurance is widely used. The legislature has made such insurance mandatory for many types of liability risk.[835] Most common forms are mandatory motor vehicle insurance,[836] professional insurance, but also the nonmandatory but in practice widely used "household insurance," covering the civil liability of family members and house personnel.[837] In principle, such insurance gives the insured that is civilly liable to compensate a victim's loss a claim against the insurer to reimburse him for the damages paid to the victim. Under Belgian law, however, a victim also has a direct claim for damages based on his own right against the third-party insurer of the person liable for his harm.[838] In many court cases dealing with civil liability questions, therefore, the defendant is an insurance company. Even if the victim—or its first-party insurer that was subrogated in its rights—brings a claim for compensation against the insured party that is allegedly liable, the third-party insurer will most often lead the defense, based on a statutory delegation of power.[839]

§2. Social Security

279. Belgium has a highly developed widely covering system of social security, including a retirement pension system, unemployment benefits, child support, yearly vacation, survival pensions for widows, widowers and orphans, health and invalidity insurance, industrial accidents insurance and a fund covering professional diseases.

833. *See* e.g. Cass. 1 April 2015 (P.13.2051.F), No. 234, *Pas.* 2015, 891, *Arr.Cass.* 2015, 921; Cass. 26 March 2003 (P.02.1609.F), No. 204, *Pas.* 2003, 638, *Arr.Cass.* 2003, 764.
834. Article 95 of the (federal) Insurance Act of 4 April 2014.
835. For a list of mandatory insurance in Belgium, *see* the website of the FSMA, the government agency superivsing het insurance market and insurance products (www.fsma.be).
836. *See also supra* para. 164.
837. While one is not required to have household insurance, every household insurance policy sold in Belgium is required to offer a regulatory set minimum coverage. *See* Royal Decree of 12 January 1984 setting the Minimum Coverage offered by Civil Liability Insurance relating to Private Life.
838. Article 150 (federal) Insurance Act of 4 April 2014.
839. Article 143, para. 2, (federal) Insurance Act of 4 April 2014.

Some of these systems cover losses for which the victim also could claim compensation based on civil liability.

280. The mandatory mutualized and partially publicly financed health insurance covers not only medical costs but also income loss because of disability. Benefits are only available to the extent the covered loss has not yet been compensated on the basis of other rules, such as civil liability.[840] Benefits are paid as advances on the compensation the victim has a right to on the basis of other rules, such as civil liability.[841] The mutual insurance company that compensates the insured cannot invoke the payment of these benefits as damage, to be compensated by the third party that is liable for the loss covered by the insurance.[842] However, the insurer is subrogated in the rights of the insured to the extent the benefits compensate the loss.[843] A third party that owes the insured person compensation, for instance based on civil liability, has to warn the insurer of his intention to pay damages to the insured.[844] If this third party compensates the insured victim without in advance informing the insurer, he will not be able to invoke this payment against the insurer that as a subrogated creditor claims compensation for the benefits it has paid to the insured victim. If this means the third liable party has to pay compensation twice, the insured victim can keep the double payment.[845]

281. The Belgian compensation system for industrial accidents is legally not based on a (strict) liability of the employer. The employer is required by law to contract insurance that covers the loss his employees and some of their dependents can suffer because of personal injuries resulting from an industrial accident.[846] This insurance is a form of first-party insurance directly covering the employee as the insured. In return for complying with this requirement, the employer receives immunity from civil liability for losses suffered by persons that can receive such insurance benefits.[847] The insurer that has paid benefits is not considered to have suffered damage that can be recovered on the basis of civil liability.[848] However, by paying the benefits the insurer is subrogated in the rights of the compensated victim against any third party who is liable.[849] As the employer enjoys immunity, the insurer will not be able to recover payments from the employer if the accident was caused by his fault or a fault of one of his servants for which he as their master would be vicariously liable.

840. Article 136, §2, para. 1, MHIA.
841. Article 136, §2, para. 3, MHIA.
842. Cass. 3 September 2003 (P.03.0256.F), No. 410, *Pas.* 2003, 1346, *Arr.Cass.* 2003, 1583.
843. Article 136, §2, para. 4, MHIA.
844. Article 136, §2, para. 6, MHIA.
845. Article 136, §2, para. 7, MHIA.
846. Article 49 IAA.
847. According to Art. 46, §1, IAA, the employer is only liable for accidents he intentionally has caused, for accidents caused by a subsistent neglect of the safety rules after the employer has been asked to comply by workplace safety inspectors, for property damage suffered by the employee, and for accidents on the way between home to the workplace and for traffic accidents (which are covered by the mandatory motor vehicle insurer).
848. *See* Cass. 9 January 2006 (C.05.0007.N), No. 22, *Arr.Cass.* 2006, 96, *Pas.* 2006, 95; Cass. 24 April 2002 (P.01.1623.F), No. 248, *Pas.* 2002, 991, *Arr.Cass.* 2002, 1104.
849. Article 47 IAA.

If the employer has failed to contract industrial accidents insurance, the employees are covered by Fedris, the Federal Agency for Professional Risks.[850] After compensating the employee or the other beneficiaries, this fund has to recover the full amount of the benefits paid from the employer,[851] who thus in effect bears a strict liability in the economic sense if he does not comply with the mandatory insurance requirement.

§3. OTHERS

282. The Court of Cassation has recognized that a third party that voluntarily helps the victim coping with the damage without the intent to permanently bear the burden of this effort, can recover the costs of such reasonable efforts from the person that is liable for the damage. Its first decision on this issue involved grandparents that claimed compensation for the costs they incurred in taking care of their grandchild from the person that was liable for the death of their daughter, the single mother of the child.[852] A second decision ruled that the State which, without being legally obliged, based merely on an internal policy, pays for the medical costs of a member of the military who wrongfully was hurt by a third party, can recover the payments as personally suffered damage from the third party that is liable for the accident.[853] In such a case, the primary victim can no longer claim compensation for the loss that effectively was already restored by the efforts of this third party.[854]

283. If, however, a third party at the occasion of the accident has paid benefits to the victim which are not strictly intended to compensate the actual damage suffered by the victim, such amounts do not have to be subtracted from the amount of damages to be awarded to the victim. Such is for instance the case for survival pensions based on social security legislation, which according to the Court of Cassation are not loss compensating benefits.[855] Notwithstanding serious criticism in the literature, the Court continues to hold that the fact that the widow of the primary victim has remarried does not diminish the amount of damages she can claim for the compensation of her financial loss as a result of losing her (previous) husband, as the contribution of her new partner toward her living expenses are not intended to compensate for the loss she suffers because of the death of her previous partner.[856]

---

850. Article 58, §1, 3°, IAA.
851. Article 60 IAA.
852. Cass. 6 November 2001 (P.99.1703.N), No. 600, *Arr.Cass.* 2001, 1856, *Pas.* 2001, 1790.
853. Cass. 4 March 2002 (C.01.0284.N), No. 154, *Arr.Cass.* 2002, 678, *Pas.* 2002, 632.
854. Cass. 25 May 2012 (C11.0494.F), No. 340, *Pas.* 2012, 1201, *Arr.Cass.* 2012, 1432, ruling that a handicapped person that effectively was helped by her sister who died because of the fault of a third person does not suffer damage, as she was in fact helped by another sister after the accident and for the whole period she could have been expected to be helped by the deceased sister.
855. Cass. 7 September 2004, (P.04.0315.N), No. 386, *Arr.Cass.* 2004, 1320, *Pas.* 2004, 1261; Cass. 15 February 2011 (P.10.1244.N), No. 133, *Arr.Cass.* 2011, 506, *Pas.* 2011, 517, allowing the surviving spouse to combine the widow pension with damages compensating for the loss of the retirement pension of the deceased husband.
856. Cass. 15 February 2011 (P.10.1089.N), No. 132, *Arr.Cass.* 2011, 504, *Pas.* 2011, 516.

Chapter 7. Other Remedies

§1. Restitution

284. The right of property gives the holder a claim of revindication (*rei vindicatio*). With this claim, the owner can demand restitution from any other person having his property under his control.[857] As this is an *actio in rem*, it does not rest on a fault committed by this other person. However, if the person by taking the property from the owner has committed a fault, the victim can choose which claim it will bring or the *rei vindicatio* can be combined with a claim based on civil liability. As civil liability gives the victim a right to restoration in kind,[858] the object of both claims is the same: the physical return of the good. The revindication has the advantage that as an *actio in rem* it protects the victim against other creditors of the person holding the good. The *rei vindicatio* also has the advantage that, contrary to a claim based on civil liability, the prescription periods of five and ten years do not apply.[859] As long as the property right persists, the owner can claim restitution. On the other hand, the claim based on civil liability might be more appropriate if the property can no longer be individually recognized among the goods under the control of the person that has wrongfully taken it or if the property right of the owner no longer exists, for instance when a bona fide third person has obtained a legally valid property right on the good.

285. A specific type of revindication exists in criminal law, in the form of a special confiscation with allocation to the victim. It is an extension of the claim for restitution of that what was taken.[860] Over the last decades, this system has been extended to all advantages obtained because of the offense,[861] so that not only the direct product of the crime itself (*productum sceleris*) but more general any advantage gained because of the offense (*lucre sceleris*) can be taken from the convicted offender. Strictly speaking, such a "taking" is really an obligation of the convicted offender to disgorge his profits from the offense. This type of confiscation can be ordered in any criminal conviction, but only if it is claimed by the public prosecutor.[862] The proceeds of special confiscation go to the Belgian State. However, the confiscated goods can be given to the civil party—a victim of the committed offense—if this person has a proprietary claim on these goods based on civil law.[863] Criminal special confiscation itself, therefore, does not grant civil parties any claims on illegally gained profits.

286. Even though it is not mentioned in the Civil Code, the Court of Cassation has recognized the *actio de in rem verso* or the claim based on unjust enrichment to

857. Cass. 3 May 1996 (C.95.0016.F), No. 145, *Arr.Cass.* 1996, 388, *Pas.* 1996, 410; Cass. 17 November 1927, *Pas.* 1928, 13; Cass. 23 January 1841, *Pas.* 1841, 124.
858. *See supra* paras. 217–218.
859. Cass. 3 June 1875, *Pas.* 1875, 219.
860. Article 44 PC.
861. Article 42, 3°, PC, inserted in 1990.
862. Article 43*bis*, para. 1, PC.
863. Article 43*bis*, para. 3, PC.

be part of Belgian positive law,[864] and nowadays considers it a general principle of law.[865] This action only lies if the defendant enjoys a gain that corresponds to or is the consequence of a loss suffered by the claimant while neither the loss nor the gain is the intended result of the application of all relevant legal rules.[866] If successful, the action gives the claimant a right to restitution. Only the value that was transferred from the claimant to the defendant has to be returned. This means that the claimant can never recover more than he has lost, even if the defendant has gained more. Also, the value to be restituted can never be greater than the gain the defendant has enjoyed.

287. In principle, civil liability can only result in an obligation to compensate for losses suffered. It cannot be a basis to claim disgorgement of illegitimate profits. However, in some cases where the victim suffered harm significantly smaller than the profit the wrongdoer has gained, one can see courts looking for ways to award damages that are higher than the loss actually suffered. This seems to be the case when the wrongdoer knowingly and willingly ignored the personality right of the victim. Occasionally, one can find court decisions awarding relatively high moral damages to such a victim, not so much as a reaction to the seriousness of the wrong committed but rather to tackle the profits the wrongdoer has realized by negating the exclusive right of the injured party.[867] Even though these judgments are formally based on reasons invoking civil liability and valuing moral damages, one could also recognize in these decisions a form of disgorgement as a remedy based on the bad faith infringed of a subjective (personality) right.

---

864. Cass. 27 May 1909, *Pas.* 1909, 272.
865. Cass. 17 November 1983, No. 149, *Pas.* 1984, 295, *Arr.Cass.* 1983–1984, 315.
866. Cass. 3 June 2016 (C.15.0423.F); Cass. 22 January 2016 (C.14.0492.F), *JLMB* 2017, 306; Cass. 5 June 2015 (C.14.0354.N), No. 376, *Arr.Cass.* 2015, 1507, *Pas.* 2015, 1496; Cass. 10 May 2012 (C.10.0707.N), No. 291, *Arr.Cass.* 2012, 1232, *Pas.* 2012, 1059; Cass. 25 maart 1994, No. 145, *Arr.Cass.* 1994, 307, *Pas.* 1994, 305, stating that the *actio de in rem verso* cannot be used by a claimant that had a claim based on civil liability that is time-barred because of prescription.
867. *See* e.g. CA Ghent 21 February 2008, *AM* 2008, 318, awarding the world famous Belgian tennis player Kim Clijsters "damages" set at EUR 790 or 10% of the return (calculated as the price times the number of circulation) the publisher of a poster-magazine had realized through the sale of an issue of the magazine including a poster with Clijsters together with fellow Belgian star player Justine Henin, after specifically noting that this was the only picture of Clijsters in the magazine, while all other pictures and posters showed Justine Henin. Clijsters had asked EUR 25,000 in damages, but the Court refused that amount as it was more than the total return of the magazine, which was circulated at 2,000 copies and sold at EUR 3.95 per copy. For another example, *see* CFI Brussels 19 May 2000, *AM* 2000, 338, awarding BEF 702,000 (approximately EUR 17,500) to a woman who had participated in the audience of a television show and whose private conversation in a bar after the apparent ending of the recordings had been secretly filmed and included in the show as it was later broadcasted, an amount the Court explicitly based on the number of viewers of the show, remarking this was appropriate "given the great importance apparently attached to television ratings nowadays."

§2. Injunctive Relief

288. As was already mentioned, civil liability in principle gives the victim a right to restoration in kind.[868] On this basis, the court can not only order the liable party to specifically restore the damage that has already occurred,[869] but also to take measures to end the situation that was created by the fact on which his liability is based and which continues to cause harm to the victim.[870] In case of a fault consisting in a zoning regulation violation, for instance, the court can order the wrongdoer to physically remove the construction that does not comply with the rules.[871] The Court of Cassation has even allowed a court to order the government to remove part of an army barrack that was built overhanging on the property of a neighbor and to remove a window that was closer to the border between the premises than allowed by law.[872]

289. Less clear is whether civil liability can also serve as a basis for preventive relief in the form of a court ordering a person to not commit a fault in the future or to take specific measures preventing a fact for which that person would bear strict liability from occurring. There is little doubt that such injunctive relief is possible in cases of fault liability based on an infringement of the victim's right. However, in such circumstances the injunction can be explained as a defensive use of that right itself,[873] so it is not really a remedy based on civil liability.[874] There are some decisions which also seem to make it possible for a court to order the wrongdoer to take the measures which are necessary to end the negligent behavior as opposed to remove the harm-creating situation caused by the negligence, but they all involve facts which can be open to another interpretation as well.[875]

868. *See supra* paras. 217–218.

869. *See* e.g. Cass. 5 May 2011 (C.10.0496.F), No. 299, *Arr.Cass.* 2011, 1157, *Pas.* 2011, 1272.

870. Cass. 29 June 2000 (C.98.0530.F), No. 420, *Pas.* 2000, 1222, *Arr.Cass.* 2000, 1245 (stating that Art. 1382 CC allows the court to order the person that wrongfully causes the loss to make the loss causing "state of affairs," as to be distinguished from the fault that has caused this "state of affairs," to stop).

871. Cass. 20 January 1993, No. 39*bis*, *Pas.* 1993, 67, *Arr.Cass.* 1993, 74; Cass. 21 April 1994 (C.93.0225.F), No. 189, *Pas.* 1994, 388, *Arr.Cass.* 1994, 392.

872. Cass. 26 June 1980, No. 686, *Pas.* 1980, 1341, *Arr.Cass.* 1979–1980, 1365.

873. Article 18 JC allows an action to prevent the infringement of a seriously threatened right, even if it only is aimed at obtaining a declaration of right.

874. *Cf.* Cass. 3 May 1996 (C.95.0016.F), No. 145, *Arr.Cass.* 1996, 388, *Pas.* 1996, 410. *See also* Cass. 29 June 2000 (C.98.0530.F), No. 420, *Pas.* 2000, 1222, *Arr.Cass.* 2000, 1245, stating that the injunction is sufficiently based on the knowing infringement of the right of privacy of the victim.

875. *See* e.g. Cass. 27 April 1962, *RW* 1962–1963, 57, *Pas.* 1962, 938, which states that the courts can order compliance with the "duty not to harm another," but which cannot be taken at its word as there is no general obligation not to cause damage in Belgian law. The case in fact turned around nuissance, and in light of the present day interpretation, the liability here was not based on a true "fault" but on a disturbance of the balance between the enjoyment of the property rights by the respective neighbors. *See also* Cass. 26 November 1974, *Pas.* 1975, 341, *Arr.Cass.* 1975, 370, which allows a court to impose construction measures on a discotheque necessary to avoid excessive hindrance for the neighbors, which bases this on the "duty not to cause hindrance that exceeds the level of normal hindrance among neighbors."

290. Specific statutory provisions create the possibility for the government or nongovernmental organizations that protect certain collective or public interests to ask the court to issue a cease and desist order, prohibiting the wrongdoer to continue the wrongful behavior in certain fields, such as the environment[876] and zoning and urban planning.[877] A cease and desist order can also be issued in case of unfair trade practices and other violations of specific economic regulation.[878]

§3. Punitive Damages

291. Belgian law does not know exemplary or punitive damages. According to the generally recognized view, the basic principle of integral compensation means that the actual loss is not only the minimum the victim should be able to recover, but also the maximum a court can grant. In setting the amount of damages, the courts are not supposed to take into account other elements such as the seriousness of the wrong or the fact that the tortfeasor obtained a gain or will be able to keep a profit even after compensating the victim for its loss (a so-called lucrative fault). The underlying idea is that punishment is not supposed to be a private matter among citizens but has to be organized and managed by the government, under more strict protective procedural rules for citizens, and is thus a matter of criminal law. Based on the principle of integral restoration, the Court of Cassation has ruled that a lump sum extra compensation over harm actually suffered by an infringement of an intellectual property right, which consists of the amount of the missed royalties, cannot be based on civil liability.[879] Another argument used is the idea that civil liability is not supposed to enrich the injured party. Financial penalties intended to punish, should not benefit other citizens, but should be collected by the government. The combination of these principles seems to leave no room for any gain-based damages based on the general rules of civil liability.

292. Careful analysis of the case law, however, has shown that court in fact sometimes do impose damages which are not directly related to the extent of the actual loss and which therefore seem to be intended to have a punitive effect. This can most easily happen with moral damages, which are supposed to compensate the victim for emotional or psychological suffering or distress. In cases of intentional infringement of personality rights, recent case law has shown a tendency of courts to awards higher damages.[880] Several commentators have interpreted these high awards as attempts of courts to punish for the wrong committed, independent of its consequences.

293. The only Belgian specific statutory provision that imposed punitive damages was a rule that liability of users of a piece of land from which wild rabbits originate which cause damage to the crop of neighboring fields results in the obligation to pay double damages.[881] This provision, however, was held to be unconstitutional by the

876. *See* e.g. (federal) Act of 12 January 1993 on an Action to Protect the Environment.
877. *See* e.g. Art. 154 Flemish Act of 18 May 1999 on the Organisation of Zoning and Urban Planning.
878. *See* Article XVII.1–2 CEL.
879. Cass. 13 May 2009 (P.09.0121.F), No. 314, *Pas.* 2009, 1167, *Arr.Cass.* 2009, 1254.
880. *See supra* paras. 106 and 287.
881. Article 7*bis* (federal) Hunting Act of 28 February 1882.

Court of Arbitration as, while there may have been specific circumstances relating to rabbit plagues that justified such different treatment at the time that rule was introduced, there is nowadays no specific problem with rabbits that could render such different treatment rational.[882]

294. Recently, a growing number of authors have pleaded for the introduction of punitive damages as a mechanism to counter lucrative faults. The Belgian literature on the subject is however rather shallow, as it does not first analyze why a lucrative fault would be socially undesirable and consequently does not specify any criteria to identify the faults that should be combatted. Lacking such analysis, one cannot determine whether punitive damages are an appropriate remedy.

882. C.Arb. No. 5/98 of 21 January 1998; C.Arb. No. 53/98 of 20 May 1998.

Selected Bibliography

H. Bocken & I. Boone m.m.v. M. Kruithof, Inleiding tot het schadevergoedingsrecht. Buitencontractueel aansprakelijkheidsrecht en andere schadevergoedingsstelsels, Bruges: die Keure, 2014, 270 p.

L. Cornelis, *Beginselen van het Belgisch buitencontractuele aansprakelijkheidsrecht*, Deel I, *De onrechtmatige daad*, Antwerp—Apeldoorn: MAKLU Uitgevers, Brussels, CED-Samson, 1989, 744 p.

L. Cornelis, Principes du droit belge de la responsabilité extra-contractuelle, Brussels: Bruylant, 1991, 779 p.

R.O. Dalcq, *Traité de la responsabilité civile*, 2 vol., Brussels: Larcier, 1959 and 1962, 667 and 821 p.

D. de Callataÿ & N. Estienne, *La responsabilité civile. Chronique de jurisprudence 1996-2007*, Volume 2: *Le dommage*, Les Dossiers du Journal des tribunaux No. 75, Brussels: Larcier, 2009, 605 p.

R. Dekkers, *Handboek burgerlijk recht*, Deel III, 3d ed. by A. Verbeke, N. Carette & K. Vanhove, Antwerp: Intersentia, 2007, 820 p.

B. Dubuisson, V. Callewaert, B. De Conink & G. Gathem, *La responsabilité civile. Chronique de jurisprudence 1996-2007*, Volume 1: *Le fait générateur et le lien causal*, Les Dossiers du Journal des tribunaux No. 74, Brussels: Larcier, 2009, 1074 p.

H. Vandenberghe, "Aansprakelijkheid uit onrechtmatige daad (2000-2008). Deel 2: Foutvereiste", *Tijdschrift voor Privaatrecht* 2010, vol. 47, pp. 1749–2145.

H. Vandenberghe, "Aansprakelijkheid uit onrechtmatige daad (2000-2008). Deel 3: Kwalitatieve aansprakelijkheid and Deel 4: Samenloop en co-existentie", *Tijdschrift voor Privaatrecht* 2011, vol. 48, pp. 349–656.

P. Van Ommeslaghe, *Les obligations*, 3 vol., Tome II in *De Page Traité de droit civil belge*, Brussels: Bruylant, 2013, 2814 p.

M. Vanquickenborne, "Aansprakelijkheid uit onrechtmatige daad (2000-2007). Deel 1: Oorzakelijk verband", *Tijdschrift voor Privaatrecht* 2010, vol. 47, pp. 283–359.

Th. Vansweevelt & B. Weyts, *Handboek buitencontractueel aansprakelijkheidsrecht*, Antwerp—Oxford: Intersentia, 2009, 935 p.

P. Wéry, *Droit des obligations*, 2 vol., Brussels: Larcier, 2011 and 2016, 1044 and 1016 p.

X., Responsabilités. Traité théorique et pratique, Waterloo: Kluwer, looseleaf.

Index

The numbers here refer to the paragraph numbers.

Index

Index

Made in the USA
Monee, IL
18 October 2026

66041399R10098